THE PRACTICE OF
MENTAL HEALTH CONSULTATION

THE PRACTICE OF
Mental Health Consultation

Edited by **Fortune V. Mannino**
National Institute of Mental Health

Beryce W. MacLennan
National Institute of Mental Health

Milton F. Shore
National Institute of Mental Health

Foreword by **Bertram S. Brown**
National Institute of Mental Health

Introduction by **James G. Kelley**
University of Oregon

GARDNER PRESS, INC., NEW YORK

Distributed by HALSTED PRESS

A Division of JOHN WILEY & SONS, Inc.

New York · Toronto · London · Sydney

Introduction Copyright © 1975 by Gardner Press, Inc.

All rights for the introduction are reserved and no
part of the introduction may be reproduced in any form,
by photostat, microform, retrieval system, or any means now
known or later devised, without the prior written permission
of the publisher.

Gardner Press, Inc.
32 Washington Square West
New York, New York 10011

This volume was originally published by The National
Institute of Mental Health.

This edition distributed solely by the Halsted Press Division
of John Wiley & Sons, Inc., New York

Library of Congress Cataloging in Publication Data
Main entry under title:

The Practice of mental health consultation.

   Includes index.
   1. Psychiatric consultation. I. Mannino,
Fortune Vincent, 1928- II. MacLennan, Beryce W.
III. Shore, Milton F. DNIM: 1. Community mental
health services—U. S. 2. Referral and consultation.
3. Community mental health services—U. S.—Bibliography.
4. Referral and consultation—Bibliography.
WM30 P894
RC455-P694 1975   362.2'2   75-25848
ISBN 0-470-56774-0

Printed in the United States of America

1 2 3 4 5 6 7 8 9

Foreword

Long before legislation made mandatory the development of preventive services as part of federally funded community mental health center programs, the Mental Health Study Center, a small NIMH community laboratory in Prince George's County, Maryland, was taking pioneering steps in cultivating community relationships toward the goal of promoting mental health and preventing mental illness. In many ways, the collaborative efforts of this small Federal laboratory and Prince George's County have provided the leadership in bridging the understanding of community dynamics with the development of national policy in the mental health area.

In reflecting on the significance of the Mental Health Study Center's program, I am reminded of some of my own early experiences in Government service when what I have called a Delphic approach was used in deciding complex public health issues. Whenever a high level official was called on to make a decision on an important issue, he usually asked his staff for two sets of information. One set had to do with the scientific merit and substance of the issue; i.e., What evidence is available to show that the program in question would, in fact, benefit those whom it was expected to benefit? The second set of information had to do with the politics of the issue; i.e., Who was interested in it and why? Then, by balancing these two sets of information, a decision would be made one way or another.

However, this Delphic approach is no longer adequate. A third leg of the stool is needed, so to speak, to clearly spell out the ethics and values which underpin both the scientific merits and the politics of an issue. The ethical value position with its critical effect on the outcome of complex mental health issues cannot be skirted in the development of policy. And this is where my thoughts about the Mental Health Study Center come in, for the Study Center over the years has provided a base of responsive continuity, a factor that is of no small importance during these times of rapid change. There is no substitute, for those who are in mental health practice or leadership posts, to having real live people in a real community to work with. This is something the Study Center has done so well over the years—dealing with people one-to-one in a community facility. If one approaches the kind of problems we must deal with from just a base of theory, research, philosophy and the like, the humanistic dimension somehow gets left out. It is this humanistic dimension with all its ramifications and implications that the Center keeps in the forefront. It is this dimension that so enriches its contributions to the national programs.

When the mental health centers legislation was enacted, one of the five essential services listed therein was consultation and education. The realization of the significance and importance of this area, as expressed in the Act, made information on a practical, theoretical and empirical basis more and more necessary. The Mental Health Study Center, for many years, has been active in trying to understand consultation within the broader context of preventive mental health. For 3 years it demonstrated a Community Mental Health Center Consultation and Education component, and it has continued to study problems in consultation and education in collaboration with other parts of the Institute. Its staff has written a large number of articles related to consultation which date back to 1951, years before consultation was identified as a specialty area. More recently, two monographs have been published: one a comprehensive cross-indexed bibliography updated in this volume; the second, a critical review of the research on consultation in mental health and related fields. Therefore, it is of particular significance that this book is generated from the rich experiences and breadth of knowledge developed by the Mental Health Study Center staff in the area of mental health consultation.

Regardless of one's interest—research, theory, practice or training—this book will have something to offer in terms of increasing understanding and fostering the development of one of the most important and challenging areas in mental health. In the final analysis, it is through the close interplay between professionals interested in the community and the community's reciprocal interest and involvement (learning from each other), that programs can be translated into operational reality. It is only through this close interweaving between the community and the practitioner, the community and the researcher, and the community and the policymaker, that a relevant, significant and meaningful mental health program can evolve.

BERTRAM S. BROWN, M. D.
Director
National Institute of Mental Health

Preface

When the Mental Health Study Center was established in Prince George's County, Maryland in 1948, a major goal was the application of public health principles and new conceptual approaches to the practice of mental health at the community level. Viewed broadly, this goal was concerned with improving the quality of the person-environment system by focusing on the interconnections between the individual and the community. Operationally it has meant seeking innovative ways to help the individual understand and utilize his environment (including the family, church, school, Government, health services, industry and recreation facilities), and to effect change in community institutions to make them more conducive to the optimal development of the individual.

A variety of methods and techniques have been used by the Mental Health Study Center toward achieving these ends. Included have been diagnostic, treatment and rehabilitative techniques, educational approaches, research, community planning and development, inservice training, program development, and program evaluation. One approach that has figured prominently in the Center's efforts from the beginning has been mental health consultation. As a major mental health practice method, consultation cuts across and intertwines with other approaches. It is believed to have a widespread impact because of its radiating effect and its applicability to a large variety of settings. Moreover, it is very appropriate for dealing with the environmental context of the individual; in fact, certain types of consultation, e.g., program consultation, administrative consultation, focus directly on changing the environment toward improving the mental health components of the person-environment system.

During the past 25 years, Mental Health Study Center staff has consulted with all of the major organizations and groups in the county. Seminars have been held to upgrade the skills of Center staff and to train other community professionals in the use of consultation. Video-tape recordings have been experimented with in conjunction with workshops and practical field training experiences. Studies have been conducted of various aspects of the operation, process and outcome of consultation. Key problems related to the planning, implementation and practice of consultation have been documented. As a result, a great deal of knowledge has been accumulated, much of which has been disseminated through staff participation in institutes, workshops, regional and national meetings and through publication in professional and scientific journals. Over 30 articles have been published by the Mental Health Study Center staff which deal with some aspect of mental health consultation.

This book is an attempt to organize and disseminate some of the knowledge we have gained in the use of mental health consultation within a community. It is meant to be a practical guide and source book, one that can be helpful in understanding what mental health consultation is and what it is not; in what ways consultation works and in what ways it doesn't; and what some of the problems and issues are in planning and implementing consultation programs in a variety of community settings.

Our hope is that the book will be of value to practitioners at both the professional and subprofessional levels. Although the descriptive articles deal with mental health consultation programs in Prince George's County, the kinds of problems faced and the settings chosen will undoubtedly be similar in many ways to problems encountered in programs developed elsewhere in the country. Hopefully, it will be useful to program administrators, both those concerned with providing consultation services as well as those seeking such services.

The book should also be useful to students and faculty in academic settings. In some ways it has certain features of a case book; but it also provides the student with a comprehensive guide to the consultation literature, as well as a review of the research which deals with the outcome of consultation. Finally, it may also be of use to the researcher, not only in terms of acquainting him with previous work, but in stimulating continued efforts in the study and evaluation of consultation as a major method of change in the community mental health field.

As can be seen from the table of contents, the book covers several areas of consultation. The first chapter deals with the definition and scope of consultation from the perspective of a community mental health center. The second chapter covers the research literature on the effectiveness of consultation. Chapters 3 through 7 are descriptive reports of consultation programs in a variety of community settings, including schools, day care centers. the police, and the new youth-oriented programs. Chapter 8 describes experiences in the training of mental health consultants. Chapter 9 offers a number of vignettes which illustrate some of the key issues and problems in the planning, implementation and practice of mental health consultation. Finally, the appendix offers a complete revision of the report entitled, *Consultation in Mental Health and Related Fields: A Reference Guide.* Originally published in 1969, the *Reference Guide* is now both outdated and out of print. The revision updates the Guide through 1973.

The book is dedicated to all of our friends and colleagues who have been affiliated with the Mental Health Study Center in some capacity over the past 25 years, and to the people of Prince George's County, Maryland, our partners and mentors for these many years.

F.V.M.
B.W.M.
M.F.S.

Contents

Contributors

Stephen B. Bernstein, M.D.
Chief, Psychiatric Inpatient and Day Hospital Service
Tufts New England Medical Center Hospital
Assistant Professor of Psychiatry
Tufts University School of Medicine
Boston, Massachusetts

C. Hal Brunt, M.D.
Assistant Professor of Psychiatry
Child Study Center
Yale University
New Haven, Connecticut

James S. Gordon, M.D.
Research Psychiatrist
Center for Studies of Child and Family Mental Health
National Institute of Mental Health
Rockville, Maryland

Stanley I. Greenspan, M.D.
Assistant Chief
Mental Health Study Center
National Institute of Mental Health
Rockville, Maryland

Beryce W. MacLennan, Ph.D.
Former Chief, Mental Health Study Center
National Institute of Mental Health
Adelphi, Maryland
Now Regional Mental Health Administrator
Office for Mental Health and Mental Retardation
Commonwealth of Massachusetts
25 Hayes Avenue
West Springfield, Massachusetts

Fortune V. Mannino, Ph.D.
Scientist Director, U.S.P.H.S.
Mental Health Study Center
National Institute of Mental Health
Adelphi, Maryland

J. R. Newbrough, Ph.D.
Professor of Psychology and
Coordinator, Center for Community Studies
George Peabody College for Teachers
Nashville, Tennessee 37203

Robert A. Nover, M.D.
Research Child Psychiatrist
Mental Health Study Center
National Institute of Mental Health
Adelphi, Maryland

William J. Polk, M.D.
Staff Psychiatrist
Mental Health Study Center
National Institute of Mental Health
Adelphi, Maryland

Robert D. Quinn, Ph.D.
Social Problems Specialist (Ret.)
Division of Mental Health Service Programs
National Institute of Mental Health
Rockville, Maryland

Shirley E. Robinson
Social Science Analyst (Ret.)
Mental Health Study Center
National Institute of Mental Health
Adelphi, Maryland

Dorothy Schroeder, M.S.S.
Professor Emeritus
The University of Michigan
Ann Arbor, Michigan

Robert Shellow, Ph.D.
Professor of Urban Processes
Carnegie-Mellon University
Pittsburgh, Pennsylvania

Milton F. Shore, Ph.D.
Clinical Psychologist
Mental Health Study Center
National Institute of Mental Health
Adelphi, Maryland

Introduction

Is mental health consultation here to stay? It is certainly an established part of the literature of the mental health professions and community mental health practice. I have an uneasy feeling, however, that the mental health professional talks, writes and reflects more about the practice of mental health consultation than actually doing it. It's unclear why with so many years of experimentation, discussions, and presentations of theoretical papers, the mainstream of mental health practice does not include mental health consultation as an important part of professional practice.

For me mental health consultation is not a major part of professional work because it is ambiguous, frustrating, and must be done for a long period of time in order to see impact. What's more, the effective consultant, in order to make a difference in the life of the consultee, will be asked to take risks, improvise, receive direct feedback, and be able to admit failure while working hard to bring about change in the consultee's organization. The consultant cannot be uptight and resist change. He must be alert, not identify with scapegoats within the organization or be seduced by pleas that the consultant is a powerful outside resource. These skills, these personal qualities, cannot be easily learned, nor learned in any one educational setting. The willingness to be a consultant, to intrude into someone else's territory to help, is a value for professional work that requires toughness, persistence and guts. Why is mental health consultation still tentative among the mental health professions? Perhaps few professionals are up to the exciting challenge for doing mental health consultation.

This useful book deals with important value issues of mental health consultation. The authors suggest that the effective consultant has a conceptual point of view, seeks out evaluative data, and organizes and reflects upon the experiences of consultation. Much of the book consists of narrative comments about the pitfalls that are a part of this important aspect of mental health treatment, including accounts of consultation in a variety of social systems, such as schools, juvenile courts, alternative services to young people, and early child care facilities.

A number of different approaches are illustrated, as well as a variety of goals. The interplay between style and personal values is also well-documented. One of the critical issues presented is how to sort out the relationship between the personality characteristics of the consultee, and the needs, values, and mission of his organization. The authors focus on the assessment process at the beginning of consultation and point out that because organizational stress is always present, unless consultants pay attention to the

ix

reactions it causes, they are likely to confuse it with personality problems. The consultant must be able to work beyond surface resistances to involve persons who are positive forces in the consultee organization, so that they can serve as role models for effective coping.

The book also includes an excellent integrative review of research on the consultation process. The authors have been expansive in their search, and selective in their detailed commentary. The chapter on evaluative research will serve as a guide for the reader who is interested in the subtleties and complexities of assessing the indirect effects of the consultative relationship. As for the literature on mental health consultation, the authors list 1,118 references, organized by topic and consultee organization. The book thus serves as an excellent resource for the new consultant, the trainer of consultants, the evaluator of the consultation process, and the consultant who is oriented to specific social settings. I enjoy getting down to cases: I like to lay out the work, focus on the issues, and take a hard look at what was done. I was not disappointed when I read this book.

James G. Kelly, Dean
School of Community Services
and Public Services,
University of Oregon

Mental Health Consultation: Definition, Scope and Effects

1

The Scope of Community
Mental Health Consultation

**Beryce W. MacLennan, Robert D. Quinn, and
Dorothy Schroeder**

Introduction

The delivery of community mental health services includes two major functions which relate both to prevention and treatment. One is to assess the mental health problems and needs in the community and to plan and develop resources to deal with them. The other is to carry out a wide variety of direct and indirect mental health services.

What agencies take responsibility for these functions varies from community to community. In some areas, planning and coordination are entirely separated from service delivery; in others they are combined. Community mental health centers, committed to the responsibility for service delivery within their communities, must include both. Even among centers, however, the concentration of effort will vary depending on their position in the community. A center which is part of a State, county or city department, often carries the formal planning responsibility of the local government for the development of community mental health services. This undoubtedly involves the coordination of all public service efforts and may include the delegation of some responsibilities to other mental health specialists and agencies.

Some private nonprofit centers, on the other hand, may operate comprehensive services for one catchment within a larger planning area and take primary responsibility only for direct services, while relying on a public agency to provide most of the indirect services. Between these two extremes the distribution of available resources between direct and indirect services will depend at least in part on the role and responsibilities assumed by the center in relation to other institutions in the community. The extent to which the community mental health center assumes a creative leadership role depends to some degree upon the social and political realities of the particular community, but even more so upon the ingenuity with which center leaders approach the problems of their communities.

Since the demand exceeds the potential for service delivery there is an urgent need to devise more effective methods of prevention and early treatment of mental health problems and more efficient utilization of available and new forms of manpower. The pressure to perform has brought increased recognition of the importance of other community caretakers in maintaining and improving the mental health of the people with whom they work. The task then of strengthening and supporting the mental health role of case workers, teachers, police, family physicians, clergymen, probation officers, and a host of voluntary agencies has become a focal point for increased activity in many community mental health center programs.

The consultation and education services component provides consultation to human service groups and individuals on the mental health dimensions of their work with people. It also includes mental health education and training for staffs of caregiving agencies, and mental health information and education for the general public. Consultation and education are the major means through which the community mental health center can share the responsibility for maintaining the mental health of the community with other agencies and with the public, and thus reduce the number of acutely disturbed and chronically ill mental patients who require direct mental health services. These services also contribute significantly to assessment of the community's mental health needs, to the development of new resources, and to reshaping of service delivery systems.

Theoretically, at least, the long-term rewards for investments in consultation and community education can be enormous. They include increased collaboration and coordination among service agencies and groups; the development of additional sources of mental health manpower; the creation of effective mechanisms for assuring continuity of care and early intervention in personal crises; an increase in the community's sophistication about mental illness and problems related to mental health; the assurance of a broad base of moral and financial support for the center's work and the enhancement of the community's general mental health.

Indeed, the 1970 Amendments (P.L. 91–211) to the community mental health center legislation specifically recognized the importance of such services by authorizing special funding for the consultation and education services which centers provide. More recently, changing patterns of Federal funding which place increased emphasis on third-party reimbursements and the use of revenue sharing have forced planners to study how best to pay for indirect services. Competition for scarce money has forced practitioners to search for ways to demonstrate the economy and effectiveness of indirect services.

This paper describes the scope of community mental health consultation and discusses some of the key issues and needs of this program today.

Definition of Mental Health Consultation

Mental health consultation is the provision of technical assistance by an expert to individual and agency caregivers related to the mental health dimensions of their work. Such assistance is directed to specific work-related problems, is advisory in nature, and the consultant has no direct responsibility for its acceptance and implementation. Consultation is offered by a mental health specialist either to other mental health workers less knowledgeable in some aspect of mental health, or to specialists in other fields who need assistance in the management of mental health and human relations problems.

Mental Health Consultation as a Component of the CMHC Program

Mental health consultation emanating from a community mental health center differs from that offered by private consulting firms or a mental health professional's office in that the consultation is oriented toward the center's programs as well as the needs of the consultees. For this reason, community mental health centers aim not only to achieve change in the functioning of individual consultees and, through them, their clients, but also to assist agencies and institutions to expand and upgrade their roles in the community's mental health maintenance system.

Consultants work with other agencies to resolve administrative difficulties, increase the skills of their staffs in understanding and managing mental health problems, and to encourage them to accept additional responsibilities in developing new programs which will affect the mental health of the community. Consequently, the disposition of the center's resources for consultation and the selection of consultation priorities are to be consonant with the goals of the center as well as responsive to the demand for consultation by community agencies.

Community mental health consultation is not only useful to the center in stimulating agencies to extend their range of mental health activities and to upgrade their mental health knowledge and skill, but it also provides a vehicle for interagency communication and liaison and for supplementing the center's knowledge of the changing needs and resources of the community.

Consultation Tasks

Any of the following activities may be included as the focus of consultation: (1) Consultation is conducted with the consultee regarding the referral or management of an individual, family or client group, or regarding the feelings of the consultee about his client. (2) Consultation also is concerned with administrative and staff organization and relationships. Problems in relationships occur in the organization of an agency, between agencies and the community, between agencies and agencies, and through conflicts between staff members and between administration and staff. (3) Consultation assists individuals or agencies to assess the nature and genesis of mental health problems and the need for new or modified programs. (4) Consultants advise on the planning and development of research, training or service programs, and on the evaluation of a program. (5) Consultants utilize consultation for the transmission of knowledge with regard to general human relations, human growth and development, social organization, and special mental health problems. (6) Consultants transmit skills in treatment, training, research, administration and evaluation, and in the preparation of written and audiovisual materials. Although consultation may focus primarily on one of these tasks, there may be several shifts in focus even in one consultation session or in regard to one problem. (MacLennan 1970)

These activities have been variously categorized by writers such as Caplan (1963), and by the Southern Regional Education Board (1970). For the purposes of this document it has seemed most functional to divide these activities into two broad categories—program consultation, and human relations and case consultation.

Program Consultation

Program consultation deals with problems concerned with the planning, development, management, evaluation, and coordination of services directly or indirectly affecting the mental health of the community. Participants in such consultations are generally administrators and planning staff. Initiative for seeking consultation may be taken by agencies, departments, associations, institutions in the community, or by the community mental health center. Such consultation may result in the development of new services or policies, in the recommitment or redeployment of manpower, and in the addition of new functions to an agency. It may assist in the creation of mechanisms for more effective continuous coordination of services and exchange of information, in the provision of training or the development of research and evaluation. Activities may include working with individuals and groups on the development of plans and proposals, ex-officio participation on committees, or advising on the writing of technical materials. As part of its consultation efforts, the community mental health center is concerned with the development of mechanisms for comprehensive and coordinated mental health service planning and monitoring. For instance, consultation may be a means of persuading the Health and Welfare Council to establish regular meetings for executives of all local service agencies, or of encouraging a local government to set up a committee to plan preventive and treatment services for children and youth with emotional or behavioral problems. (Hunter 1968; Libo 1966)

Program consultation differs from other kinds of community organizations in that the consultant's role remains advisory and he does not take direct responsibility while in that role.

Although the consultant may have much interest in the outcome of the consultation, the initiative for action remains with the consultee. This is in contrast to the direct administrative and program development activities of the center, where the staff may themselves set up a planning committee, organize community activities, or act as equally responsible partners in negotiating interagency collaboration. Some examples of program consultation are: A city demonstration agency director requests consultation and technical assistance in planning the mental health components of a Model Cities program; the head of a city health department seeks advice in setting up a mental health program within his service; a hospital administrator requests help in establishing a psychiatric wing; a personnel director in a factory needs advice on dealing with a high rate of absenteeism; a civic group seeks assistance in organizing preschool nursery programs as an antipoverty measure; or a legislator seeks aid in drafting a mental health service bill. These are among the kinds of program challenges a mental health consultant can expect to meet.

Human Relations Consultation and Case Consultation

Human relations consultation and case consultation are concerned with the day-to-day functioning of an agency or service and its clients, and deals with the interpersonal relations of agency staff and the relationship between the consultees and their clients. In regard to the latter, focus may be on the feelings and reactions of the consultees, on the needs and management of the clients, or on the interaction between client and consultee. (Berlin 1960; Caplan 1970)

Such consultation arrangements not only assist the consultees to manage day-to-day problems, but also provide a vehicle for liaison between the direct service staff of community mental health centers and other community agencies and for the dissemination of knowledge and skill in regard to mental health matters to the staff of collaborating agencies. Case consultations sometimes stimulate new mental health interests and capacities on the part of other service personnel and overlap into program consultation; for instance, when public health nurses, after consulting on a number of cases, decide to add after-care to their services for mental patients or a parent education program at the well-baby clinic; or when welfare foster care administrators come to expect some of their foster parents to cope with seriously disturbed youngsters as a result of case consultation and then develop training to increase the competence of their staff.

In case consultation, the consultant is always in an advisory position. However, the fact that the consultant is also a representative of the community mental health center, which offers a variety of direct services, may place him in many different roles, and he may in his work with any particular individual or agency find himself having to shift from the role of consultant into some other role. For instance, he may move from advising on referral into accepting the case as an agent of the center or for treatment as the therapist. He may assist in planning training and then become one of the trainers assuming program responsibility. He may advise on program development but later find himself as a collaborator in a joint interagency program endeavor. (MacLennan 1968)

The consultant at times also seeks consultation from his consultee. For instance, a consultant from a community mental health center to a school principal often takes the opportunity to draw on his consultee's knowledge of the community regarding key leaders or teenage problems (Kazanjian 1962; Rapoport 1963)

Differentiation Between Consultation and Other Activities

There is frequently a very narrow line between consultation and other activities. Consultation differs from supervision in that the supervisor has an administrative responsibility for outcome, must assure that the work is completed, evaluate it, and transmit organizational expectations. The consultant's responsibility is advisory.

Consultants train through the examination of problems. They do not take formal responsibility for training, nor do they utilize formal educational arrangements and methods, although such programs may be the outgrowth of consultation. Training through consultation, because it arises out of what the consultee brings into the sessions, is impromptu in nature. Inservice and professional training are more organized. The former, like consultation, is concerned with increasing competence on the job. Professional training prepares potential practitioners for work in a particular discipline. It aims to develop not only knowledge and skill, but also a professional identity in trainees.

Consultation differs from collaboration in that the consultee retains responsibility for the management of the program, situation or case. Collaborators carry joint responsibility. Mental health consultants sometimes find their roles changing to that of program administrator and collaborator, once programs have been formulated and responsibility for action allocated. Sometimes it is hard to distinguish when consultation becomes collaboration, as when a consultant is a member of a planning committee or task force which moves from advice-giving to the implementation of proposals for action.

Consultation may resemble psychotherapy and casework very closely when the focus is on the feelings and relationships of the consultees. However, the aim of consultation is always work-related, which sets a clear focus and limit to the discussion. Consultation aims to improve work functioning and is not primarily embarked on for the private motives of the individual consultee, such as personal advancement or increased enjoyment in the work situation, although these may be secondary gains.

As extensions of their roles, consultants may choose to see a client directly for evaluation purposes, or may develop a demonstration of a particular method in which they include consultees as collaborators. However, these arrangements are in fact combinations of consultation and direct services, or of consultation, direct service and training, in which consultants play multiple roles.

The Organization of the Consultation Services

A primary decision for the community mental health center is the amount of center resources which will be devoted to consultation. Some centers have made consultation the major vehicle for contact with the community, through which they have endeavored to help existing communities deal with mental health problems (Haylett 1969; Hunter 1968; Libo 1966; MacLennan 1968). These centers are either interested in reducing the number of designated patients or in providing efficient service in spite of a shortage of mental health specialists. Through consultation they mobilize community resources and strengthen existing informal mental health systems. These centers take the initiative in developing consultation arrangements. At the other end of the scale, centers view consultation only as an indirect service to the community to be provided as need arises, and have waited to be called in by community agencies for case and human relations consultation and for training through consultation.

An important question is whether consultation should be conducted by a separate staff or combined with direct services such as the outpatient program. The advantages of the latter arrangement are that where programs are decentralized, travel is reduced and consultation provides a vehicle for case referral, for intimate understanding of local agencies and their programs, and for the development of close relationships between center and agency staff. It is also possible to better understand, when clients are referred, whether the problem lies with the patient or the agency. Case and human relations consultations also demand many of the same skills as those utilized in diagnosis and treatment, and there are advantages in integrating programs which combine consultation, training and treatment in response to specific problems. For instance, in addressing the mental health problems of foster care, a child mental health specialist can consult with social service personnel, train foster parents, and treat children whose problems have been identified in consultation as requiring more than care from foster parents and schools. However, program and administrative consultation, undertaken between administrative personnel, may demand skills not always possessed by clinical staffs, and it makes sense in some situations to differentiate organizationally between program consultation and human relations and case consultation. In small centers, shortage of staff often will necessitate a combined program. In all situations, responsibility for the coordination of consultation should be assigned to one staff member.

Consultation services may be offered directly by center staffs, or they may be contracted for with individuals or groups who work as independent professionals, or as members of federated ˙ or collaborating agencies. Occasionally, if a consultation is particularly designed to confront an agency or part of an agency with the need for change which may arouse anger, it may be helpful to employ a consultant who is not a member of a community agency, but who can enter from outside to stimulate changes and accept the negative reaction which does not jeopardize local relationships. Other times, working through conflicts brings agency staffs closer together. (Levenson 1969)

Another organizational difference lies between consultants who specialize in working with a particular kind of agency, such as the clergy or the schools, and those who are generalists and who, particularly at the local level, attempt to use consultation as a medium for increased interagency communication or for coordination of community efforts related to particular problems. Consultants working with a particular agency become expert in problems of that agency and can utilize special knowledge in the consultation, but they may be less aware of the need for broad collaboration between human service agencies.

Priorities in the Establishment of Consultation

When a center begins to consider the development of a consultation program, enough information must be obtained to give the center some idea of the major problems in the community and the resources available to deal with them. The center should know the nature of the community, its physical layout, population composition, institutional structures and dynamics, and the specific mental health values and problems of its community. Decisions regarding which consultations to develop will be conditioned by the directions of the overall program, for consultation is one of the resources through which the center tackles mental health problems, as well as a service it offers to the community. For instance, if the population in a community consists largely of families with very young children, it will likely be desirable to place more emphasis on consultation with well-baby clinic, day care center and elementary school staffs than with high school staffs, if a choice has to be made.

The center also will need to determine how it plans the role of consultation in its program so that it can select consultees through whom the maximum impact can be achieved. If the center wishes to concentrate a major effort in prevention, working with principals and teachers in the schools may be more effective than working with special pupil services which deal only with the child who is identified as a problem. If the center wishes to affect the administration of a system, it usually is not effective to consult only with line personnel.

The center also must obtain a picture of the most urgent needs which are expressed by the agencies and citizens and plan its program so that it can be responsive to these. In beginning a program it is very important that the first efforts succeed. Consequently, consultees should be selected who are interested and accepting of consultation. (MHSC 1968, 1969)

The Consultees

There is a mental health and human relations dimension to all human activities; consequently, almost anyone in the community may seek consultation from a community mental health center. Choice of consultees will depend on their interest and willingness, and on the priorities of the community and the center. The most frequent consultees are community service personnel such as school staffs, clergymen, physicians, public health nurses, vocational and occupational workers, welfare workers and court and correctional staffs. Other professionals such as policemen, firemen, recreational and youth group workers, sanitarians and agricultural extension agents also have extensive community contacts where consultation programs could be developed.

However, many others may seek consultation or be sought out as consultees. Lawyers, for instance, have access to partners in marital conflict and many people who are suffering from bereavement. Executive and legislative members of the Government play very important roles in the promotion of mental health and the prevention of mental illness. They set policies and priorities, facilitate the development of service, and appropriate money. Mental health associations, PTA's and other citizen organizations are influential in obtaining community support, in keeping the public informed on mental health problems and resources, and in the formation of public opinion on central community mental health issues. They may seek consultation on the direction or implementation of their programs. Employers and employment agencies, real estate developers and property managers, labor organizations, and public utility planners all structure and maintain situations and climates which will facilitate or impede community mental health. They often also must make decisions about the mental health problems of their personnel or clientele and may seek consultation and guidance on these matters. Administrative and program staff of radio and TV stations can affect the quality of programs relating to mental health issues.

Employment policies regarding opportunities for job satisfaction and advancement may have great effect on the mental health of the community. The capacity to spot a worker's state of tension may prevent accidents. The skilled management of disturbed employees may enable them to stay on the job. The policies and practices of property and resident managers may determine the fate of a neighborhood. They are key people in the reduction of conflict in changing communities. They are often called on to deal with personal crises, such as suicide threats, a death in the family, or a case of drug taking. The physical relationships between services and people may be crucial in the mental health climate of a town. Transportation is sometimes the greatest barrier to service delivery. Consequently, planners of public utilities and zoning regulations may seek mental health consultation. Some individual citizens, such as bartenders, cab drivers, CAP workers, may be very important members of the informal mental health maintenance system of a community. Bartenders, for instance, are frequently the first line of defense in the treatment of alcoholics. All workers who have to deal with crowds in the course of their work, such as ballpark and amusement park attendants, policemen, movie house managers, and rock festival managers may need both consultation and education on group dynamics and the management of mental health problems.

Citizen organizations concerned with special problems or age groups also may seek expert assistance in developing their programs. Youth groups, senior citizen organizations, parent associations or self-help groups may require consultation on their special needs.

Consultation may be offered also to mental health professionals and non-professionals in other mental health agencies whether affiliated with the center or not. These consultations may be related to advanced techniques, special methods, or intra-agency conflicts.

Consultation may be conducted with individuals or groups of individuals, the latter belonging to the same organization or to a number of organizations. They may be of the same rank or of varying ranks. Group consultation has both advantages and limitations. It provides opportunity for the development of a nondefensive problem-sharing atmosphere in which learning from one situation can be carried over into others. It provides opportunities for cooperative planning and communication and for the resolution of interlocking and conflict-ridden relationships. Groups reduce the use of the consultant as a weapon between staff members. On the other hand, some consultants lack the skills to understand and manage group interaction and certain consultees may have difficulty speaking freely in a group. Some administrative situations could not appropriately be examined in a group setting. When problems discussed have high relevance for all group members, then group consultation saves considerable time; however, when there is low relevance, it may be less expensive to work with consultees individually. In group—as in individual—consultation, the consultant is not responsible for the administrative arrangements of the consultation. Staff remain responsible for effective utilization of the consultant's time and skills. (Altrocchi 1965)

Even when the initiative for consultation originates with a consultee agency or organization the choice of specific consultee does not need to rest solely with that agency. Consultants are always parties in deciding how, with whom, and on what they will consult. When an approach is made by a staff member in an agency, it may be very important also to consult with the supervisor and administrator either in a group or separately, or at least to meet these officials and have free access to them. When an administrator seeks consultation on a problem, it may be necessary to bring in the line personnel. These are matters which consultants consider in developing a contract with a consultee agency. They have to devise ways of getting to know organizations well enough so that they can make informed decisions. Initial success is important, so every effort should be made to ensure that the consultants who initiate a center's program are able to relate to the particular consultees who have been selected and that the first problems are not too hard to solve. (Gibb 1959)

Gaining Access

Consultation does not begin spontaneously, but arises out of perceived needs and competences. Initiative for establishing an arrangement may be taken by consultant or consultee. Consultants take several factors into consideration in the development of program. Who sponsors the center in the community will be important. Too speedy alliances may block off access to relationships which may later be very desirable. Historical accounts, community agency reports, census data and other statistics, and newspaper articles all will be useful in offering background information on the community. If staff members are new to the area, a series of meetings with community agencies to become acquainted and to learn about their programs and problems probably will be very profitable. Community agencies are usually very knowledgeable about the community even though they undoubtedly will define the needs and problems in terms of their own perspectives. Independent professionals and citizens' associations may be useful informants. Initial consultation probably will be involved on the basis of expressed agency and community needs. As center staff talk with agencies, useful areas for consultation will become apparent. Some centers have devised needs assessment questionnaires which can be used by the agencies with whom they consult. Each consultation should be clearly defined between consultant and consultee, and care taken that access to and consent from all relevant parties have been obtained. For instance, if administrators are not aware that their line personnel are receiving consultation, they may become antagonistic and obstructive at a later date, and the consultant may be vulnerable to being used as a tool in battles between administration and staff. If administrators impose consultation on line staff, they may subtly sabotage it and allow it to wither away. The maintenance of multilevel relationships is complicated by problems of communication and sanction to which the consultant needs to be particularly sensitive.

In developing community mental health programs, center staffs usually see themselves as having the primary responsibility for mental health efforts in the community, but others, such as welfare councils, county and State health departments, and mental health associations may already view themselves in a similar role. When a new structure is created, existing roles and territories may be active as consultants. For instance, school psychologists may act as mental health consultants to the school system and may view center staff as undesirable competition. In such a situation center staff seek to work out a relationship so that each reinforces the other.

Each agency also has its own priorities. Consultee staff have to perform their primary functions. They are interested in the community mental health center to the extent that it can help them improve their program, solve their problems, or take their problems off their hands. They have limited time and resources and try to use these to best advantage. Successful consultants relate to the consultees' needs as well as to their own and modify their approaches accordingly.

Nonmental-health people are often uneasy with mental health specialists. Effective community mental health consultants, while demonstrating their expertise and usefulness, respect their consultees and take care not to present themselves as superior. The relationship should be that of colleagues, with authority based on knowledge and expertise. Time is often needed before consultees will feel confident enough to reveal their needs, and the fruits of a relationship may not be immediately apparent.

Consultees often have preconceived ideas of the roles and functions of mental health specialists, and these may need redefinition before a useful working relationship can develop. Generally, the first request from clinical personnel is for direct treatment because that is what the community understands. It is useful for consultants to be able to provide direct service back-up from their agency if this is necessary and appropriate, but they have the prerogative of determining whether this is the most appropriate management of the problem and the most effective use of their time. They often have to sell their program. Consultation often has developed out of the conduct of specific training programs or mental health education, just as the need for these is often identified in consultation.

The choice of consultees will depend on the goals of the consultation. The organization of the consultee agency and the functions of staff are taken into consideration. Thought is given to whether supervisors or line staff or both will be most effective consultees. Such decisions, however, usually are not made unilaterally but in collaboration with the consultee organization. Sometimes, several organizations or groups may have to be involved if the purposes of consultation are to be achieved. (For an interesting discussion of some of the problems related to gaining access, see Glidewell 1959.)

The Course of Consultation

Consultation is essentially a dynamic process which is carried out through the establishment of a relationship between the consultant and his consultees. Each consultation arrangement, as it is established, should declare its purposes, focus, frequency, duration, expectations and responsibilities of consultant and consultee. Essentially a contract is established. This undoubtedly will require redefinition and review from time to time. The beginning phase then is concerned with the establishment of the contract, the setting of goals and objectives, the development of initial trust and an acceptance of the need for change. As the consultation develops, the body of the consultation will be occupied with the sharing of ideas, identification of problems, consideration of alternatives, and coming to grips with possible solutions. Throughout the consultation arrangement there may be changes in focus, from process to content and from client to consultee, to administrative arrangements or to an examination of the nature of the program. Some consultations will concentrate in one area, others may fluctuate.

The speed with which a consultation develops will depend on the defensiveness of the consultee and the skill and capacity to inspire confidence on the part of the consultant. Because consultation is also a process, a relationship has to be developed between consultant and consultee and time is required before trust and confidence are established. Consultation is normally conducted within a positive relationship and at a level of support, guidance and clarification similar to casework. Consultation directed toward major changes in institutions or programs or the development of staff may take several years to achieve its ends. As a consultation arrangement draws to a close, achievements should be evaluated and decisions made whether to terminate, renew or reorganize the arrangement.

The aim of consultation is to enable the consultees to function independently in a more efficient manner so that long-term dependency will not be fostered. However, it may well be that long-term, inter-agency collaboration will be an important aspect of the community mental health network and consultation between staffs may be of continuing duration although varying in nature over time.

Because consultees become attached to their consultants, attention is always paid to the resolution of the emotional aspects of the relationship at termination. Often the consultees experience a sense of loss. If a transfer is contemplated, they may be reluctant to establish a new relationship, just as in psychotherapy or in private life. Successful consultation is based on a relationship of mutual trust and confidence, and consultants are not immediately interchangeable. This is important to recognize, for many CMHC's are plagued by staff turnover, and new consultants have the task of reestablishing agency relationships.

Authority and Power in Consultation

In most consultations, direct authority rests with the consultees. The consultants' power to influence rests in their expertise and their ability to be of help, in their need to demonstrate their competence and in the consultee's wish to vest them with capacity for assistance. However, in some situations the consultant's organization well may have authority to veto or approve programs or to recommend funding, in which case the consultant's opinions and advice are extended from a base of direct authority and power. In these situations, consultants need to be particularly sensitive and responsive to the consultee's opinions and feelings.

Consultant Goals

The consultant's task is to help consultees in one or more of the following ways:

1. To *understand* the mental health dimensions of their program and problems. This includes their own and other people's intra-psychic and inter-personal reactions and the appreciation of appropriate mental health alternatives for action, both in specific and general work situations.
2. To *resolve* interpersonal conflicts and program crisis on the job.
3. To *acquire and improve skills* in dealing with the mental health dimensions of their work.
4. To *research, plan, develop, and evaluate* programs related to mental health.

General Knowledge and Skills

Consultants must possess basic professional skills before they attempt to become consultants. Just as importantly, they should be able to exude an aura of confidence, competence and concern for their consultees. Prior experience as a supervisor is useful so that the mental health professional is already able to gain understanding of individual, family and group behavior at second hand and to transmit this understanding to others. Consultants need to be knowledgeable about the identification and treatment of mental health problems relevant to proposed areas of consultation. They also should be able to analyze the organizational structure of the consultee agency and understand the process of program development and decisionmaking in order that their advice and opinions can be relevant and useful to the consultees.

Competent consultants are responsive to the needs of consultees. They analyze and appraise their consultee's position, their mandate, their needs, their capacities and resources, their power, and their particular biases. They present their knowledge in a way which is usable by the consultees and they can "speak their language." In developing a program, experienced consultants know how to gain access to and acceptance by a consultee and are able to develop relationships of trust. They also understand their own biases and reactions in the variety of situations where they will serve as consultants. Consultants possess techniques for quickly acquiring knowledge about the community, the institutions and the population with which they are concerned. If they are responsible for program development, they set program priorities and consider strategies for the development of the program. They need to know how to present themselves and whom to contact for what purposes. In the consultation itself, whether it is case or program consultation, they must listen and question in order to be able to extract the essence of the problem and help their consultees examine and deal with it.

The Training of Consultants

Becoming a consultant, at least for clinicians, requires an identity change (Signell 1971). Instead of directly delivering services, consultants must be able to understand the problem at second hand and to adapt interventions for the consultees to use in their own manner. Consultants must often reach out to consultees and work with them in their institutions and not in the center offices. These reductions in direct action, control and security often create anxiety and confusion in novice consultants. Training must help the professionals deal with these feelings.

Specific training for consultants should also teach: (1) how to assess the most pressing needs for consultation in the community; and (2) how to manage a consultation relationship.

1. The Assessment of Need for Consultation

The community. Consultants, when moving into a new community for the first time, should take time to get to know something of the area, its vital statistics, its physical layout, the people and situations in the news. It is a good idea to drive and walk around in the area to get a feel for it, to see what the houses, stores and amusements are like, to shop and eat in the neighborhood, and then discuss with members the needs of their community.

The population. If the consultation is concerned with a subculture with which the consultant is unfamiliar, he will read any materials available on that population, talk with people who are familiar with the group, meet with indigenous workers, and take part in activities where such a population is active.

The institutions. A consultant who is setting up a new program in an area makes contact with the key people in the agencies and institutions and determines how they see the needs and resources of the community. Combined with his knowledge of the community, he will begin then to set some priorities and to work out consultation arrangements which are related to pressing community needs. A beginning consultant has to learn how to assess agencies and institutions and to make appropriate contacts. He will study their tables of organization and try to find out who has formal and informal power and responsibility. If a community mental health center has an ongoing relationship with an agency or institution, it usually is possible to create a learning situation for the beginning consultant and to arrange for him to observe his future consultee at work. He accompanies a public health nurse on some visits, reads cases and sits in on some case presentations.

In a school setting he may be permitted to observe in the classroom, sit with a counselor, and attend building conferences. At first he only observes. When he begins to understand what is going on, he gradually joins in and makes comments. Lunching informally with staff members, he becomes aware of the areas of difficulty, the concerns of the staff members and begins to understand their particular styles. At the same time, he learns how to analyze the institution, and to explore the functions and roles of different staff members. He will read the current literature related to his field of interest. If a novice consultant has to create a new consultative relationship, he may need assistance in learning how to make access.

2. The Management of Consultation Relationships

Consultants must be able to develop relationships of trust with consultees, to understand and manage group phenomena, to recognize that there is an ongoing process from beginning to termination. They learn how to utilize basic professional skills, to facilitate the expression and identification of problems, clarify confused feelings, lead the consultees toward relevant and appropriate solutions and to generalize from specific situations. Beginning consultants should familiarize themselves with basic theories of consultation and use the literature to gain from other consultants' experiences. Where possible, it may be helpful for novices to act as consultants where they can observe a senior consultant at work. An ongoing workshop on consultation where beginners may present their programs is a most useful vehicle for learning as it serves both for assistance and support and as a model of a consultation from which the participants can learn. If new consultants are part of a larger program, they can participate in meetings where senior staff are present and analyze their problems in consultation. Wherever possible, regular supervision, or at least consultation, should be provided for beginning consultants. (Mannino 1969) In all these activities, the anxieties of the consultant should be recognized and dealt with.

Selection of Consultants

Probably most important in the selection of consultants is their basic personality and competence, their capacity to relate to people, which enables consultees to develop trust and confidence in them. However, other factors may have to be taken into consideration. Sometimes a consultee will have strong feelings about the profession, religion, race, age or sex of a consultant from the same profession or to have a consultant who is or is not an M.D. Sometimes the consultant must be from the same ethnic group. Most times this is irrelevant. Some people find it easier to accept advice and assistance from a man; others from a woman. Most frequently these initial preferences can be overcome by a competent consultant. Very occasionally the consultee insists on predetermining the qualifications of the consultant.

Occasionally more than one consultant will work on a consultation. This is expensive for the center but it sometimes can be justified. It may be a useful device for training an inexperienced consultant. Two consultants from different disciplines or who have special expertise occasionally can provide, through a team approach, exactly the assistance required by the consultee.

It should be noted that as consultation is a dynamic process, the ways in which consultees relate to two consultants are not identical and the consultants are not interchangeable. Consideration also must be given to the relationship between the consultants for, as with cotherapists, consultants may work well or poorly together.

Locus, Duration, and Frequency of Consultation

Consultation may be undertaken in any setting—at the office of the consultant or consultee, in a neutral setting, over a meal, in a car, over the telephone. Most regular consultations are held in one place. Sessions held in the consultee's agency have the advantage of keeping the consultant in touch with that agency's changing climate. Some interagency consultations rotate between agencies. Consultations may be offered ad hoc for one or two sessions to deal with a specific nonrecurring problem or crisis. They are most frequently conducted regularly over a set and limited period of time, although consultation does sometimes develop into a permanent service offered by one agency to another, or even by a staff member of one department to another within the same agency. The "permanent" consultant is particularly useful when there is high turnover in the consultee agency, and the consultant assumes the added role of staff trainer. He is sometimes retained on an "as needed" basis to assist in the management of specific problems when they arise. Most consultation arrangements seem to be conducted on a weekly, twice monthly, or monthly basis. Length of session varies from a few minutes to a stay of several days or even months to study a particular problem. Some consultants visit outlying localities for 1 day every 3 or 4 weeks and carry out several consultations within that day. However, the average community mental health consultation session probably lasts 1 or 2 hours.

Payment of Consultation

While some community mental health center consultations may be paid for out of continuing local or State appropriations as an ongoing and permanent service to the community, many community mental health services are only partially or even temporarily funded out of public monies. Preferential funding for consultation is included in the 1970 CMHC Amendments (P.L. 91–211). However, the problem of obtaining payment for consultation services is a very real one for most centers. When a need is rapidly perceived by the consultee, and the consultant is clearly acknowledged as an expert, there is generally no problem in obtaining payment from the consultee even if it only means a transfer of funds between two public agencies. Most frequently, the need has to be established and the expertise demonstrated before the consultee agency will pay for this service. Under these circumstances, it may be useful to offer a time-limited service stating clearly the center's financial position. If the need becomes established and the consultee can obtain funds, then the question remains to be settled whether consultation will be bought from the center or elsewhere. Some centers have obtained contracts for consultation services from school districts, for instance. Others, having obtained recognition of the need for consultation and demonstrated its usefulness, may be content to encourage the utilization of private resources if they are available. In these cases, centers' consultants can turn their attention to the development of new areas. In the future, more efforts will have to be made to obtain reimbursement for consultation in view of the reduced amount of Federal funding. A relatively unexplored possibility is to include reimbursement for case consultation in public and private health insurance packages. Such inclusion will have to be justified by the demonstration of cost benefit because of its preventive capacities, its use of less expensive manpower, or its greater effectiveness.

The Recording and Evaluation of Consultation

All community mental health center programs make an effort to keep adequate records (Kane 1966; Lippitt 1959; MacLennan 1968; Singh 1969). Consultation records are no exception. It is essential to know what was intended and what has taken place in order to monitor and control for cost of the ongoing services and to evaluate their effectiveness and efficiency.

Consultation has impact on two populations, the consultees and their clients. For completeness, an initial description is written on each consultation arrangement delineating the purposes and goals for both populations and plans for the conduct of the consultation. A regular record is then kept of contacts, of time and attendance of consultees, and brief notes of the problems presented. A summary is made from time to time of the progress and cost of consultation. Records are kept on individual clients considered in consultation and a method devised for following them if they enter the direct service delivery system. In evaluating the effectiveness of consultation, it is necessary to ask whether the purposes of individual consultation arrangements are achieved, and whether they actually contribute to the mental health of the community. If consultation is offered on case management, are decisions carried out, and do they resolve the problem? Routine feedback on the implementation and effect of decisions on the client's adjustment enhances the importance of the consultation and increases the confidence of the consultee in the consultant.

If there is staff or organizational conflict, is this worked out? If the purpose of the consultation is directed toward increasing the skills and knowledge of the consultee does this happen, and if so, does it increase the impact of the consultee on the clients? Testing the increased knowledge of the consultee is possible through questionnaires and observation as well as through the expressed satisfaction of the consultees.

If the purpose of consultation is to change institutional systems, does this happen, and if so, does it decrease the problems or improve the mental health of the community? If a network of consultation, with or without direct service, is designed to reduce a particular mental health problem, does this happen? Is it seen as relevant and does it meet the expectations of the consultees? Is consultation less expensive and more effective than training or direct treatment for a particular kind of problem or population? These are questions which must be addressed in the evaluation of a program of community mental health consultation. Only an adequate recording and monitoring system can permit such analysis and refinement of the program.

Comprehensive evaluation is very expensive. However, some simple tools have been devised which monitor the program and assist in its assessment. No program is perfect initially, and the capacity to learn from mistakes is one of the hallmarks of a successful program.

References

Altrocchi, J.; Spielberger, C.; and Eisdorfer, C. Mental health consultation with groups. *Community Mental Health Journal*, 1(2):127–134, 1965.

Argyris, C. Explorations in consulting-client relationships. *Human Organization*, 20(3): 121–133, 1961.

Basico. Mental health consultation to the schools: directions for the future. Behavior Science Corp. No. 645–02, 1973.

Berlin, I.N. The theme in mental health consultation sessions. *American Journal of Orthopsychiatry*, 30(4):827–828, 1960.

Berlin, I.N. Mental health consultation in schools as a means of communicating mental health principles. *Journal of the American Academy of Child Psychiatry*, 1(4):671–679, 1962.

Bindman, A.J. Mental health consultation: theory and practice. *Journal of Consulting Psychology*, 23(6):473–482, 1959.

Caplan, G. *The Theory and Practice of Mental Health Consultation*. New York: Basic Books, 1970.

Caplan, G. Types of mental health consultation. *American Journal of Orthopsychiatry*, 33(3):470–481, 1963.

Claiborn, W.L., and Cohen, R., eds. School intervention. Vol. 1. New York: Behavior Publications, 1973.

Gaupp, P.G., Authority influence and control in consultation. *Community Mental Health Journal*, 2(3):205–210, 1966.

Gibb, J.R., The role of the consultant. *The Journal of Social Issues*, 15,(2):1–4, 1959.

Glidewell, J.C., The entry problem in consultation. *The Journal of Social Issues*, 15(2): 51–59, 1959.

Haylett, C.H., Issues of indirect services. In: Lamb, H.; Heath, D.; and Downing, J.J., eds. *Handbook of Community Mental Health Practice*. San Francisco: Jossey-Bass, 1969. pp. 305–321.

Haylett, C.H., and Rapoport, L. Mental health consultation. In: Bellak, L., ed. *Handbook of Community Psychiatry and Community Mental Health*. New York: Grune & Stratton, 1964. pp. 319–339.

HumRRO, *Preliminary Handbook on Procedures for Evaluating Mental Health Indirect Service Programs in Schools*. Alexandria, Va.: Human Resources Research Organization, 1971.

Hunter, W.R., and Ratcliffe, A.W. The Range Mental Health Center: Evaluation of a community-oriented mental health consultation program in northern Minnesota. *Community Mental Health Journal*, 4(3):260–267, 1968.

Iscoe, I.; Pierce-Jones, J.; Friedman, S.T.; and McGehearty, L. Some strategies in mental health consultation: A brief description of a project and some preliminary results. In: Cowen, E.L.; Gardner, E.A.; and Zax, M., eds. *Emergent Approaches to Mental Health Problems*. New York: Appleton-Century-Crofts, 1967. pp. 307–330.

Kane, R.F. Social work consultation to the Priest. *Catholic Charities Review*, 50(8):4–10, 1966.

Kazanjian, V.; Stein, S.; and Weinberg, W.L. *An Introduction to Mental Health Consultation*. U.S. Public Health Service Publication No. 922, Public Health Monograph

No. 69, Washington, D.C.: Superintendent of Document, U.S. Government Printing Office, 1962. p. 13.

Latimer, N. et al. *The Protection and Promotion of Mental Health in Schools.* Bethesda, Md.; U.S. Dept. of HEW, National Institute of Mental Health, 1964.

Levenson, A.I., and Brown, B. Social Implications of the community mental health center concept. In: Zubin, J., and Freyhan, F.A.; eds. *Social Psychiatry.* New York: Grune & Stratton, 1968. pp. 117–127.

Levenson, A. Organizational patterns of community mental health centers. In: Bellak, L., and Barten, H.H., eds. *Progress in Community Mental Health.* 1. New York: Grune & Stratton, 1969, pp. 67–90.

Libo, L.M. Multiple functions for psychologists in community consultation. *American Psychologist,* 21(6):530–534, 1966.

Libo, L.M., and Griffith, C.R. Developing mental health programs in areas lacking professional facilities: The community consultant approach in New Mexico. *Community Mental Health Journal,* 2(2):163–169, 1966.

Lippitt, G.L. A study of the consultation process. *Journal of Social Issues,* 15(2):43–50, 1959.

Lippitt, G.L. Operational climate and individual growth; The consultative process at work. *Personnel Administration,* 23(5):12–19, 43, 1960.

Lippitt, R. Dimensions of the consultant's job. *Journal of Social Issues,* 15(2):5–12, 1959.

MacLennan, B.W. "The Systematic Development of a Consultation Program in a Comprehensive Community Mental Health Center." Paper presented at St. Elizabeth's Medical Society Annual Institute, Washington, D.C., 1968.

MacLennan, B.W.; Montgomery, S.L.; and Stern, E.G. *The Analysis and Evaluation of the Consultation Component in a Community Mental Health Center.* Laboratory Paper No. 36. Adelphi, Md.: Mental Health Study Center, NIMH, 1970.

Mann, Philip A. Establishing a mental health consultation program with a police department. *Community Mental Health Journal,* 7(2):118–126, 1971.

Magner, G., and Briggs, T. *Staff Development in Mental Health Services.* New York: National Association of Social Workers, 1966.

Mannino, F.V. *Consultation in Mental Health and Related Fields: A Reference Guide.* Rockville, Md.: National Institute of Mental Health, 1969.

Mannino, F.V. Developing consultation relationships with community agents. *Mental Hygiene,* 48:356–362, 1964.

Mental Health Study Center. *Annual Report—July 1, 1967 to June 30, 1968.* Adelphi, Md.: MHSC, National Institute of Mental Health, HEW, 1968.

Mental Health Study Center. *Annual Report—July 1, 1968 to June 30, 1969.* Adelphi, Md.; MHSC, National Institute of Mental Health, HEW, 1969.

Murphy, L.B. The consultant in a day care center for deprived children. *Children,* 15 (3):97–102, 1968.

Newman, R.G. *Psychological Consultation in the Schools.* New York: Basic Books, 1967.

Nitzberg, H., and Kahn, M.W. Consultations with welfare workers in a mental health clinic. *Social Work,* 7(3):84–93, 1962.

Parker, B. *Psychiatric Consultation for Non-Psychiatric Professional Workers.* Public Health Monograph, No. 53, DHEW. Washington, D.C.: Superintendent of Documents, U.S. Government Printing Office, 1958.

Quinn, R., and Magnuson, L. W., eds. *Mental Health and Learning.* DHEW Pub. No. (HSM) 72–9146. Washington, D.C.: Superintendent of Documents, U.S. Government Printing Office, 1972.

Rapoport, L., ed. *Consultation in Social Work Practice.* New York.; National Association of Social Workers, 1963.

Scheidlinger, S.; Sarcka, A.; and Mendes, H. A mental health consultation service to neighborhood organizations in an inner city area. *Community Mental Health Journal,* 7(4):264–271, 1971.

Seashore, C., and Van Egmond, E. The consultant-trainer role in working directly with a total staff. *Journal of Social Issues,* 15(2):43–50, 1959.

Signell, K.A., and Scott, P. Mental health consultation. *Community Mental Health Journal,* 7(4):288–302, 1971.

Singh, R.K.J., and Thompson, D. "Evaluation of a Program of Community Mental Health." Flint, Mich.: Community Mental Health Services, 1969. (Mimeo.)

Southern Regional Education Board. Definitions of Terms in Mental Health Retardation and Alcoholism Programs. 2nd ed. Atlanta Ga.: Definitions and Classification Committee, Southern Regional Conference on Mental Health Statistics, 1970.

Spielberger, C.A. A Mental Health Consultation Program in a Small Community with Limited Professional Mental Health Resources. In: Cown, E.L.; Gardner, E.A.; and Zax, M., eds. *Emergent Approaches to Mental Health Problems.* New York: Appleton-Century-Crofts, 1967. pp. 214–238.

Stringer, L.A. Consultation: Some expectations, principles and skills. *Social Work,* 6(3):85–90, 1961.

2

Effecting Change Through Consultation

Fortune V. Mannino and Milton F. Shore

Although consultation as a method for dealing with human relations problems is very popular among professionals in the human service fields, research on its effectiveness is still minimal. Moreover, there continue to be great chasms between theoretical rationales, research, and practice. This is particularly true of the mental health field which has long been dominated by clinicians and individually oriented theoretical models. In general, this clinical-individual emphasis has resulted in either a common sense approach utilized by mental health clinicians with no special training in consultation, or the development of semi-closed systems by isolated theorists who develop and teach their methods to new consultants. The new consultants then often accept the theories as sacred and pass them on to their students with little or no input or feedback from other sources.

However, there are trends in the consultation field which point to important changes and promising new developments. One such change is the application of new theoretical models which take into consideration the man/environment interface to a much greater extent than have conceptual approaches previously. These include the application of a systems approach to consultation (Goldmeier 1971; Miller 1973); the use of organizational theory (Bennes 1965); the application of behavioral modification principles (Randolph 1972; Meacham 1971; Woody and Woody 1971); and the application of an ecological approach (Simmons 1960; Kelly 1970). In each of these approaches, environmental factors are stressed. Other changes include greater specification of target populations, attempts to more precisely define activities performed under the consultation label, and measuring specific kinds of techniques in more reliable and objective ways. With such changes, one hopes that the gap between theory, research, and practice will begin to narrow.

There is some evidence that bridging theory, research and practice is already beginning. In reviewing the research related to consultation outcome from 1958 (the first published report we were able to find) to 1972, the increased sophistication of the studies through the years is apparent. More and more care is being given to an operational definition of consultation within a conceptual frame with increasing use of control groups and the testing of hypotheses. It is now rare to find a study in the consultation area that does not either use a control or some type of comparison group. There is still, however, a very long way to go toward refined methodologies. Also, too many researchers and practitioners still do not refer to what has been done in the field when they set out to initiate a new research project or develop a new program.

The purpose of this article is to review those studies reported during 1958–1972, which attempt to measure the effect of consultation practice, i.e., outcome studies. Studies which do not relate to outcome, such as process studies, surveys, etc., are not included. Hence, this is not a comprehensive review of all the reported research in consultation, but rather a review of those studies which bear on the question, "Does consultation work?"

Studies of outcome are basically studies of goal achievement and are naturally dependent upon being able to clearly define the goals one sets out to accomplish. In mental health consultation, defining goals is extremely difficult. Who is it that one expects to change through consultation, and what kinds of change are anticipated? It would appear that there are at least three major areas of outcome that can be measured. First, there is the immediate objective of effecting change in the knowledge and skills of the consultee so that he will work more effectively with the client he serves. Second, there is the long-range objective of bringing about positive change in the client group itself. Finally, there is what might be spoken of as an intermediate goal—that of effecting change in the institutional structure, or the system, aimed at improving the mental health components of its services and activities. The studies included here generally focus on one or more of these levels in the same study. The material discussed in the text is summarized in table I.

The paper is organized as follows:

I. Studies of Change in the Consultee
   A. Changes in Group Behavior
   B. Changes in Individual Professional Development and Functioning
      1. School Personnel
      2. Police
      3. Clergy
      4. Nurses

II. Studies of Change in the System

III. Studies of Change in the Client
   A. Changes in Academic Performance
   B. Changes in Behavior

IV. Studies of Change on a Combination of Levels
   A. Changes in Consultee, Client, and System
   B. Changes in Consultee Functioning and Client Behavior

Table 1.—Outcome studies

Author	Date	Kind of consultation	Controls used	Positive effect reported in		
				Consultee	System	Client
Eisenberg	1958	Psychiatric	Yes	*	....	Yes
Foster & Hartman	1959	Dietary	No	....	Yes	....
Mariner, Brandt, Stone & Mirmow	1961	Psychiatric	No	Yes	....	....
Teitelbaum	1961	Educational	Yes	Yes	....	....
Ginther	1963	Educational	Comparison Group	....	....	Yes
Cutler & McNeil	1964	Mental Health	Yes	Yes	....	Yes
Dorsey, Matsunaga & Bauman	1964	Mental Health	No	Yes	....	....
Payne	1964	Educational	Comparison Group	....	....	No
Chapman	1966	Mental Health	No	....	....	Yes
Kellam & Schiff	1967	Mental Health	Yes	Yes	....	Yes
Trione	1967	Psychological	Yes	Yes	....	Yes
Pierce-Jones, Iscoe & Cunningham	1968	Mental Health	Yes	No	....	....
Friedlander	1968	Behavioral Science	Yes	Yes	....	....
Schmuck	1968	Behavioral Science	Yes	Yes	No	No
Townes, Lytle, Wagner & Wimberger	1968	Mental Health	No	Yes	....	Yes
Hunter & Ratcliffe	1968	Mental Health	Comparison Group	....	....	Yes
Bolman, Halleck, Rice & Ryan	1969	Psychiatric	Yes	....	....	No
Lewis	1969	Educational	Yes	....	....	Yes/in part
Whitley	1970	Educational	Yes	No	....	Yes
Bjork	1970	Educational	Yes	Yes	....	Yes

Table 1.—Outcome studies (cont)

Author	Date	Kind of consultation	Controls used	Positive effect reported in		
				Consultee	System	Client
Caplan	1970	Mental Health	Yes	Yes	....	....
Ulmer & Kupferman	1970	Psychiatric	No	No	....	No
Young	1971	Mental Health	Yes	No	....	....
Keutzer, Fosmire, et al.	1971	Behavioral Science	Yes	Yes	Yes	Yes
Zacker, Rutter, Bard	1971	Mental Health	No	Yes/in part	No	....
Berk	1971	Mental Health	Yes	....	....	....
Thurlow	1971	Educational	Yes	....	....	No
Tyler	1971	Psychological	Yes	Yes	....	....
Deloughery, et al.	1972	Mental Health	No	Yes/in part	....	....
Conner & Thoresen	1972	Mental Health	Comparative	....	....	No
Fisher	1972	Psychological	Yes	No	....	....
Davis	1972	Educational	Yes	....	....	No
Linoff	1972	Educational	Yes	No	....	....
Hommen	1972	Mental Health	Yes	Yes/in part	....	....
Newfield	1972	Mental Health	Yes	Yes	....	....

*Not applicable to particular study.

I. Studies of Change in the Consultee

Fourteen studies have focused on the effects of consultation on some aspect of consultee behavior. These studies can be divided into two general areas: Those that use group consultation in an effort to change the behavior of the consultee within the group setting (four studies); those that focus around aspects of change in the individual consultee's professional functioning (10 studies).

A. Changes in Group Behavior

Helping consultees develop decisionmaking skills, problem-solving techniques, etc., through a type of group reinforcement consultation was the focus of four studies. Though similar in their use of a group approach, there were variations in what was done. Friedlander (1968) studied three separate styles of consultation: one was sensitivity training; a second was preliminary work followed by training on specific work-related problems; a third, similar to the second, had an extensive relationship with the consultant prior to and following the training sessions. Young (1971) used a laboratory approach within a field setting, consulting with Sunday school teachers. His laboratory task was a NASA simulated task. Deloughery et al. (1972) worked with a small group of nurses, aiming to improve their problem-solving ability through group discussion of problem-solving efforts. Fisher (1972) studied a group of students and teachers working together in problem-solving discussions where the consultant focused on facilitative and diagnostic activities aimed at helping teachers and students deal with their relationship difficulties. All but one of these studies (Deloughery et al.) used control groups.

Two of the four studies reported positive results in social behavior. Friedlander, using a questionnaire developed from open-ended interviews which were factor analyzed, studied six general areas (group effectiveness, leader approachability, mutual influence, personal involvement and participation, intragroup trust, and the worth of the meetings). He found that the greatest impact of consultation in all six areas was in the group that combined prework, followup, and continuously problem-oriented group activity. Despite greater consultant time needed for this approach, the payoff seemed to be considerably greater than any of the other approaches.

Fisher, using four groups of teachers and students randomly assigned to control and experimental groups, found significant increases in the complexity of the students' perceptions within the group, but not in the positiveness of their perceptions or their orientations to be involved in and to improve relationships in the group.

Negative results were found in two studies. Young, using three groups— one a helping group, one an information group, and one a combination of the two—found that decisionmaking was not improved with the help of a consultant; in fact, it was worse in one of the groups. However, despite his careful laboratory procedure, Young's study may not be a valid test of consultation because of the contrived test situation and the absence of conflict necessitating the need for consultation.

The pilot study reported by Deloughery et al. aimed at improving the problem-solving ability of work groups of nurses, had an extremely small sample and no control group. Nevertheless, the results suggested a trend in the direction of a progressive increase in problem-solving ability brought about by the groups' use of consultation. It was doubtful, however, whether significant differences in problem-solving would have been found even had the sample been enlarged in size.

Thus, the picture of the effect of consultation on behavior in a group is a mixed one. The greatest effect occurs when the group is motivated for change, and when the technique used involves the group in a combination of problem-solving and sensitivity-type experiences. Methods that focused on intellectual types of activities, some of which were contrived, had very little effect.

B. Changes in Individual Professional Development and Functioning

Another way of evaluating the effectiveness of consultation is to study the changes in the individual consultee and certain aspects of his personality structure or function. By far the largest number of consultee-focused studies are in this area. Since there are differences for the different professional groups, the section will be divided by professional disciplines.

1. *School personnel.* A very popular area of mental health consultation has been in the schools. About one-seventh of all the studies of the effects of consultation focused on changes in school personnel. Mariner et al. (1961) consulted with counselors, administrators and public school teachers. Four studies were found which focused only on teachers.

The study by Mariner et al., lacking a control group, used school personnel, almost all of whom had volunteered for the consultation. The aim of consultation was to increase the awareness of the influence of motivation and other aspects of personality dynamics on the learning process in children. To measure this, a test of "psychological mindedness" and a rating scale were used. Results showed that the psychological mindedness test changed significantly. The participants also rated the discussions as stimulating, meaningful, and beneficial to their work.

In 1961, Teitelbaum studied the effectiveness of consultation given to a group of teachers who were assigned to matched schools in the lower-class black and Puerto Rican neighborhoods of New York. Each consultant worked with 15 teachers on their handling of the children in class. Monthly logs were kept by both the teachers and the consultants and rating forms were completed by the principals on degree of teacher growth. The results showed that teachers who had consultation were more confident in their ability to function and showed greater professional growth than those who did not.

Tyler (1971) was particularly interested in the effect of time spent with teachers on the effectiveness of consultation. He divided teachers into three groups of 40, giving one group intensive consultation, a second limited consultation, and the last group no consultation. Before and after paper and pencil reports by the teacher and psychologist consultant were analyzed. Results showed that teachers who received intensive consultation changed significantly more than teachers in either of the other groups, with the control teachers changing the least. The teachers who had the intensive consultation, unlike those in the other two groups, changed significantly in their understanding of the child in the direction of that of the school psychologist. But, as with other studies reported here, this study failed to control for the effect of nonspecific attention to the control group. How much was the result a function of the intensity of attention, and how much was it the skill of the consultation?

A study by Linoff (1972) compared a consultation model which stressed understanding of student behavior with a behavior modification model, comparing both of these with an untreated group. No significant differences were found between the two models with regard to teacher-student behavior, open-mindedness, unconscious motivations of teacher behavior, and teacher perceptions about student behavior. However, the consultation group had poor attendance, as well as many changes in consultants.

The most comprehensive consultee-focused study of school consultation was the major study reported by Iscoe, Pierce-Jones, Friedman and McGhearty (1967), and Pierce-Jones, Iscoe and Cunningham (1968). The aim of the study was to improve the skills of the teacher and to encourage the use of school resources. Evaluation was done by studying changes in the teachers (consultee) and changes in various elements of program functioning. Fourteen schools participated in the program, and an equal number were selected as controls. A large number of measures were used to evaluate the changes in the teacher, many of which were specifically designed for the study: (1) dimension of teachers' opinions (110 items set up to measure teachers' orientation to child behavior); (2) need for assistance scale (50 items identifying classes of problems which school personnel need help in managing); (3) behavior classification checklist (92 item-scale designed to determine what the child does in the classroom and how much it irritates the teacher); (4) what is an ideal pupil scale (comparing the responses of teachers in this group to other geographical areas); (5) child attitude survey (a survey of teachers' attitudes with regard to aspects of child behavior); (6) assessment of consultation service (a questionnaire given to determine how much was known about the consultation service and how much it was used); (7) school and community survey (to determine the teacher's perception of the interaction of the school and community at the beginning and end of the academic year). In addition, other data collected were biographical materials on the teachers, consultant reports in which an objective reporting device was used to get demographic data and identify the nature of the consultant-consultee relationship, the origins of the case, the way the case was handled, and the general assessment of the problem. Hypotheses stated that consultation would produce significant changes in the mental health orientation of teachers, and that the differential use of consultation would be associated with differences in the measures of the teachers' mental health orientation. The results showed no statistically significant difference that would support the hypotheses. The only statistically significant finding was an increase in rapport between consultant and consultee, which occurred between the beginning and the end of the consultation program.

2. *Police.* A study in which a group of graduate psychology students consulted with police officers was reported by Zacker, Rutter, and Bard in 1971. Consultation was held weekly for 14 weeks and focused around discussions of interpersonal conflicts in which the police had intervened. Attitude measures were administered prior to and following the consultations. No change was found in the consultees (police officers). However, the attitudes of the consultants toward the police changed in more realistic directions. There was no control group, and there was also a question as to whether the changes that occurred were due to changes in the behavior of the police officers or resulted from a dissolution of the consultants' stereotypes about police officers, which often change when one has been exposed to and works with individuals that one has stereotyped. Nevertheless, such a study as this one is rare, for few studies have focused on changes in the consultants.

3. *The clergy.* Hommen (1972) investigated the changes in pastoral care and mental health attitudes of a group of parish clergymen following a consultation program which included laboratory training, education, and consultation. In 46 sessions of 1 1/2 to 2 hours each, 11 experimental and 12 control subjects were interviewed, using a bereavement scale constructed for ministers (Everest Bereavement Ministry Instrument). In addition, the clergymen were administered an information questionnaire, the Community Mental Health Ideology Scale, and the Semantic Differential. The results indicated that clergymen significantly improved in their abilities to be aware of and to respond to the affective needs and communications of those who were grieving. There were no significant findings in relation to mental health attitudes or in the overall balance of the use of affective, interpersonal, and meaning-integrative approaches in the clergymen's work with their bereaved parishioners. Independent effects of consultation in the study could not be isolated.

4. *Nurses.* Three studies have investigated the effects of consultation on nurses, two of them using Caplan's conceptual model. Dorsey, Matsunaga,

and Bauman (1964) studied the effects of consultation on public health nurses over a 5-month period. Unfortunately, they did not have a control group. Public health nurses met with a psychiatric team (psychiatrists, psychiatric social worker, and psychiatric nurse) to discuss cases. Change was assessed by evaluating the process notes of the consultation, the sequences of referrals over time, anecdotal observations of the psychiatric team, before and after self-ratings on an interpersonal checklist, before and after ratings on the effectiveness of the course as obtained through a special scale, and the review of the notes by a nonparticipant observer, focusing on the understanding of cases and changes in the understanding of these cases by the nurses over time. The findings were statistically significant. Nurses in the program showed an increased awareness of family involvement and family interactions in the cases described at the end of the consultation as compared with prior to consultation. Greater emphasis was shown on prevention. The nurses, after the course, were closer to a mental health view and seemed to have a better idea as to why they were referring cases. However, the greatest effects, as reported by the nurses, were in the areas of nursing knowledge, nursing practice and attitude toward a patient, with the least effects in the areas of professional relationship, private and social life, and the attitude of the patient toward the nurse. Reviewing cases presented toward the end of the course as compared with the beginning showed greater understanding of the case. The interpersonal checklist used to obtain a picture of changes of self-image in the nurse did not change. Thus, increased skill in early case finding, the ability to utilize psychiatric consultation more effectively, and the ability to integrate results into an improved understanding of cases were demonstrated.

The two investigations of Caplan's conceptual model of consultation were by Caplan himself and Newfield. Caplan (1970) found that when compared to a control group, the consultation techniques of theme interference reduction, unlinking, education and support/reassurance increased the nurses' objectivity in cases. The technique of theme interference reduction improved objectivity in significantly greater numbers when compared to other consultation techniques.

Newfield (1972), using a very sophisticated research design—eight a priori hypotheses, control groups, multitract-multimethod validity analyses —studied six consultation groups (total of 42 members), which were led by four consultants using a Caplan model for 1 1/2 hour sessions over a 5-week period. Measurements were made in four areas: knowledge, skill, confidence and objectivity. Six tests were administered on a prepost basis to measure the above areas. Self and supervisory ratings were also used. The results showed that data on the pre-post measures were in the expected direction with four of the six measures changing significantly. However, the supervisors rated the nurses in the control group as significantly more improved than the nurses in the experimental group. The conclusions drawn by the author were that all the nurses improved over time, but consultation seemed to accelerate the process in the areas of objectivity, skill and application of knowledge.

In summary, eight of the ten studies which focused on consultee functioning demonstrated some type of change in professional functioning. By and large, the studies seem to have shown that consultation is effective in the areas of increasing sensitivity and understanding and in improving skills related to functioning on the job.

II. Studies of Change in the System

Studies which focus on change in the system are rare. Even though there seems to be greater emphasis placed upon system change through consultation in recent years, evaluation of such change poses considerable problems and is a definite challenge to the ingenuity of the investigator. For the purposes of this review we have classified two studies as investigations of change in a system even though they are on markedly different levels with one far removed from the mental health area.

Foster and Hartman (1959), through "voluntary" consultation to dietary and personnel administrators in 33 general hospitals, attempted to raise the quality of dietary services using a checklist to assist dietetic administrators. They evaluated the hospital before and after the consultation program. They also tried to compare the voluntary consultation with consultation services given by State agencies and by private service firms. (The authors indicated that the voluntary consultation lacked the financial involvement through fees that the private service firm had, and the sanction of licensing implied by governmental regulatory agencies.) Although there was no control group, the authors felt that the consistency of the changes suggested more than circumstantial evidence of the program's value. They also concluded that voluntary consultations were at least as effective as those given by State agencies or private firms.

The second study is by Berk (1971) who looked at changes in teacher-child interaction after a 4-month consultation period. Two models of consultation were employed: The first was Caplan's consultee-centered case consultation; the second combined the Caplan approach with results of projective test data on the child which were made available to the consultant. There was a control group. Consultation was provided by two school psychologists to four eighth-grade teachers who had six classroom groups of Mexican-American children. Observations of teacher-child dyadic classroom interaction were obtained at the beginning, middle and end of the consultation period using the Brophy-Good coding system. The findings failed to show that either consultation method had a significant effect on teacher-child interaction.

III. Studies of Change in the Client

Demonstrating change in client behavior is more difficult than that of demonstrating change in the consultee, inasmuch as the client is one step removed from the primary help-giving source being investigated, i.e., the consultant. However, studies in this area are crucial in determining whether the ultimate objectives of consultation are realized. The main areas of change studied were academic performance or some type of behavior change ranging from specific change (anxiety level) to more general personality change. Some studies have combined the two.

A. Changes in Academic Performance

Ginther (1963) and Payne (1964) in similar studies tried to evaluate the effectiveness of two different methods used by science consultants in elementary schools. The criterion of change was improvement in the students' achievement tests. Two groups were used, one where the science consultant worked only with the teachers in planning the unit, and the second where the consultant talked to students directly once a week, with the regular teacher following up the consultant's work during the remainder of the week. In the first study, the author found that there was greater learning in the students when the consultant worked only with the teacher. In the second study (Payne 1964) neither method had any advantage over the other in terms of student achievement. These conflicting results may have been due to two differences in the studies: (1) In the second study the roles of the teachers were reversed from the first study, i.e., the teachers who originally worked only with the consultant in the planning of work now followed up the consultant after he worked directly with the students, and vice versa. This may have had an effect on teaching effectiveness, particularly if one role was preferred over the other; (2) in the first study the subject matter content was "light" and in the second it was "electricity." Hence, there may have been a change in the complexity of the subject and in the teacher's familiarity with it.

In a college setting, Bolman, Halleck, Rice and Ryan (1969) set up a consultation program that consisted of group meetings between house fellows in university dormitories and university psychiatric and psychological counseling faculty. Their aim was to increase the house fellows' sensitivity to problems in the dormitory. The experimental dormitory contained 567 women and 567 men, mostly freshmen and sophomores. A dormitory not given this service was used as a control. The effects of the program were measured by comparing academic performance, number of visits made to a variety of campus service agencies, withdrawals, and dropouts. Although no significant differences were found, the intervention did intensify a conflict between the house fellows and the administrative personnel (who were not included in the program). The authors felt that this negative affect caused by the intervention program may have neutralized any positive gains. This study clearly points to the necessity of working with the entire social system in planning and implementing a consultation program.

Davis (1972) investigated the effect of consultation as well as other techniques on student computational and reading skills, on attitudes of students toward school, peer social acceptance, teacher ratings of student behavior, and on student self-esteem. The experimental consultation group received 20 biweekly, 45-minute presentations of selected mental health materials from the classroom teacher who received consultation from a guidance specialist. A pre-post design was utilized with a control group which received no mental health presentations. The results revealed that the consultation group was significantly higher than the control group on peer social acceptance, but there were no significant differences on any of the other measures.

B. Changes in Behavior

Eisenberg's (1958) study of what he termed psychiatric consultation to the welfare department was the first evaluation of a consultation program found in the literature. The specific nature of the consultation was diagnostic. Highly skilled mental health personnel were employed to diagnose the child, but the treatment was left to others in the agency. The clinical staff who had done the diagnostic (with the psychiatrist as head of the team) were also available to help in determining strategies for treatment. Forty-eight children were studied during the first year. A comparison was made of the outcome of the cases where the treatment plan was not followed and in the cases where the treatment plan was followed. The results showed that the number of cases that improved was significantly greater for those in which the plan was carried out. Despite certain limitations in measurements, such as the imprecise clinical distinction between the categories ("improved"—"unimproved"), the authors were extremely impressed by the significance of this combination of direct and indirect service.

Two evaluations of what was called unit group mental health consultation in the military service have been reported. In the earliest, Chapman (1966) followed the performance of enlisted men who had received unit group mental health consultation. However, no control group was used. (Unit group consultation was consultation in which mental hygiene technicians functioned as consultants to unit commanding officers, assisting them in coping with behavior problems in their command.) The study attempted to determine the subsequent performance of 316 enlisted men. Six to 12 weeks after the consultation, the military performance of these men was reported as satisfactory or better in two-thirds of the cases. The second study, reported by Conner and Thoresen (1972), evaluated the effects of unit group mental health consultation and a comparison group given a traditional type service program (primarily psychiatric screening and referral). It was believed that the consultation program would significantly reduce unit rates of AWOLs, court martials, Article 15s, and requests for mental health service. After 6 months the evidence was inconclusive in support of the program's predicted impact. This technique, i.e., unit group consultation, appears to be midway between consultation as defined by the mental health professions and direct service.

Hunter and Ratcliffe (1968) did a 1-year followup of cases seen in mental health consultation at a community mental health center. The consultee was asked to rate whether the social adjustment or symptomatic behavior was better, the same, or worse at the end of the consultation than upon referral. The aim was to base the rating on the client's observed behavior toward people in his environment: family members, peers, friends or caretakers. Despite the lack of checks on reliability, the data showed that the distributions of the outcome (better, same, worse) were not significantly different from the results of direct clinical service: fewer than 10% were rated "worse." Although further research is needed to substantiate this finding, as the authors point out, the results are encouraging. If consultation is found to be as effective as direct clinical services, the advantages of consultation are clear since it is less expensive, as well as more efficient in the use of scarce professional manpower.

Finally, two studies investigated the relative effects of counseling and consultation on elementary school children. After a 12-week experimental period, Lewis (1969) found that consultation had a positive effect upon teachers' perceptions of the achievement-oriented behavior of students. However, it was not effective in changing sociometric status or personal adjustment variables. The second study, by Thurlow (1971), had a 7-week experimental period. His findings showed that neither the counseling nor the consultation groups differed significantly from the control group in their ability to lessen anxiety in the student.

The studies discussed above all show that the positive effects of consultation on the client are far from clear. Neither academic achievement nor behavior was changed in any consistent way as a result of consultation. Whether this is due to the problems inherent in conducting research on subjects who are not directly influenced by the experimental variable, to our lack of understanding of the linkage between the consultant, the consultee and the client, or to actual difficulties in effecting change indirectly is unclear at the present time.

IV. Studies of Change on a Combination of Levels

Nine studies investigated the effect of consultation on a combination of elements. As one might expect, most focused on the consultee and the client.

However, there are two excellent studies that dealt with changes in all three elements—consultee, client and system.

A. Changes in Consultee, Client, and System

Schmuck (1968) undertook a very careful study of the effects of consultation on classrooms, teachers, and students. The consultants (mental health personnel), who unfortunately had little experience with consultation to teachers, attempted to assist teachers with classroom coping through small group discussions, visits to the classroom, and individual conferences. All contacts were problem-oriented and centered around classroom processes and how the teachers might improve group interactions within the classrooms. The consultants were assigned one to a school for half a day each week for 15 weeks. Forty teachers (in the experimental group) received consultation, and 20 teachers (controls) from another school did not. The problems around which discussions were focused were primarily problems of self-esteem, learning difficulties, and interpersonal problems.

Schmuck evaluated changes in the teachers (the consultees), changes in the students (the clients), and changes in the classroom (the system). Changes in teachers were determined through anecdotal materials and through four questionnaires. The anecdotal material showed that the teachers at the end of the program were better able to ask each other for help and use each other to talk over problems, trade materials, and respond to the new ideas. They also developed a strong group feeling with a new sense of challenge and interest, and reported greater leeway in accepting students' behavior and in dealing with individual differences. The questionnaire results revealed significant changes in the experimental teachers' perceptions of themselves as teachers, their cognitions of mental health categories (greater realization of the emotional problems and their diversity), and better views on how problematic situations in the classrooms could be handled. There was no significant change in categorizing students when the experimental teachers were compared with the controls.

Changes in the students in the classrooms were also studied. In both the consultation and comparison groups the students were administered four questionnaires to determine whether group processes in the classrooms changed and whether their attitudes toward school and self improved. No improvement was found in any of the student areas as a result of the consultation. Group processes also were unaffected by the consultation process. Thus, cognitive and attitudinal changes did occur in the teachers, but it was clear that there were no accompanying behavioral changes, changes in the classroom group processes, or changes in the students' attitudes. Schmuck's study brings up a very important issue. What is the relationship between cognitive and attitudinal change in teachers and overt behavioral changes in students?

A second study, which focused on change in consultee, client and the system, was that of Keutzer, Fosmire, Diller, and Smith (1971). These authors were concerned with changes similar to that of Schmuck and were alert to the fact that changes in self-perceived teacher behavior are not necessarily translated into observable behavior. Using a new high school scheduled to open in the fall of a particular year, the authors involved all staff in a 2-week summer workshop. In the first week the focus was on skill building and personal growth through participation in inquiry groups and general sessions aimed at imparting communication skills. During the second week the focus was on real-life problems and consisted of analyzing decisionmaking styles, force-field analysis, problem-solving task, representative decisionmaking, developing alternatives to traditional school structure, and equalizing levels of participation among group members. A similar school also scheduled to open for the first time in the fall, served as a control. A 25-item Situation Prediction Questionnaire was administered to the staff, as well as the student body four times during school year, including once before the workshop began. This instrument allowed the staff to predict their own behavior in several areas, such as dealing with co-workers in a candid manner, attempting innovations in teaching, encouraging open expression and management of conflict, etc. The results showed that when compared with the control school, teachers in the experimental school exhibited significantly greater interpersonal openness and acceptance of conflict. To examine more closely the perception-behavior relationship, students were asked to observe and describe the teaching environment of the two schools to determine if actual behavior changes had occurred. In addition, a 40-item Environment Description Questionnaire was administered to assess the expectations and preferences of students regarding various aspects of school life. These findings, which also turned out to be significant, revealed that students saw the faculty as more receptive. They also saw themselves as more responsible and co-active with the staff in making decisions affecting their learning, developed stronger feelings of responsibility toward fellow students and faculty, and developed stronger student-enforced norms bearing on behavior in unsupervised areas. Observations and anecdotal data in such areas as intra-faculty relationships, student-faculty relationships, student-student relationships, and general staff-school relationships tended to confirm the results of the tests.

B. Changes in Consultee Functioning and Client Behavior

Seven studies combined consultee change along with client change. The approaches in these studies are similar to those described above which dealt with these two factors, consultee and client, separately. Of these seven, two large scale, comprehensive studies were in school settings, three studies were directed specifically at teacher functioning and student behavior, and two studies focused on community agencies.

The two comprehensive studies, Cutler and McNeil (1964) and Kellam and Schiff (1967) were similar in that they both worked with a variety of school personnel, such as teachers and administrators, as well as students and parents. Although the actual physical settings were very different (one being a planned, suburban community, and the other an inner-city, poverty area), their goals were similar. Cutler and McNeil aimed at helping school personnel handle classroom problems and improving the general mental hygiene atmosphere of the school. Theirs was an extraordinarily intense program covering many levels of functioning of the school. Parents, children, teachers and administrators were given questionnaires to evaluate the effectiveness of the program. There were no control groups for teachers or parents. However, a small group consisting of ten teachers, eight special services personnel and six administrators, were identified as being more intensively exposed to consultation and were compared to a larger matched group. Analysis showed that for the school personnel in general, 16 of the 43 variables changed significantly. Improvement was noted in the staff's understanding of personal relationship with colleagues, and in their self-described overall effectiveness. Teachers seemed to have a stronger, more assertive and forceful view of themselves and appeared to have achieved greater general comfort and self-satisfaction. Although the findings regarding the participants who were more exposed to consultation were presented mainly in tabular form without statistical tests of significance, the authors thought that these participants benefited substantially more than the larger groups, especially in increased flexibility in their relationships with children, increased openness in interpersonal relationships, and in their tendency to judge fewer children as serious classroom problems. For the parents, 12 of 56 variables showed significant positive change in the direction which seemed to reflect a more mature parental role. Comparisons between children in the experimental group and those in a control group on 19 variables indicated more children with significant positive change in the control group than in the experimental group.

Kellam and Schiff had three main elements to their program which was focused on the first grade: (1) School staff meetings which involved meetings of mental health professionals with the principal, assistant principal, adjustment teacher, and all the first grade teachers in the six experimental schools. The goal here was to consider issues having relevance to a first grader's capacity to advance to the second grade; (2) Classroom meetings with a mental health specialist, the first grade teachers, and a group of severely maladapted students. Here the aim was to involve the children in discussions regarding the importance of the first grade and the importance of being as successful as they could on first grade tasks; (3) Parent meetings which included all of the parents of the first grade children in the experimental schools. Focus of these meetings was to introduce the parents to the nature of the tasks of first grade, to talk about the importance for the child to be as successful as possible on these tasks, and to discuss any problems they or the school had with the class.

To evaluate the program, teachers from the experimental schools and control schools (matched on selected criteria) rated their students' adaptation to school. Ratings of three successive first-grade classes showed that the teachers from the experimental schools developed higher expectations for their students, while the ratings of teachers from control schools showed no such change. The authors' interpretation of their findings was that the consulting program had helped teachers to become more sensitive to maladaptive behavior. A followup after 2 years indicated that there was a significant change toward greater adaptation in the experimental schools, while the control schools moved toward greater maladaptation.

Another approach to studying both consultee and client change focuses only on teachers and their students. Two studies were concerned with helping teachers deal with classroom problem situations: Trione (1967) used school psychologists to help teachers assume an attitude of psychological exploration, while Whitley (1970) tried to assist teachers in learning to use social reinforcements. In a third study, Bjork (1970) attempted to change the curriculum implementation practices of teachers. His focus, however, was on student achievement and learning rather than on behavior problems in the classroom. All three of these studies used control groups.

Trione found significant differences in achievement tests and a guidance scale between the experimental and the control classes in both teachers and students. His results seemed to reflect the systematic and intense efforts made to encourage the teachers to make their own evaluations in light of new knowledge, rewarding new attitudes aimed at understanding the psychological reasons for a specific student's behavior, rather than seeing student behavior as personal threats or willful and vicious attempts to disrupt the classroom. Whitley used an innovative approach in his study. Teachers viewed videotapes of their interactions with students while receiving consultation. The control group also reviewed tapes but without the benefit of consultation. Change was measured by analysis of behavior in new videotapes made subsequent to the consultation experience as compared with the first taped session. The results indicated that teachers in both the experimental group and the control group significantly increased their reinforcement of desirable student behaviors. However, neither group significantly reduced their reinforcement of undesirable behavior, although more such reduction occurred in the experimental group than in the control. Nevertheless, students in the experimental group significantly reduced their undesirable classroom behaviors, while those in the control group did not.

Bjork studies the effectiveness of a curriculum consultant who provided consultation to teachers during a 6-week science unit of instruction. Data were collected by means of an observational checklist, a questionnaire, and a post-test of pupil learning. The findings showed that the experimental teachers implemented their curriculum to a significantly higher degree than teachers in the control group, and had significantly higher perceptions of their curriculum implementation practices. Also found was a significant difference in pupil achievement in the experimental as compared with the control groups.

Two further studies combining change in the consultee and change in the client took place in community agency settings. Townes, Lytle, Wagner and Wimberger (1968) studied the effectiveness of brief, intensive diagnostic evaluations of children done by a mental health team. Twenty-seven cases referred by general practitioners were seen by the diagnostic team who made recommendations for help. A questionnaire was then sent out to the referring physicians and to the parents (father and mother separately) to determine the effectiveness of the program. Ninety-five percent of the physicians who returned the questionnaire felt that the program was helpful; although they felt it was least effective in teaching techniques for the handling of the child and his parents. A large number of parents found the diagnostic consultation helpful. The parents' report of the degree of assistance to the child was independent of the child's age, the family's socio-economic status, or the presenting symptoms. The parents felt that the consultations were less helpful to the child than to themselves, and that they wished for more information on etiology, what to do with their child's problem, and where to go within the community. The child was not seen independently to determine if there indeed were any changes in his behavior. Rather, all information on the child was obtained from the parents. No independent measures were taken of either the practitioners' handling of cases or the possible changes in the parents. All the questions focused on whether or not the service was perceived by these individuals as being helpful. Thus, it was more a measure of satisfaction than change. No control groups were used. A secondary finding, in conflict with the feeling of being helpful, was that over half of the patients never returned to the physician for further treatment after they were seen for diagnostic evaluations, despite the need for further help. Thirty-seven percent received no treatment elsewhere in the community. Thus, measurements of satisfaction may have little or no relationship to behavior.

Ulmer and Kupferman (1970) looked at psychiatric consultation in a vocationally-oriented social welfare agency over a 3-year period. Seventy-one consultations with one psychiatrist were studied, and a detailed followup was made of 11 males and four female clients. Their report was mainly clinical-impressionistic and did not use a control group. The findings failed to show that consultation was of any value either in improving the caliber of professional functioning of consultees, or in helping those clients who were discussed in consultation.

In summary, the above studies were far more successful in demonstrating change in both the client system and the consultee system than were those that focused separately on these areas. All but one showed change in the consultee, and five of the nine showed change in the client. Furthermore, one study was able to demonstrate change in all three areas—the consultee, the system, and the client.

Summary

A look at all of the studies listed in table 1 reveals that the change evaluated breaks down as follows:

Focus on consultee	14 studies
Focus on client	10 studies
Focus on system	2 studies
Focus on consultee, client and system	2 studies
Focus on consultee and client	7 studies

Of the total of 35 studies, positive change of some kind was demonstrated in 24 or approximately 69%. Out of the 23 studies that focused on consultee change either separately or in combination with other factors, 17, or approximately 74% showed statistically significant changes. Of the 19 studies that focused on change in the client, either separately or in combination with other factors, 11, or approximately 58% reported positive change. Finally, positive change was shown in two of the four studies which focused on system change, either alone or in combination with other factors.

In summary, the evidence available indicates that consultation as a method of professional practice has been shown to effect change. Moreover, the changes have been brought about on several levels—the consultee level, the client level, and the system level.

Conclusion

Although in the studies reviewed above there are often wide differences in the situations labeled as consultation with wide diversity of definitions, the evidence appears to indicate that consultation as a technique of intervention does have a positive effect. While there continues to be a dire need for studies which build cumulatively on earlier ones so as to provide comparable data instead of a conglomerate of isolated findings, there is much to suggest that progress is being made in the evaluation of consultation.

The more recent studies, as mentioned earlier, are becoming increasingly sophisticated. The use of controls or a comparison group of some sort is now more the rule than the exception. There are more theoretically-based studies, and more studies which test hypotheses. There is a gradual attempt to apply conceptual gains, such as in the area of defining different types of consultation. As a result, the questions asked are no longer broad, but instead are more narrow and more meaningful from a research point of view. Although not reviewed in this paper, there are a few studies which are beginnning to link process variables to outcome variables (Norman and Forti 1972; Mannino 1972; Robbins, Spencer, Frank 1970).

All these facts indicate that progress is being made, although such progress has been slow. However, minor gains are preferable to major fallacies. We see a need for more in-depth studies that could attempt to delineate process variables and relate these to change variables. Also, we continue to see the need for multivariate studies to evaluate different levels of change in relationship to other factors, such as how the consultees' views and expectations of consultation affect outcome, or how experienced consultants and inexperienced consultants have different effects, etc. In the final analysis, the more we can delimit the population studied, specify the activities performed, and use multilevel outcome variables, the more meaningful, and therefore more valuable, the results.

References

Bennis, W.G. Theory and method in applying behavorial science to planned organizational change. *Journal of Applied Behavioral Science,* 1(4):337–360, 1965.

Berk, M.R. Effects of mental health consultation on teacher-child interaction. *Dissertation Abstracts International,* 33(1):186–A, 1972.

Bjork, W.E. A study of the influence of the role of the curriculum consultant on curriculum implementation. *Dissertation Abstracts International,* 31(7):3404–A, 1971.

Bolman, W.M.; Halleck, S.L.; Rice, D.G.; and Ryan, M.L. An unintended side effect in a community psychiatric program. *Archives of General Psychiatry,* 20:508–513, 1969.

Caplan, G. *The Theory and Practice of Mental Health Consultation.* New York: Basic Books, 1970. pp. 308–327.

Chapman, R.F. Group mental health consultation—Report of a military field program. *Military Medicine,* 131:30–35, 1966.

Conner, D.R., and Thoresen, A.R. Observations of a mental health command consultation program. *Military Medicine,* 137(4):152–155, 1972.

Cutler, R.L., and McNeil, E.B. *Mental Health Consultation in Schools: A Research Analysis.* Ann Arbor: Department of Psychology, University of Michigan, 1966.

Davis, K.M. An experimental study of group procedures using the elementary guidance worker, consulted teacher, and nonconsulted teacher to present selected mental health materials to rural fourth grade students. *Dissertation Abstracts International,* 33(2):566–A, 1972.

Deloughery, G.W.; Neuman, B.M.; and Gebbie, K.M. Mental health consultation as a means of improving problem-solving ability in work groups: A pilot study. *Comparative Group Studies,* 3(1):89–97, 1972.

Dorsey, J.R.; Matsunaga, G.; and Bauman, G. Training public health nurses in mental health. *Archives of General Psychiatry,* 11:214–222, 1964.

Eisenberg, L. An evaluation of psychiatric consultation service for a public agency. *American Journal of Public Health,* 48:742–749, 1958.

Fisher, R.J. Third party consultation between high school students and teachers. Vols. 1 and 2. *Dissertation Abstracts International,* 33(11):6447–A, 1973.

Foster, J.T., and Hartman, J. A project in voluntary consultation for hospitals. *Public Health Reports,* 74:607–614, 1959.

Friedlander, F. A comparative study of consulting processes and group development. *Journal of Applied Behavioral Science,* 4:377–399, 1968.

Ginther, J.R. Achievement in sixth grade science associated with two instructional roles of science consultants. *Journal of Educational Research,* 57:28–33, 1963.

Goldmeier, J. Applying a general systems approach to consultation in public welfare. *Public Welfare,* 29(3):316–319, 1971.

Hommen, D.L. An assessment of the effects of a community mental health center laboratory training-education-consultation program in bereavement ministry for parish clergymen. *Dissertation Abstracts International,* 33(4):1818–A, 1972.

Hunter, W.F., and Ratcliffe, A.W. The Range Mental Health Center: Evaluation of a community oriented mental health consultation program in Northern Minnesota. *Community Mental Health Journal,* 4:260–267, 1968.

Iscoe, I.; Pierce-Jones, J.; Friedman, S.T.; and McGehearty, L. Some strategies in mental health consultation: A brief description of a project and some preliminary results. In: Cowen; E.L.; Gardner, E.A.; and Zax, M., eds. *Emergent approaches to mental health problems.* New York: Appleton-Century-Crofts, 1967. pp. 307–330.

Kellam, S.G., and Schiff, S.K. *Adaptation and Mental Illness in the First-Grade Classrooms of an Urban Community.* Washington, D.C. American Psychiatric Association, Psychiatric Research Report #21: Poverty and Mental Health, 1967. pp. 79–91.

Kelly, J.G. A quest for valid interventions. In: Spielberger, C. ed. *Current Topics in Clinical and Community Psychology.* New York: Academic Press, 1970. pp. 183–207.

Keutzer, C.S.; Fosmire, F.R.; Diller, R.; and Smith, M.D. Laboratory training in a new social system: Evaluation of a consulting relationship with a high school faculty. *Journal of Applied Behavorial Science,* 7(4):493–501, 1971.

Lewis, M.D. A study of the relative effects of counseling and consultation upon personal and social adjustment, sociometric status, and achievement-oriented behavior of third grade children. *Dissertation Abstracts International,* 31(2):609–A, 1970.

Linoff, M.G. An investigation of attitudes of teachers toward student problem behavior using behavior modification and consultation groups. *Dissertation Abstracts International,* 33(4): 1517–A, 1972.

Mannino, F.V. Task accomplishment and consultation outcome. *Community Mental Health Journal,* 8(2):102–108, 1972.

Mariner, A.S.; Brandt, E.; Stone, E.C.; and Mirmow, E.L. Group psychiatric consultation with public school personnel: A two-year study. *Personnel Guidance Journal,* 40: 254–258, 1961.

Meacham, M.L. The school psychologist: "Classroom Consultant in Behavioral Techniques." Paper presented to American Psychological Association, Washington, D.C., September 3–7, 1971.

Miller, W.B. Psychiatric consultation: Part 1. A general systems approach. *Psychiatry in Medicine,* 4(2):135–145, 1973.

Newfield, N.L. An evaluation of mental health consultation for public health nurses. *Dissertation Abstracts International,* 33(5):2352–B, 1972.

Norman, E.C., and Forti, T.J. A study of the process and the outcome of mental health consultation. *Community Mental Health Journal,* 8(4):261–270, 1972.

Payne, A. Achievement in sixth grade science associated with two instructional roles of science consultants. *Journal of Educational Research,* 57:350–354, 1964.

Pierce-Jones, J.; Iscoe, I.; and Cunningham, G. *Child Behavior Consultation in Elementary Schools: A Demonstration and Research Program.* Austin: University of Texas, 1968.

Randolph, D.L. Behavioral consultation as a means of improving the quality of a counseling program. *School Counselor*, 20(1):30–35, 1972.

Robbins, P.R.; Spencer, E.C.; and Frank, D.A. Some factors influencing the outcome of consultation. *American Journal of Public Health*, 60(3):524–534, 1970.

Schmuck, R.A. Helping teachers improve classroom group processes. *Journal of Applied Behavioral Science*, 4:401–435, 1968.

Simmons, A.J. "Consultation Through a Community Mental Health Agency." Paper presented at the American Psychological Association, Chicago, Illinois, 1960.

Teitelbaum, D.I. "An Evaluation of an Experimental Program of Assistance for Newly Appointed Teachers in Certain Elementary Schools of New York City." Doctoral dissertation, New York University, New York, 1961.

Thurlow, B.H. A comparative analysis of the elementary counseling role and the elementary consultant role with selected anxious fifth grade students. *Dissertation Abstracts International*, 32(8):4362–A, 1972.

Townes, B.D.; Lytle, C.E.; Wagner, N.N.; and Wimberger, H.C. The diagnostic consultation and rural community mental health programs. *Community Mental Health Journal*, 4:157–163, 1968.

Trione, V. The school psychologist, teacher change and fourth grade reading achievement. *California Journal of Educational Research*, 18:194–200, 1967.

Tyler, M.M. A study of some selected parameters of school psychologist-teacher consultation. *Dissertation Abstracts International*, 32(10):5626–A, 1972.

Ulmer, R. A., and Kupferman, S.C. An empirical study of the process and outcome of psychiatric consultation. *Journal of Clinical Psychology*, 26(3):323–326, 1970.

Whitley, A.D. Counselor-teacher consultations including video analysis to reduce undesirable student responses. *Dissertation Abstracts International*, 31(10):5142–A, 1971.

Woody, R.H., and Woody, J.D. Behavioral science consultation. *Personnel Journal*, 50(5):382–391, 1971.

Young, C.E. The effects of three consultation models on individual and group decision making. *Dissertation Abstracts International*, 32(4):2413–B, 1971.

Zacker, J.; Rutter, E.; and Bard, M. Evaluation of attitudinal changes in a program of community consultation. *Community Mental Health Journal*, 7(3):236–241, 1971.

The Practice of Mental Health Consultation in a Variety of Community Settings

3

Working With the Juvenile Police—A Possible Role for the Psychologist in Community Mental Health*

Robert S. Shellow and J. R. Newbrough

This paper describes a working relationship between two psychologists in a community mental health agency and the six juvenile officers of a local police department. We will not only illustrate what specifically transpired over a 2-year period of participant observation, but will also attempt to articulate the insights to which these field observations led us.

From the very beginning, we have been impressed by the difference between the philosophies underlying mental health activities and law enforcement. In the mental health movement, as in psychotherapy, the basic value is a humanistic respect for the individual and his capacity to assume responsibility for his actions. In contrast, the police are concerned with maintaining an ordered society. They are representatives of societal authority which takes control away from the nonresponsible, nonsocial person, as well as others who threaten the social order.

Police officers learn to assume an authoritarian, dogmatic, moralistic posture, which is always available as a response to the complex, socially disturbing human action encountered in their everyday work. Reinforcement of a moralistic stand comes from fellow police officers who voice the prevalent societal reaction to criminality, i.e., anger, righteous indignation, and demand for retribution.

On the other hand, it has been our experience that police officers are sensitive to the plight of the individuals they apprehend. With two divergent responses available, a value conflict may be experienced to some degree by all policemen. Ordinarily, an officer can keep this conflict out of con-

*Presented at the Seventh Inter-American Congress of Psychology, Mexico City, December 1961.

scious awareness by assuming a suppressive approach in his role as policeman. There are, however, circumstances which make avoidance of the conflict difficult.

One such circumstance, we have learned, is when the police officer is confronted by a mental health worker. Mental health evokes the stereotypes of sympathy and do-goodism which threaten to reawaken the value conflict.

Another situation activating the conflict is when a police officer is assigned to special work with children. The juvenile officer, as he is called, not only is charged with protecting society, but must also deal effectively and appropriately with children and their families. Children, unlike adult offenders, evoke hope; that is, they are seen as yet able to learn responsibility, they are not easily typed as criminals. This places the juvenile officer in the midst of the value conflict which the regular officer can easily sidestep by fulfilling his securely structured role.[1]

In addition, we have observed that the mental health worker, for his part, is threatened by the policeman. The use of force as opposed to verbal, intellectual means as legitimate aggressive outlets for hostility may create considerable anxiety, if not confusion, in the mental health worker. As a result, he may not be clear as to the necessity for law enforcement action, especially where individuality may be threatened by suppressive action.

In the face of this mutual threat, how is it possible for these two camps ever to join forces? One point of communality between the two is that the juvenile police officer and the psychologist in community mental health are deviants from the mainstream of their respective professions. They deviate toward each other.

The psychologist has stepped out of the office, the clinic, and the laboratory;[2] the juvenile officer has stepped into the realm of family counseling and the preventive use of his interpersonal skills. Both find a common

---

1. One finds in looking at police work a curious dualism. On the one hand, there is the military structure of the station organization, and, on the other, the very unstructured area and situations within which the individual officers operate.

The very fluidity of the police officer's everyday work seems to lead him to search for anchors (symbols of absolutes such as gun and badge) and ways of structuring things (whistle-blowing, lining people up, etc.). His major fear is loss of control.

The structuring of situations (categorizing, stereotyping) enables him to deal with many situations, whether he understands them or not.

2. The psychologist, exploring the implications of the community mental health philosophy, finds himself closer in his concern to the juvenile officer than his more traditional colleagues. He is no longer exclusively committed to helping people by psychotherapy, but has begun to experiment with social intervention. This has proceeded from an increasing conviction that society is the relevant backdrop for deviant behavior; that responsibility for dealing with the socially deviant is shared by a number of societal institutions. It is, therefore, appropriate to relate directly to the police as one such institution. This trend is documented in a reference guide by the Harvard Medical School and Psychiatric Service, Massachusetts General Hospital.

ground in their interest in the family; and, perhaps, it is here that they speak the same language.

The Development of a Relationship

In the case of the program under discussion here, the following events are significant in the natural history of the development of this apparently unique relationship.

A psychologist from the Mental Health Study Center met with the Chief of Probation to discuss the county police department. Unlike the police of large metropolitan centers, county police departments must cope with the mushrooming populations of suburbia. Though they are organized along the lines of a metropolitan force, the county police deal with a unique situation. The psychologist was particularly interested in how children were handled in such a department.

The Chief of Probation who had been, along with the Inspector of Police, a prime mover in the establishment of a juvenile squad within the police department, encouraged the psychologist's interest and suggested that he meet the six officers of the newly formed squad in the county. The Chief served as a go-between, describing the psychologist as a sympathetic, interested person to the officers and describing the officers as equally interested in the psychologist and what he had to offer.

At the first meeting, the officers appeared to be quite impressed by this "doctor" who showed interest in them. They had popular stereotypes about what such an expert could offer them. There were many comments such as: "We certainly could learn a lot from you, doc." "We sure need someone like you around to tell us about these crazy kids."—and so on. The psychologist insisted that he had come to learn; that he wasn't at all sure they could use his understandings or techniques in their special situation. His experience had been in making therapeutic and administrative decisions about youth in a correctional setting, and to some extent in an outpatient psychiatric clinic; but this, he felt, did not qualify him in the handling of delinquents at large. For the moment, at least, the officers brushed this disclaimer aside as a modest gesture.

Nevertheless, he was invited to ride along in the police car, to observe and, specifically, to tell the men how they were performing. The invitation to ride was accepted, and over a period of 15 months, on some dozen separate occasions, he accompanied the officers on their daily and nightly duties. Trouble spots, street corners, parking lots were checked and rechecked. Dances and teen clubs were visited. Gang fights were anticipated and skillfully averted. Suspects of car theft, housebreaking, robbery, assault, and arson were interrogated. Family after family was seen at the police station and at home for conferences about their child in trouble. Arrangements were made for abandoned children and infants. The list continues and each visit revealed a broader perspective of this special officer's responsibilities.[3] During these extended contacts with the officers, the following observations were made:

One fact became evident immediately. The officers perceived a considerable gap in status between themselves and the psychologist. If these men were to feel comfortable enough to reveal their personal feelings and thoughts about their work, and expose their competencies as well as their felt inadequacies to the psychologist, this status gap had to be overcome in some way. It was up to the psychologist, with his higher status, to take responsibility for closing the gap without being either patronizing or condescending.[4]

Early contacts with the officers were marked by their attempts to determine whether the psychologist really was sympathetic; whether he would be easily shocked by their language or their often callous character assassinations of the children they were supposed to be understanding and helping. In this manner, the officers behaved somewhat like adolescents toward the psychologist. Here the relationship between officer and psychologist hung in the balance; for had the psychologist responded with moral indignation to what he might describe as the uncouth sentiments of his new associate, the status gap would have been rapidly reinstituted and the distance between the two camps widened.

As the months passed, initial testing abated, and the interactions between the psychologist and the officers became much more informal and friendly. The psychologist sensed that it was something of a distinction to have the "Doc" riding in the squad car. A great deal was learned about the county and the social habits and habitats of its youth. The psychologist was often asked to observe an officer interviewing a child and comment on the "technique." The problem was to choose what comments would be appropriate, and where to make a contribution.

The men seemed to be experts in interrogation of children as well as in anticipating group movements, gang fights, and where to expect trouble in a community. The officers were also unusually adept in relating quickly to adolescents and gaining their confidence. Against all this, it seemed inappropriate to try to train these policemen in the image of psychologist; to teach and develop diagnostic and therapeutic skills.[5]

---

3. For more extensive discussion of the recommended roles, duties, and training of the child specialist in police departments, *see* Kenny and Pursuit (1954).

4. In an analysis of American English as used in American plays, a Boston business firm, and by business executives from various sectors of the United States, Brown and Ford (1961) conclude that "in the progression towards intimacy of unequals (in status) the superior is always the pacesetter initiating new moves in that direction."

5. Caplan (1959) in his discussion of mental health consultation makes a strong point that mental health workers should help the consultee to solve problems in his own way, and not to teach him the values of the mental health worker which will likely be inappropriate in his setting.

Travelling with one officer and then another, the psychologist became involved in lengthy discussions of children, community problems, and the officers' struggles with their unique role. Their usual communications were informal and never came to grips with these basic issues.

Perhaps here was a place where a contribution could be made. Drawing upon an academic frame of reference, the psychologist suggested the establishment of a "seminar." All six officers were warmly in favor of it. The mechanics of setting up such a discussion group was another matter, fraught with the seemingly insurmountable obstacle of time. Time, to police officers working long hours, is no easy matter. In addition, and more important, the one indispensable sanction for the development of the seminar was lacking; the approval that had to come from top police administration. The relationship had been established, but only on an informal basis. A formal, time-consuming, "official" activity required approval by superior officers within the police department. The seminar, therefore, was not immediately realized.

Surprisingly, the idea appeared several months later in a meeting of the advisory board of the county mental health clinic. The Inspector of Police mentioned that his juvenile officers could use a seminar on how to deal with families. The associate director of the Mental Health Study Center, present at this meeting, brought the information back to the psychologist. He, and an interested colleague, contacted the inspector and made arrangements for a planning session.

The Seminar Takes Shape

After two such planning sessions with the Inspector and the Sergeant of the Juvenile Squad, details for a series of discussions were agreed upon. There were to be ten meetings attended by the juvenile officers and their Sergeant, ending with an evaluation session.

Each group approached these planning meetings with rather different notions. This difference in expectation proved to be a recurrent theme throughout the entire experience. For example, the Inspector envisioned a seminar as a series of lectures for a group to include not only himself, but also a number of officers from other departments. Our intention was to create a climate in which free discussion could develop. This meant that the group should be kept small and free from the inhibitions engendered by the presence of superior officers. We sensed, though did not fully realize, that at the basis of the Inspector's interest was a concern about maintaining administrative control over six of his officers. In sensing this we struck a compromise. The Sergeant would be included and the Inspector, though not to be a participant, would be kept apprised of our dealings with the men.

Several weeks after the planning meetings, we met with the officers to determine what they wanted and how it should be presented. We attempted to go about this democratically, even to the point of arranging the chairs in a circle. This was no easy matter since it turned out that the officers expected a lecture. They found discussions of how-to-begin foreign. They just began!—by asking direct questions and discussing cases.

Despite all this, a time was agreed upon and the seminar took shape as a weekly occurrence. Such was our first encounter with the difficulty that vague, indefinite structure would present to the technique-oriented, rule-conscious police officer.

The Seminar

The program was carried out in 12 meetings over a 13-week period. The group met for the first few sessions at the police department and alternated with the Mental Health Study Center thereafter. It began with case presentations in which the officers were concerned with techniques for dealing with the situations. Our purpose was to set action aside, for the moment, and try to understand why children and families behave as they do. The general themes of mental illness, insanity, sexuality, dependency, and violence were always part of the case discussions. The cases themselves changed from the dramatic with a murder-suicide of a boy's parents and his subsequent extreme dependency, to the more everyday instances of a runaway girl.

Two films, *Ask Me; Don't Tell Me* and *Booked For Safe Keeping* were shown about mid-way in the program.[6] Both presented the use of patience, firmness, and understanding with delinquent gangs on the one hand, and psychotic violence on the other. The showing of the films, especially *Booked For Safe Keeping* which depicts police handling of a paranoid schizophrenic, led to a discussion of whether the squad could make a film of their own. This, in turn, led to a searching examination of those characteristics and skills unique to juvenile work.

The 12th session, originally planned for evaluation, was much like the first planning meeting; it didn't go according to design. There was an initial statement by the Inspector, echoed by the Sergeant, that the seminar should be discontinued for the summer months. Following this, they began to push us for a formula or a set of techniques for dealing with people; as if they sought to squeeze the last drop from the sponge of knowledge. They asked us whether they had, and we had, gotten any-

---

6. *Ask Me; Don't Tell Me* may be obtained free for loan through the American Friends' Service Committee, 160 N. 15th Street, Philadelphia, Pennsylvania. *Booked for Safe Keeping* is available free for loan from the U.S. Public Health Service's Communicable Disease Center, Atlanta, Georgia 30333.

thing out of the sessions. They never *were* able to be reflective and to respond to our desire to have their evaluation. Things ended rather abruptly. The Inspector excused himself early and the conversation turned from the serious to a raucous good joke about the sexual exploits of three young ladies. Sometime later our bewilderment over this abrupt ending subsided and we realized that they had had enough.

Reflections

Anxiety: the risk of a relationship. As in all new relationships, everyone involved suffered his share of anxiety—the officers, their superiors, and the psychologists. In this case, perhaps the police suffered more than their share, since not only did they have to contend with a considerable status-gap, but also a peculiar mixture of ambiguity and specific threat which we presented at different levels within the department. To the administrators, our presence was a feather in their caps, although the image of us as almost mystically expert and potentially persuasive proved disquieting. How far would our skills and influence take us with the men? Did we threaten to control them? Would the seminar get out of hand? The officers, for their part, were suspicious of our motives for stepping down the status ladder to them, and were vaguely distressed by our personification of humanistic values. This served only to intensify the role-identity conflict between, as they put it, being a "police officer or a welfare worker."

Since at first we were not quite clear ourselves how to relate to the officers, our uncertainty and inconsistency must have presented an ambiguous image to them. Along with anxiety this ambiguity netted for us their projections of what they wished to believe about us, as well as what they dreaded most. They wished that we had all the answers. They dreaded the fact we might, and especially that we might understand their hidden motives. And it was the *ambiguity*, over which we had some control, that served to heighten their anxiety. The officers' response to the first and the last sessions clearly demonstrates this point. They expected us, more than in any other sessions, to tell them what the seminar was about and where it had been. In our preoccupation with insuring a democratic expression of their feelings and preferences, we clearly let them down.[7] The demanding quality of their questions about techniques as well as the abrupt, highly charged ending were their way of handling the anxiety we had produced.

---

7. Maintenance of an ambiguous role during a therapy session encourages the patient to respond to the consequent anxiety with projections onto his therapist. The analysis of these transferences is widely accepted as the bulwark of psychotherapy. If, however, he is to work with people in the community who have not made the commitment to a therapeutic relationship, the mental health worker would do well to suppress this natural therapeutic inclination.

The anxiety engendered in the superior officers led, we now believe, to a competition for the leadership of the men. At the time we thought it reflected competition between the two ideologies. The Inspector had sensed the need to provide an appropriate model for the officers' work with children. This was a model which the Inspector felt neither he nor the Sergeant could provide. It was probably for this reason that he turned to the mental health groups initially for assistance. It was only after a study of our notes that we realized how intuitively this delicate matter had been handled.

To illustrate, the Sergeant missed several sessions midway through the program. On one occasion, when there was no agenda, the discussion swung towards ridicule of a Sergeant in another squad. This eventually led to criticism of the absent Sergeant. We deliberately avoided the role of psychotherapeutic listener which could have led to the elaboration of further dissatisfactions.

The following meeting, the Sergeant was 45 minutes late. One psychologist became so angry that he delivered a lecture on psychotherapy and its basic tenet, mutual respect. The Sergeant, upon arrival, was pointedly chastised. Instead of the dire consequences which we imagined would happen, the Sergeant arrived 10 minutes early the next time and everyone was relieved.

This was not only a powerplay between the two men, but it held different meanings for each group. They saw us to be a potential threat to the officers' identification with the structured police system. Freedom to express personal dissatisfaction with the system represented a Pandora's box. We saw the seminar and the carefully constructed relationship to the police department threatened with collapse. We were alarmed by this state of affairs symbolized by the Sergeant's abdication of leadership and the tendency to turn the men completely over to us. It was indeed fortunate that we countered this move by reinforcing the Sergeant's leadership role with his men.

Management of anxiety: The essence of a relationship. Due to the military nature of police organization, and the necessary sanction of the administration for any relationship with the department, it becomes imperative that superiors be kept not only informed but also actively involved in the relationship process. This is especially true where having a mental health person around has become important to the prestige of the department. In these circumstances, the mental health worker may be given considerable latitude in the determination of his role. This is precisely the situation in which one must proceed carefully with one eye to the degree of ambiguity in his role and the other to the level of anxiety generated in the police.

Our management of anxiety was directed mainly toward the involvement of the superiors. We recognized the Sergeant as the formal leader of the squad, and included him in as many sessions as possible. The Inspector was originally excluded from the group which served to heighten his curiosity about what took place during the meetings, He was occasionally informed by us, but never to the extent to which we had originally intimated to him. It was with the Inspector that we probably did not follow through adequately, and which, therefore, prompted him to visit a seminar session unannounced. The Inspector seemed never completely assured that we were providing the proper experience for his men, but was satisfied enough to allow us to continue.

Based on our experience and the points made in the preceding discussion we would structure subsequent programs with the police as follows. Since it appears that ambiguity has considerable anxiety-arousing potential, programs should have clear goals and straight-forward means to achieve them. The programs should be of much shorter duration to provide a focused, intensive experience, rather than a diffuse, extensive one. There should be more demonstrations and more active participation by the leaders in the sessions. Two to four sessions could be held on each of the following topics: (1) how to interview a child to determine his way of viewing the problem and his feelings about it; and (2) uses of the family conference to understand the atmosphere of it and to change attitudes within it.

In short, we should move much closer to their expectations and, only later, begin to provide them with the experience that flexibility and ambiguity do not necessarily lead to loss of control.

The maintenance of the relationship, in the future as in the past, will be based on periodic riding in the squad car. It was here that the psychologists proved their mettle to the men, and it is fitting that this activity continue as a symbol of our interest in the squad and as a testimony to its importance.

References

Brown, R., and Ford, M. Address in American English. *Journal of Abnormal Social Psychology*, 62:375–385, 1961.

Caplan, C. *Concepts of Mental Health and Consultation: Their Application in Public Health Social Work*. Children's Bureau Publication No. 373. Washington, D.C. Superintendent of Documents, U.S. Government Printing Office, 1959.

Harvard Medical School and Psychiatric Service, Massachusetts General Hospital. *Community Mental Health and Social Psychiatry: A Reference Guide*. Cambridge: Harvard University Press, 1962.

Kenney, J.P., and Pursuit, D.C. *Police Work With Juveniles*. Springfield, Illinois: Charles C Thomas, 1954.

Working With the Juvenile Police:
Reflections of the Authors Fourteen Years Later

In reading this article, after an interval of many years, I have several reactions to the observations we made and reported at the time. First of all, the divergence in philosophies between mental health worker and police officer are still somewhat apparent. However, I now regard the police as playing a more critical, potent role than the psychologist in capitalizing on crisis and conflict situations to bring about changes within families and individuals. Police have always occupied a unique vantage point with reference to immediate psychological stress induced by the breakdown in human relations. Being on the spot as they are during the height of personal and relationship instability, how they behave, what they do and say may very well have a far more profound influence on the ultimate resolution of a conflict than the efforts of mental health workers in carefully metered therapeutic sessions strung out over time.

Secondly, the status differences, so poignantly experienced at that time, still exist but the gap is closing between police officer and psychologist. Police are moving toward a professional identity (albeit without great haste) that encompasses the innovative use of human relationship skills formerly the exclusive province of their mental health advisors. Nevertheless, the cautious respectful approaches described in the paper to gain access to police trust are still valid. The task, however, is becoming somewhat simpler due to two important developments. Police administrators are increasingly recognizing that the bulk of the peacekeeping function does not involve strict enforcement of laws, but rather the prevention of serious destructive conflict that has its origins in the run of the mill service call for neighborhood or family disputes. These events, though still considered by some "hard line" police officers as "garbage" calls, are more and more seen as early warning signals that criminally deviant behavior may be about to follow. Police administrators are not only providing the time for their men to get special training in this area and consultation on a case-by-case basis, but are insisting upon it. Indeed, the very type of seminar described by the authors in the paper has been woven into the operational fabric of many departments. In addition, more and more behavioral and social scientists are following the path along which we embarked more than 14 years ago. It is now recognized that to comment on the role of the police in society, the social scientist must base his analyses on as broad a first-hand contact or experience with police work as possible.

And finally, the beginnings of a close working relationship described in this paper ultimately led to a variety of collaborative efforts during the ensuing 5 years. The Juvenile Squad did realize its hope to make a film. It became both the subject and acting cast for a police training film "Headed for Trouble," produced by Potomac Films for the NIMH that still enjoys wide use in police academies and inservice training programs throughout the country. One of the authors went on to assist the department in forming a civil disturbance unit and to participate regularly in inservice training. And these subsequent experiences are described in two articles: "Reinforcing Police Neutrality in the Face of Civil Rights Confrontations" *(J. Applied Behav. Sci.,* Vol. 1, No. 3, 1965, pp. 243–54), and "The Riot that Didn't Happen" *(Social Problems,* Vol. 14, No. 2, Fall 1966, pp. 221–33). If anything, this author's experience, over one and one-half decades, with police personnel and organizations, reinforces his original contention that the most effective conveyors of social and behavioral science knowledge and approaches to the police field are the social scientists themselves. Quick studies, occasional expert consultations, dramatic exposés serve only to feed the natural suspicion with which police tend to regard the highly educated mental health professional. Only a continuing commitment to work with police on incredibly difficult human problems by some mental health workers can neutralize that suspicion and repair the damage inflicted by others.

ROBERT S. SHELLOW

This project got me into work with police which has continued to date. After moving to Nashville, I was invited (in 1968) by the Metropolitan Police Department and the Metropolitan Human Relations Commission to design a human relations training experience for all the uniformed officers (for 8 hours). This was occasioned by a civil disturbance in the spring of 1967 (which became part of the National Commission on Civil Disorders study) yielding considerable community concern about police behavior in the field. Following the in-service training, a week-long experience was invited to be part of the newly instituted 13-week recruit training program. Since 1969, a team of social scientists has worked with each group of new recruits. This program and an evaluation of it were reported by Bartlett.[8] Our approach has been to emphasize the professionalization of the policeman and to help him manage field situations effectively.

We have continued our training efforts to establish a means of concrete trust and regular contacts with the Department. In some ways, the recruit training has served as a means of entry into a relationship with the Department. In 1974, we were invited to help with another evaluation of the training program and to help again with the in-service training. This is

---

8. Bartlett, D.P. (in consultation with J.R. Newbrough, N. Greenberg, J. Miller and W. Moore) *Human relations training for police in Nashville: History, analysis and prospects.* Nashville: Center for Community Studies, 1972.

expected to expand the ways in which our group will work with the Police Department.

A major issue for us has been whether our work can affect the field behavior of policemen. The impact has not been as apparent as we would have hoped and probably will only become so as we are able to work with them on organizational matters. We have needed to think in 5-year blocks in our work and to be prepared to stay with it, as Shellow indicated.

J. R. NEWBROUGH

4

Program Development and Gaining Access in Community Mental Health Consultation to the Schools

Beryce W. MacLennan *

Most private consultations develop out of the initiative of the consultee who perceives a need and seeks a suitable consultant. However, this is not necessarily the case with the consultant who works out of a community mental health center and who adopts consultation as one of the methods which the center will use to improve the mental health of the community and increase mental health services.

Community mental health centers share responsibility with the school system in their communities for the psychosocial development and mental health of the children and their parents who live there, and many centers seek to develop partnerships with the schools. They use consultation as a major tool in the expansion of mental health resources in the schools. Through consultation, center staff can assist school personnel to understand and deal with human relations problems which occur in the course of their daily work, to identify and refer the seriously disturbed, and to maintain children, suffering from lesser emotional problems, in their normal classrooms. Center consultants also encourage the schools to develop new programs which will serve the emotionally disturbed and to examine their normal institutional environments to ensure that they do not increase the stress, tension and frustration amongst those they serve. Consultants use their consultation as a method for staff training, problem-solving, and crisis management. They assist school administrators to increase the mental health resources and manpower in the school system and to improve the quality of school environment.

In order to achieve these ends, community mental health consultants may have to try to reach educators who have only a vague idea of what mental health consultation is all about and who only think of mental health

* Acknowledgement is made to Drs. Robert Abramovitz, Walter Bradshaw, Gordon Cohen, Richard Gross and William Polk for descriptions of their experiences in consultation.

personnel as offering direct treatment in a clinical setting. Consultants, therefore, frequently find themselves taking the initiative in establishing a consultative relationship and in interpreting the functions and utility of consultation to the prospective consultee.

Gaining Access

When community mental health consultants contemplate a collaborative partnership with a school system or particular school, they must consider how best to utilize their limited manpower and to make access. They should first of all review what they know about the community, its problems and resources, and about the functioning of the schools. It is useful to know whether there is a consistent educational philosophy and, if so, what are the primary educational goals of this particular system. Is emphasis placed on academic learning or preparation for adult life? Does the system have a reputation for special competence in one or another area? How is it organized; is it an open or closed system? Is it directive, or does it encourage free and open communication? How does the system relate to the community? What educational approaches does the system use? What is its reputation in the community? Are there marked differences between schools? Which schools serve high risk populations? How does the system as a whole deal with problems and what resources does it have?

A table of organization is a useful tool. Although it cannot show who really makes important decisions, or where the power in fact lies, it can enable one to see where responsibilities are formally placed and what personnel the system has at its disposal. Does the system have a department of special education and, if so, what does it offer? What pupil services are provided? Are there school psychologists, guidance counselors, pupil personnel workers? What about school social workers and nurses? Does the school system have its own psychiatric clinic and health care unit or does it rely on the resources in the community? The availability of services will make a difference in what consultants will be asked to undertake for the schools, and to whom they will seek to relate. For instance, if school psychologists have been encouraged to serve as therapists or mental health consultants, they may resent the intrusion of community mental health personnel in schools where they are active. Consultants must avoid competition and conflict with school special services and must discuss how they can put their resources together.

Whether the community mental health staff take the initiative or not, because mental health resources are limited, they have to consider which consultees will serve their purposes best, and as negotiations proceed, explore how the consultee's and their own ends can be fulfilled. The choice of consultee must always be relevant to the goals of the consultation.

If mental health consultants are most interested in serving the emotionally disturbed children in the school, they may well relate primarily to the psychologists, pupil personnel workers, guidance counselors, and the special education department. If they wish to influence the overall functioning of the system, they will need to relate to the superintendent and his central administration, to the Board of Education, and perhaps even to the local and State legislatures. If they are interested in influencing, changing, or supporting the day-to-day climate of the school and the classroom, then they must develop contacts with the principal and his teaching staff.

Whatever goals the consultants have, when they are asked, or wish to work within the school system, top level administrative consent must be obtained, and then agreement and acceptance obtained from all levels with which the consultant needs to work. For example, when the Mental Health Study Center initiated a 3-year community mental health demonstration in the southern half of Prince George's County, Maryland, (MacLennan 1973a) the director and the chief of the consultation service met with the superintendent of schools to explore how the two systems could work together most effectively. Consultation and direct service chiefs then met with all the school program directors and exchanged information about mutual resources. With sanction obtained to contact local supervisors and principals, the clinical chiefs then called on the principals of the schools in their subareas and on the psychologists and pupil personnel workers who were attached to these schools. Because the Center staff were becoming acquainted with their area, they could make introductory calls on a relatively neutral basis without immediately committing themselves. This enabled them to find out the needs as well as the resources of their area, and the receptivity of the school system to consultation and collaboration. They used these visits not only to obtain information, but also to interpret their skills and services and to try to find areas of mutual interest and concern.

Even where a prospective consultee was not ready to use the consultant, Mental Health Study Center staff found that a continuing relationship could be developed on the grounds that both had a responsibility toward the community and a need to keep in touch. Occasional informal interchanges, such as over lunch, sometimes flowered into effective consultation or collaboration.

If at least informal, contractual agreements and understandings are not clearly worked out, consultants are likely to encounter difficulty later. For instance, a consultant is asked to assist a school counselor or teacher with identifying emotionally disturbed children and helping the consultee work with them on a day-to-day basis. If it becomes clear that new administrative arrangements have to be made, the principal or the director of special personnel will have to be approached. These administrators may not be at all happy at suggestions coming from a consultant outside the institution about what is essentially their program if they have not already agreed to his presence. Even if sanction has been obtained, it is probable that now the contact will have to include administrators as well as line personnel if consultation is to be continued.

Consultants seek to develop a positive relationship at each level of decision-making with which they have to deal. Sometimes conflicts between levels impede their work. Sometimes there is conflict between the Board of Education and the chief executive of an agency or system. Consultation on the system as a whole will not be effective if this goes unrecognized and is unaccounted for.

If staff are happy, competent and trustful of each other, access is easy to gain—up, down and across the system—if consultants handle themselves well. However, if there are conflicts between colleagues and between staff levels and departments, then consultants may have a hard time avoiding being caught in the crossfire. This is why it is important for a consultant to try to obtain as much information as possible about a community or an institutional system before making a move and to continue to study and supplement this information as the consultation proceeds.

Consultation to Principals and to Individual Schools

The development of consultation is a process. The consultant will not be told at the start all he needs to know. He will need to use his clinical judgment in assessing the situation and the people with whom he will have to work and adapt his approach accordingly. Time may well be an important factor. The consultant in a school should be able to spend time in the teachers' lounge, lunch informally with staff members, or chat with the principal as he walks around the school.

The consultant can be very helpful to the principal and his staff during the exploratory phase. As he gains an understanding of the strengths and difficulties of students and staff, he often gives the principal a new perspective on the school. The consultant will not only want to know the nature of the disturbed children in the school, but also, over time, gain an understanding of the range of performance and behavior in the school, the student and staff cliques, the home and community situations to which all return at the end of the day. He will gradually come to recognize those who support him and those who may resist his efforts. No two consultations are alike and consultants and consultees together will make different choices in each situation.

In one subarea in Prince George's County, (MHSC 1968) the Mental Health Study Center staff contacted the administrator who supervised a number of elementary school principals and arranged a meeting with his group to explore how the mental health team and the principals could best work together. At this meeting, the principals decided they would like the help of the team in dealing with the everyday problems of children with whom they had difficulty but for whom they did not feel specialized help was needed. Such children were angry or easily frustrated children, children who were overly competitive, shy, withdrawn, or children who came from homes where both parents worked or where one parent was an alcoholic.

Two sessions were held. The first was a 3-hour discussion on the shy, withdrawn child, and the second, a month later, was on the aggressive child. For these meetings, the principals had their teachers prepare descriptions of the criteria which they used in defining a shy, withdrawn, or aggressive child, and provide examples of problems they experienced with each. The principals then discussed the materials with the consultants, explored the dynamics of each situation, and worked together to find solutions from which they could draw general principles.

As a result of these meetings the principals invited the consultants to work with them and their faculties. A program was arranged for a school release day in which a mental health staff member led a discussion at each of 10 elementary schools. The teachers presented specific problem situations and the consultant and principal helped them understand the situation and work out a means for resolving the problem. This testing of the consultants led in many cases to a continuing relationship with the principals and their staff. Consultants helped teachers manage disturbed children and classroom problems, taught the teachers how to work more effectively with parents, and consulted with the principal on problems with his staff.

Once contact is made with the schools, a wide variety of programs can be developed. In one school, the teachers expressed interest in continuing discussions on such problems as disobedience, fighting, lying and stealing. The psychiatrist-consultant, who had found role playing effective as a teaching method, developed instruction sheets on commonly experienced problems and had the teachers adopt the roles and act out the problems. For instance, for one skit the instruction sheet described a teacher called over to a disturbance on the playground resulting from one child "butting in" at the head of the line. Instructions for the roles of the various children indicate that the tattle-tale should pester the teacher, demanding the offending child be punished and report other misdemeanors the child has committed. The instructions suggest that other children standing in line get "itchy" and fight amongst themselves. Several alternative personality descriptions were provided for the role of the child butting in. In one the child is an intelligent, articulate but fresh, smart aleck. In another, the child is a manipulator who bursts into tears and has a tantrum to get his own way. In a third, the child is sullen and bitter against all authority and unresponsive to the teacher's approaches. Thus, with the use of these alternative personalities, the same theme could be enacted three or four times, each time highlighting a different type of child, and accordingly, eliciting different reactions from the teacher.

Similar instructions were developed for a teacher holding a parent conference about a child who cheats, also providing for several different types of parents (hostile, passive and helpless, withdrawn and defensive).

When the role playing was carried out with the faculty group, it provided the teachers with a vivid experience in which they could become involved, and stimulated surprisingly intense discussion among the group. The role playing itself took a relatively small part of the time.

In a low key approach, two child psychiatrists (MHSC 1967) were interested in consulting with a special school. They visited the principal and presented their interest as an opportunity for mutual learning. They began by observing in the classrooms to learn what the children were like, what the teachers were trying to do, and what problems they were encountering. They sat in on weekly staff meetings to hear what the principal and teachers were concerned about. Gradually, they were able to make a few suggestions and to demonstrate their usefulness in other ways. For instance, one child was constantly disturbing the class by asking the teacher apparently irrelevant questions. The consultants suggested that this child really wanted the teacher's attention and if she could make some opportunity to work with him at her convenience he might well be less demanding at other times. This suggestion was put into practice and the child relaxed. In another situation, a boy had a very short attention span. When he became bored, he grew restless, moved around aimlessly and then turned destructive, hitting other children or throwing things. The teacher's attention was directed to the danger signal of restless behavior and new activities were introduced at that point which reduced the destructive episodes and enabled the child to be managed in the classroom.

As confidence in the consultants grew, staff brought other problems to them. For example, the principal, a permissive person, had some difficulty in enforcing her authority when it was realistically necessary. The consultants encouraged and supported her. Another time, toward the end of the year, staff and students were upset because one or two staff were leaving and some students were being transferred. The consultants helped the faculty deal with their own feelings of loss and difficulties in separation and then showed them how to help the students work through their need to mourn and their unwillingness to part from a loved teacher.

One problem, which Mental Health Study Center consultants have frequently found to be at the heart of many of the conflicts between members of a school community, is that of scapegoating (MacLennan 1969). Anyone—teacher, administrator or student—may serve as scapegoat or act as scapegoater, and it is important that those involved be able to recognize it for what it is. An example of this problem occurred in discussion between teachers and mental health staff in an elementary school. A fifth grade teacher had expressed particular concern about a boy, who, although a conscientious, bright pupil, seemed very unpopular with his classmates. Whenever he started to answer questions, the other students snickered and made derogatory remarks about what he had to say. When the class was assigned group projects, no one wanted to work with him. There seemed no special reason for the class's attitude except, perhaps, that the boy was new to the group and extremely conscientious. He didn't make any fuss in the class, but in the halls, cafeteria or playground he was continually getting into arguments with teachers or fights with younger children. These disagreements seemed to be related to the anger he felt toward his class-mates.

The consultant was aware that to adequately understand the situation, it was not only necessary to consider this boy and his problems, but also to analyze the total situation. She suggested then that the group take a look at what was going on with the class as a whole.

The teacher pointed out that two of the boys seemed to be the ringleaders. They were the strongest and largest boys in the class and tended to bully all the children. Both did poorly in their school work and had strict fathers who beat them if they brought home poor report cards. One was described as being not particularly bright, and the other as defiant and a poor reader who had difficulty concentrating. It appeared as though they were both taking their anger out on the new boy, who, because of his newness, had no friends or allies in the group. The other children were afraid to stand up to these boys and instead joined their attack on the newcomer. Each one would rather see him be the scapegoat than themselves.

The teachers thought of ways to correct the situation. They suggested that both boys might benefit from the teacher's showing more friendly interest and encouraging them to employ their leadership qualities in a more positive way. They also indicated the need for counseling and remedial help for the boy with the reading problem, and the possibility of arranging work for the other that was more geared to his ability level, so that he might be able to earn better grades and, consequently, be in less trouble with his father.

The teacher also discussed ways to effect changes in the class as a whole. Someone suggested taping a series of incidents demonstrating how the children had been unkind not only to the new boy, but to each other. The class could listen to the tapes and discuss the importance of encouraging and helping one another.

Another teacher suggested that the class might divide into regular sub-groups for projects in which leadership would rotate, but everyone was expected to work together. If the three boys mentioned above were separated, the rest of the children might learn to stand up better to the larger boys and the newcomer might begin making friends in his subgroup.

The discussion returned to the new boy, who was also displaying his anger. He was angry at his classmates for bullying him and at his teacher for letting them, yet he was too weak in the face of group pressure to deal with his problems in the classroom. Instead, he expressed his anger by annoying others who were less able to fight back or who had less influence over his life. The teachers decided to wait and see whether reduction in group pressure and a general discussion of human relations in the classroom would be sufficient before taking further steps.

Collaboration in School Program Planning

In the Mental Health Study Center demonstration mentioned above, as trust developed, Center consultants had a number of opportunities to assist the schools in planning programs for the general mental health of the schools, for the development of programs for emotionally and behaviorally disturbed children and for the management of the human relations aspects of systems change. Two of these to be described relate to the development of collaborative programs between the Center and a school. One was a multiagency effort which resulted in a collaborative program between the county mental health authority and the school system and the other related to planning for changes in one or more schools.

In the first situation a mental health consultant (Bradshaw 1972a) working with a senior high school, assisted the principal and his counsellors in reviewing all 250 incoming students to the 10th grade class to identify those who showed serious behavioral, learning or emotional difficulties. After screening out those who had organic problems or who were mentally rather than functionally retarded, a team of three teachers, one counsellor, the mental health consultant and a special education supervisor designed and carried out an individualized program of education and group counselling for the remaining 26 students. The mental health consultant worked primarily with the teachers and the counsellor, observing in the classroom, meeting with the educational team and training the counsellor to work with groups. He also consulted with the principal on the problems of sustaining such a program in regular school during the initial period when the students tested the good intentions of the staff. Although at the end of the first semester the project teachers were almost in despair, and the rest of the faculty were complaining about the behavior of the students outside the classroom, by April only 2 out of 26 students had dropped out of school and the remainder had settled down and advanced their basic achievement levels from second to seventh grade. These results were much better than would have been expected as assessed by Lloyd's Drop-Out Expectancy Scales (Lloyd 1967) used to evaluate the project.

In the second case a psychiatrist was consulting with a special school for retarded children. He initially met with the principal and with the psychologist and pupil personnel worker separately to obtain an understanding of the school and then began to attend the school's "building conferences" where problem situations were discussed with all involved.

Early in the year the case was presented of a 14-year-old boy with a history of psychotic episodes who was again beginning to act in a bizarre fashion. He was only functionally retarded and really did not belong in this school. He required placement in a program for the treatment of emotionally disturbed children and the consultant agreed to help find such a setting although on a residential basis. There was no treatment program in the county at that time.

Before any arrangements could be made, the school psychologist mentioned that there were several such children in the school and eventually five severely emotionally disturbed children were uncovered, two boys and three girls, ranging from 9 to 14 years of age. Three of the five children had speech problems. One boy could not speak, one was just learning to say a few words, and one could speak but preferred not to. Only one of the children could read. All were in different classes. These children required special programing with frequent and clear definition of reality, firm structure and limit-setting, and, in general, more advanced curriculum. The principal was unhappy about having them in the school. The teachers were made anxious by their behavior but there was no other program for them.

The principal, the pupil service personnel and the consultant faced this problem realistically and devised a plan in which the children worked with a special education teacher for one period each day and the psychiatrist met with all the regular class teachers, the special teacher, the psychologist and the speech therapist once a week to plan program and discuss the management of the children.

The period with the special teacher each day seemed to relieve the tensions of the children and gave them feelings of friendship and caring. The discussions each week helped their regular teachers understand these children and deal more effectively and sympathetically with their problems. Although perhaps not an ideal program for the children, they did settle down, they could stay in school and they made progress in their work. Thus it did provide a workable model in a school situation where resources were limited.

Decisions frequently have to be made as to whether the treatment of seriously disturbed children should be undertaken within or outside the school system. Wherever possible, the principle has been upheld that children should be educated within the regular school. However, for some a more relaxed setting with specialized program is more effective. In Prince George's County an Inter-Agency Task Force, consisting of all agencies serving children and youth was able to plan and obtain funding for a therapeutic treatment center for emotionally disturbed children. The county community mental health authority took responsibility for the program and the school system took responsibility for the educational component. Consultation to such planning committees is another aspect of program development. Participation may include not only attending meetings, but gathering supporting data and assisting in proposal development.

In the early phases of collaboration between community mental health agencies and school systems, requests are likely to be for direct treatment, consultation on cases or staff interpersonal relationships and staff training on mental health matters. However, as confidence grows, mental health consultants are likely to be included more frequently in administrative consultation and school human relations planning.

Planning for Change in the Schools

During the last year of the Mental Health Study Center's community mental health center demonstration, the Prince George's County school system had to complete its secondary school desegregation. Because of the conflicting feelings of students, faculty, parents and community this was a highly charged operation. Eight junior and senior high schools were involved in the desegregation, and the superintendent appointed a staff coordinator and a school-community committee to work out the logistics. Two staff consultants from the Study Center were appointed to the committee. Decisions regarding teacher and student transfers and the curriculum scheduling and other technical problems were primarily dealt with by the central office of the school system. Mental health staff worked with neighborhood associations in smoothing out community conflicts (MacLennan 1973b).

As an aid to planning the human relations aspects of the transition, the committee decided to hold a charrette. (Prince George's Co. Bd. Ed. 1970; Bradshaw 1972b). This is a planning workshop which usually lasts a week to 10 days and which brings all those who are involved to study and work out necessary changes. A community leader was designated charrette director and two educational consultants experienced in charrettes were employed to provide technical guidance. A steering committee, consisting of school administrators, pupil service personnel, students, community residents and one mental health consultant, was called together 6 weeks prior to the scheduled dates for the charrette. It was decided to include 20 students, 5 parents, 5 teachers and administrators from each school and to assign 2 consultants to each group. Each school group would meet by itself during the day and then the groups would congregate and report to each other in the evening. The charrette would last for 6 days. Six members of the Study Center staff agreed to serve as group facilitators and resource persons.

At the urging of the mental health contingent, two meetings of the consultants were held to plan the structure, process and basic content of the charrette. There was some disagreement in this group as to whether the charrette should focus primarily on procedures for achieving a smooth desegregation and to deal with the specific human relations problems created by the transfer of students and faculty or whether to study more globally the functioning of the school system as it affected the eight schools and to set more general educational goals. The consultants also had some concern about their roles. They were to provide initial group leadership until school members emerged as leaders, at which point the consultants would revert to the role of resource persons in the groups. A further problem which disturbed the consultants was the lack of clarity regarding the relationship between the charrette and the school system. It was difficult to estimate how much authority was delegated to the charrette to deal with problems associated with the desegregation plan or who would be responsible for carrying out recommendations. In practice, it was found that the presence of the principal in each group and the principal's acceptance of recommendations were vital factors in their implementation. School members carried over into the group their customary hierarchical relationships and were conscious that they would have to continue these relationships after the charrette was over. These were natural inhibiting factors in the free functioning of the workshop.

Thus, the mental health consultants were very conscious that a clear contract had not been negotiated, that authority and sanction for change had not been fully delegated to the charrette and that the plans and the recommendations which resulted from the charrette were likely to be considered advisements which would be dependent for their adoption on the acceptance of the permanent authority at each level. The authority structure within the workshop was also not clear, for the consultants were not sure to whom they were supposed to report (Prince George's Co. Bd. Ed. 1970).

In spite of these deficiencies, obvious at the end of the planning period, the mental health consultants decided to continue to take part in the charrette. The six consultants worked in four schools. Each school had a different experience. In one, the absence of the principal (on a long-planned fishing trip) was a severe drawback in that staff and pupils could not estimate whether their plans would meet his approval. In this group, staff were also very anxious, fearing the possibility of the students entering into violent confrontations. Nevertheless, this group did provide an opportunity for students to explore differing points of view and to experience confrontation of differing cultural values without violent conflict. They were able to form a working group which advised the principal after the charrette. They also developed a set of recommendations, although without a plan for their implementation. In this group, the consultants used a transactional method for assisting the members to understand how the group process and their anxiety maneuvers interfered with the task of planning. Educational resource persons were drawn from other groups.

In a second school group, a mental health consultant and an educator were somewhat overeager to develop continuing school leadership. As a consequence, it seemed students were permitted to take over leadership prematurely. Students and adults polarized and the two factions split apart and began to plan separately. However, by the end of the week staff and students were working together and produced a well-organized set of recommendations.

In a third group, a mental health consultant and an educator utilized a more structured educational approach which felt comfortable to the school members and which, while it prevented any conflicts being confronted did provide a friendly working experience and an excellent plan which was later carried out with the full support of the principal.

In the fourth school the students and principal confronted each other in a very negative way which tended to harden attitudes on both sides.

While the plans and some of the relationships developed during the charrette were positive and useful, the extent to which the workshop affected school relations during the next year depended very much on the extent to which the principal was involved and accepting. There is no doubt that the planning around the opening of school was very helpful in eliminating conflict at the beginning of the school year.

As a result of the charrette, school principals and their staffs began to realize that some of the general human relations problems they were experiencing in their schools might be relieved by more effective long-range planning. One of the mental health consultants was invited to work with the principal of a high school and its feeder junior high schools in identifying the problems and needs of the school community. After several meetings with the principals, an all-day workshop was held which included teachers, parents, students, pupil service personnel, public health nurses, community recreation workers and librarians, who served the neighborhoods surrounding the schools and representatives of the local shopping center employers' association and security force. Almost 100 people attended the meeting and during the first hour they met in plenary session to identify problems. These included inadequate after-school activities; trouble with teenagers in the shopping center; problems with the work-study vocational program; poor communication between teachers and parents; lack of orientation in transferring from junior to senior high school; and problems which foreign students had in adjusting to the schools (about 10% of the school population was from Spanish-speaking and Asiatic countries).

The workshop then broke into small groups, each designated to discuss one of these problems, and at the end of the day came up with a number of recommendations. It was decided to form a student committee to work with an employer-security group from the shopping center to understand and handle problems with students there. It was found that there was considerable overlap between the recreation, library and after-school programs. The recreation program and library would in the future be represented in the school's extracurricular planning committee. Employers agreed to meet with the administrator responsible for vocational education and the work-study program to plan a more effective program. Parents complained that teachers had rigid hours when they could meet which made it very difficult for some parents to come to school. It was agreed that these could be relaxed. Changes were agreed upon to facilitate the transition from junior to senior high school and a task force established to explore how to improve programs for foreign-born students.

The high school identified some special problems in regard to the motivation and performance of the students and in regard to discipline in the school. After this workshop a group of 30 teachers continued to meet with the principal, one or two representatives of the central office administration, student representatives and the mental health consultant. They reviewed the performance records of the classes over the last few years. They recognized there had been a change in the type of student in the school (markedly fewer were college-bound), as well as a growth in numbers. They analyzed the structure of the school and found there was not a clear statement of the role and function of the various student and faculty bodies, such as the student council. They identified such problems as the number of students who were cutting classes, the amount of disorder in the halls and the fact that drug-taking was seen as a problem in the school. This was a large school and teachers felt isolated from each other. They could not even recognize all their students, and students felt they had no one to whom they could go for advice.

Plans were developed to divide the school into smaller units so that students and faculty could know each other better. Faculty were encouraged to socialize so that they could be more supportive of each other. Faculty teams within and across specialities began to work on modernizing the curriculum. Student-faculty volunteers established a rap room where students with problems could informally seek advice. The mental health consultant agreed to provide training for this group. A drug education program was begun and procedures established for the management of drug emergencies with linkage to the county drug treatment program. The student-faculty organizations were restructured to provide more effective communication with the principal and his assistant administrators.

In all of this planning activity four principles were observed: (1) involving those who would have to sanction and carry out recommendations; (2) gathering data, analyzing problems and setting goals before embarking on actions; (3) exploring alternative means of making the most effective use of resources; and (4) making sure all persons understand the nature of their responsibilities and the extent of their authority.

Sometimes in planning program the most effective solutions may not lie in the agency where the problem rests. School dropouts may require interventions such as the stimulation of job opportunities and work training through employment and rehabilitation agencies, as well as primary intervention in the school. Absorbing recreation programs and adequate street lighting may be the solutions of choice for vandalism rather than consultation with the police and the courts. Increased family allowances may be preferable to school breakfasts for hungry children who are apathetic, inattentive or restless in class.

In developing program, the mental health professional and the schools have hard choices to make. Resources are always limited. Shall the consultant spend a large part of his time in one or two schools, or shall he spread himself over many, making brief or group contacts with principals or special personnel? How much time will the professional spend in direct treatment, training or consultation? Can he aid in developing integrated programs in which treatment, training and education reinforce each other? Can he help the school reorganize its resources so that pressures are less, curriculum more relevant, and crisis counselors lend support to classroom teachers in order to keep difficult children in school and learning? More and more we see that community mental health is everyone's business, and education and mental health must develop a partnership in which each uses his training to best advantage in support of a quality environment and a stimulating school for children to learn and develop their psychosocial and cognitive skills.

References

Bradshaw, W.H. "An Education-Therapeutic School Program for Problem Ninth Grade Students." Paper presented at AGPA Annual Conference, New York, 1972a.

Bradshaw, W.H., et al. Mental health consultants in an educational charrette. *Psychiatry*, 35(4):317–335. November 1972b.

Lloyd, D.N. "Multiple Graduation Analysis of Antecedent Relationship to High School Dropout or Graduation." Lab Paper 21, Rockville, Md.: National Institute of Mental Health, Nov. 1967.

MacLennan, B.W. Scapegoating. *Today's Education*, 58(6):38–40, Sept. 1969.

MacLennan, B.W. A collaborative program of mental health and education in rural and suburban Maryland. In: Quinn, R., and Wegner, L.M., eds. *Mental Health and Learning*. DHEW No. (HSM) 73–9111. Rev., Reprinted. Rockville, Md.: National Institute of Mental Health, 1973a. pp. 55–60.

MacLennan, B.W. Community mental health professionals assist in school desegregation. In: Clairborn, W.L., and Cohen, R. *School Intervention*. New York: Behavioral Publications, 1973b. pp. 208–221.

Mental Health Study Center. *MHSC Annual Report 1966–67*. Rockville, Md.: National Institute of Mental Health, 1967. p. 18.

Mental Health Study Center. *MHSC Annual Report 1967–68*. Team II. Rockville, Maryland: National Institute of Mental Health, 1968. pp. 31–34.

Prince George's County Board of Education. *The Charrette 1969*. Upper Marlboro, Md.: the Board, 1970.

5

Consultation With Alternative Services for Young People

James S. Gordon

For the last 2 years I have served as a consultant to groups—a hotline for youth, two group foster homes for adolescents, a "runaway house," a "free high school"—which provide what may loosely be called alternative social services for young people. In the paper that follows I want to share some of my experiences, examples of how one person trained as a psychiatrist has worked with new kinds of social service workers and the young people they serve. This is an outline, a working paper for more detailed narratives, but I think it conveys the substance and the feeling of their and my work.

This account of my involvement is part of the larger story of alternative services. And it, in turn, may be seen as a chapter in the history of the way our society has viewed and dealt with its young. I will begin by presenting a historical perspective which I—and many of the people I work with—have found to be helpful in understanding my work. Afterwards I will present a brief sketch of two of the alternative service projects I have worked with. Then I will proceed to the actual description of my work as a consultant to these two projects.

A Historical Perspective

A hundred years ago a person of 13 or 14 was well on his or her way to adulthood (Bremner 1971; Handlin and Handlin 1971). Already a worker in field or factory, an apprentice or scholar, a young man was accorded the dignity and prerequisites of an adult; young women—then as now relegated to a second-class citizenship—were being educated by mothers and aunts and grandmothers to serve their future husbands and children. If a young person chafed against the oppressiveness or restrictions of home, he or she could seek solace or advice from an older member of the extended family or from some adult in the community who was known to be sympathetic. If the situation became intolerable—or the lure of distant places too strong—the young person could leave.

In 19th century America a boy or girl could still, like Huck Finn, "light out for the territory"; or else he or she could begin life in another town or city. There, according to temperament, skill and luck a young person could make his own way, find support from his elders, or be exploited—by white slavers, cruel masters and oppressive factories.

Only toward the end of the 19th and the beginning of the 20th centuries did adolescence come to be regarded as a separate stage in a young American's life, a time of biological adulthood and social immaturity. Three changes in the legal structure (Bakan 1971)—as much the consequences of industrial development and its economic necessities as of humanitarian concern—signified and reinforced this change in attitudes: The passage of laws prohibiting child labor, enforcing compulsory education and creating a separate juvenile justice system.

Compared to the losses in social status, the gains for adolescents in humanitarian treatment were negligible. Economic considerations remained preeminent in determining whether labor and education laws were enforced: Factories which had already found child labor to be inefficient were content not to employ young people; but parents who depended for their economic survival on their children's labor could hardly afford to heed either child labor or compulsory education laws. Young people who were confined in juvenile institutions were now not exposed to "hardened adult criminals," but, in return, they forfeited virtually all of their rights: Not only could they be confined without a jury trial, but they could be convicted of a whole new class of "crimes" including "stubbornness," "truancy" and "running away." Behavior that was tolerated or criticized in adults, that had once been similarly tolerated in young people, became subject to legal as well as social scrutiny and constraints.

The new sciences of psychology and psychiatry developed and over the years amplified a perspective on adolescence which justified this intrusive and patronizing treatment. From Stanley Hall's (1904) text on *Adolescence* to present-day psychoanalytic papers, and popular magazine articles on "How to Get Along With Your Teenager," adolescence in America has been regarded as a time of turmoil and psychopathology; and adolescents themselves have been seen as "difficult" or "troubled." Ignoring anthropological data such as that accumulated by Margaret Mead (1928, 1930), many writers on adolescence have made the effect (the difficulty of being a young person in 20th century America) into the cause (adolescence is a time of great stress).

Adolescents, like mental patients, blacks and women were assumed not to know what was good for them. Adults, and increasingly adults who had degrees which certified their expertise in the "problems of adolescence," were to tell them. In the chambers of judges, in the offices of guidance counselors, social workers and psychiatrists, adolescents who were at odds with family or school or community were labelled sick or delinquent or deficient—in any case, problems.

Already treated as a special class and labelled as problems, adolescents had their difficulties compounded by rapid social and economic change. The casual oppressiveness of a society rapidly expanding toward its geographic and economic limits was supplanted by the oppressive concern of a society which demanded ever-greater degrees of technical specialization and higher levels of consumption. Young people were asked to set aside more and more years to prepare for a life of work which was increasingly removed from their experience at home or at school.

At the same time, the increasing mobility of nuclear families and the resulting breakdown of the extended family and multigenerational community made it harder and harder for young people to understand and participate in the history and traditions from which their parents' beliefs and style of life seemed to emanate. Often there were no adults to talk to— no aunts or grandparents, no ministers or policemen known since birth and trusted—except for the very parents who participated in the conflict. Cut off from the past, isolated from their parents' lives as adults and dubious about their own future, adolescents turned more and more to one another for comfort and support.

In contrast, their parents turned increasingly to professionals, especially to professionals who could help them figure out what exactly was going on with their children. Parents might expect a sympathetic reception from these experts, but their children rarely did. To go to see one of *them*—a guidance counselor, minister, social worker, doctor or policeman—was by definition to admit to sickness or guilt, often to forfeit the integrity of one's own experience or point of view to a perspective grounded in psychopathology and criminality. As if that were not bad enough, adult professionals shared the power of parents as well as their point of view: The guidance counselor was paid by the school and might report to the principal; the police could jail you for running away or using drugs; the psychiatrist, silent, forbidding, could label you crazy and lock you up; and the social worker who spoke demeaningly of "acting out" or "poor impulse control" could remove you from your home.

In the late 1950s black people in America began to demand their civil rights, began also to insist that the larger society treat them with respect. In the wake of the civil rights movement and of the third-world struggles which nourished and were fed by it, other oppressed groups, including women, ethnic minorities, mental patients, and old people became more assertive and demanding. Young people too became conscious of themselves as a social entity and a political force. Since their shared isolation from the concerns and lives of adults had made them cling less tightly to the dominant values of the American society, it was easy for many of them to see in the powerlessness and anger of the American blacks a reflection of their own situation.

The palpable contradictions between the American ideals of truthfulness

and peace, of democracy and self-determination and the American actions
in the Indochina war drove a deeper wedge between young people and
their parents (Gordon 1972). Revulsion at the televised slaughter—and
in some young people an unsuppressable fear that the murderousness
vented on the Vietnamese might eventually be directed toward them—
was the first step toward the rejection of the moralism and materialism
which seemed to sustain it.

The "youth culture" that evolved in the mid-1960s was at once a "coun-
ter" or "alternative" to the dominant adult culture and a parody of its worst
fears about its young people. Calling themselves brothers and sisters, large
numbers of young people drew on a common store of democratic ideals
and utopian hopes. They rejected—verbally and often in action—war, rac-
ism, materialism, privatism, competitiveness, hypocrisy and fastidiousness.
And, in so doing, they confirmed their parents' and society's suspicions
that adolescents were lazy, sex and dope-crazed and unrealistic or dangerous and delinquent—"hippies," or "radicals," or both.

Young people gathered in urban neighborhoods and college communities—
the Haight-Ashbury in San Francisco; the East Village in New York
City; Dupont Circle in Washington, D.C.; Ann Arbor; Madison; and
Cambridge. There they evolved new styles of dress and music, politics
and art, interpersonal relations and intoxication—amalgams of past and
present, of technological innovation, economic necessity and imaginative
fantasy. They found heroes and heroines of their own, revolutionaries and
rock musicians and revolutionaries who were rock musicians.

Building on the interests and talents of members of each community,
local groups formed to provide a network of human services. In San
Francisco, the Diggers, borrowing their name from the English egalitarians
of the 16th century, improvised daily bread and soup for thousands of
Haight-Ashbury residents; Switchboard directed telephone callers to crash
pads, free clothes and legal services; the Haight-Ashbury Free Clinic,
staffed by street people and local physicians, dealt with the ailments of a
young and transient population that experimented with its limits of physical and mental endurance; and church-sponsored Huckleberry House took
in those young people who wanted the security that the street did not offer.

In contrast to the doctors and social workers, the schools and hospitals
of the larger society, these counter-institutions and those who worked in
them were responsive to and respectful of young people and of their right
to independence and experimentation. A girl who wanted a ride to Colorado
was not lectured about the dangers of hitchhiking; a boy who had run
away from his parents was not forced to return home or harangued about
his "future." Young people with venereal disease were treated without
smirks or moralism and those on bum trips were gentled down in quiet
rooms, not jabbed with mind-numbing doses of tranquilizers.

Even more important the barriers between helper and helped were breached and often discarded. The boy who last night was bummed out on acid might help talk someone else down the next day. The kids who received free food from the Diggers donated their extra clothes. The doctor who prescribed an antibiotic might learn about an equally effective herbal tea from his patient. For many young people these counter-culture service groups provided an opportunity—sometimes the first they had ever had—to be humanly useful to others; for some professionals, young and old, they provided a new kind of working experience relatively free from the posturings and strictures of professional roles.

Over the last 5 years many of the service groups which formed in response to a sudden influx of young people have simply disappeared. But many others have grown and changed with the times, expanding their services to deal with new needs, developing new structures, integrating themselves more completely with a community which they are helping to build..A runaway house with which I have worked was founded 5 years ago to provide a safe living space and an opportunity for reflection for young people who migrated in search of action or in flight from parents to the city's hip community. A year later, some of its staff members opened group foster homes to provide more permanent places for those young people who could or would not go home; and others started the free school, a new kind of educational setting where high school students— those who stayed at home as well as those who ran—could learn and be, without being regimented or infantilized.

In the last 2 or 3 years young people in the suburbs and older people sympathetic to their situation have set up similar projects. Responding to the blandness and isolation of subdivisions and to the anonymity of large schools, young people and their older allies have opened "drop-in centers," "crisis counselling services," "coffee houses," and suburban runaway houses. Towns and counties in every State have developed their own hotlines, telephone answering services which link lonely young people to other young people who can tell them, in their own language, about birth control, abortion or drugs; to peers who can hear their needs and urges without judging them.

Workers in all of these projects have in common some understanding of the insensitivity and inadequacy of traditional social services for young people. They feel that they can be—without professional degrees of certification—helpful to others and believe that people—even troubled and confused young people—can run their own lives and make their own decisions. They share the desire to make the world, and, in particular, their corner of it a better place, and the conviction that such change is shaped by and inseparable from the way people treat one another. In projects that are run by the people who work in them they hope to create humane and humanly manageable alternatives to the institutions and services that have constrained and labelled them and their younger brothers and sisters.

The Hotline and the Group Foster Home

There are, however, differences among the various projects. The kind of neighborhood they are in; the source of funding; the age, background, experience, interests and ideology of the staff, and those whom they serve: All of these shape each project. For the account of consultation which follows, I will discuss two projects which are at different places on the alternative service spectrum in terms of neighborhood, age of workers, structure of organization, and type of service.

The Hotline: Many of the phone aides at the suburban hotline live at home in the subdivisions of white, middle and lower-middle class neighborhoods. They are generally in their late teens and early 20s and attend— or are temporarily on leave from—local high schools and colleges. They operate a 24-hour-a-day telephone answering service which deals mostly with teenagers and provides everything from casual conversation to legal and medical referrals to counseling in crisis situations. Twelve to fifteen paid staff receive $2.00 an hour to work on and supervise two 8-hour phone shifts a week; in addition they generally put in extra volunteer time in organizational activity and on committees. Sixty volunteers also work on the phones, under paid staff supervision; they contribute at least 4 hours a week. The hotline's coordinator has a master's degree in social work and is paid by the County Mental Health Association which is nominally in charge of all hotline activities.

The Group Foster Home is located in a "hip" white enclave in a larger, mostly black urban neighborhood. The workers or counselors in the Home are in their mid-to-late 20s. They try to live collectively with five or six teenagers who have left or have been forced out of their parental homes; these young people have all been classified as "psychotic" and/ or "delinquent" and/or "in need of supervision." The workers receive $50.00 plus room and board for a week during which they are to be available for 5 days, 24 hours a day. The Home is one member of a group of alternative service projects—including a runaway house, another group foster home, a job cooperative, and a free high school—which attempt to function as a collective, sharing economic resources and decisionmaking.

The Consultant

A "mental health professional" who works as a consultant to young people on their projects must understand not only where they "come from," what their ideals and needs and aspirations and expectations are, but what he or she is about. The professional training that "qualifies" a person to comment authoritatively on unconscious meaning or group process guarantees neither acceptance nor usefulness in alternative service projects. If the professional does not share many of the values of the people with whom he is consulting, if he does not respect what they are trying to do, if he is not open to engaging them on their terms, then all his knowledge is worse than useless. Observations, interpretations, open-ended questions, all become weapons in the arsenal of an unwanted and destructive interloper.

If the consultant thinks of the young workers as "kids" and their work as "nice but not professional," then he is being both ignorant and condescending. Alternative services have arisen precisely because our communities and the helpers in them have *not* served these young people. The concerns and biases of teachers as well as psychiatrists, parents as well as police, have prevented them from being helpful to large numbers of young people. The condescension of the consultant, silent or spoken, simply perpetuates and confirms the previous experience of the workers and the young people who seek their help. The consultant must always remember that the services are alternative and that they belong to the people who live and work in them.

I believe that it has been possible for me to be useful to alternative social service workers because I recognize with them the impoverishment of traditional services; because I sense that alternative services, controlled by the people who work in them, not by a bureaucratic or professional hierarchy, offer a new and better way for people—including professionally-trained people like myself—to help and work and simply be with one another.

Since my work is subsidized by a salary that I receive from the United States Public Health Service, I need not ask for money from the groups that I work with. This is a mixed blessing. Though financial security could conceivably make me less sensitive to the rigors of working in an alternative service project, it has the great advantage of allowing me to spend time with people whose work I respect, rather than those who can pay. I have some distance, not only from the day to day hassles that arise out of full-time work in one project, but also from the chronically stressful struggle for financial survival.

My experience as a therapist and as a mental hospital ward administrator and my personal psychoanalysis have all been valuable in my work as a consultant. From my own therapy I have learned to be sensitive to my reactions to what is happening around me, at once observant and self-critical. My psychiatric training—and in particular the time I spent as a ward administrator—make it easier for me to move from one frame of comprehension to another, from an empathic understanding of an individual's words to an evaluation of their communicative effect in a group to an estimation of the influence of that person's previous experience on his point of view. And, not least, I can feel moderately confident about the limitations of specifically therapeutic ideologies and approaches. I know—with the young people who have often enough been victimized or insulted by therapists' techniques and institutional coercion—that "introspection," "encountering," and analyses of "group dynamics," as well as a variety of psychiatric "treatments," can all be used to obfuscate and maintain inequities of power, privilege or economics which ought to be redressed.

First Meetings

People have generally contacted me—a young psychiatrist, with free time, who published writings on "madness," (Gordon 1971, 1972) and with something of a reputation of a "radical therapist"—to help them with what they believe to be psychiatric problems. This has meant most often that people in an alternative service project have felt that one of their group or one of the "kids" they work with was acting "crazy." At other times the group as a whole has decided it needed perspective on an apparently irreconcilable conflict; and occasionally one or more members have felt that the group needed supervision or instruction or information—about adolescence, or "mental illness"—to help it do its work better.

In general I have been first contacted by a person in a position of power and authority—the coordinator of the hotline, the director of the runaway house, the most active of the counselors in a group foster home. Sometimes the situation is viewed as a crisis, sometimes not; but always, in contacting me the group is opening itself to an outsider; confessing to a need; soliciting the services of a member of a powerful profession of which there is great distrust.

The way I respond to an initial request for help begins to shape my relationship to the alternative service group. If, in a psychiatric clinic, one simply listens to an individual patient's account of her difficulties, one may proceed very differently than if one insists on seeing her with her husband and her children; and, differently still, if one visits her in her home, gets acquainted with her children and meets her close friends. Similarly, in the case of my consultation with groups, what I find out and deal with differs with the setting and the persons making up the group.

In general, my approach is ecological and political. Almost always I first meet with my caller on his or her turf. I want to understand the entire situation of which the "caller" and "the problem" are but a part, to begin from the beginning to see the project's neighborhood and feel its physical dimensions and constraints. At the same time I want to affirm—at a time when discouragement or anxiety may have led the workers to question themselves and their purpose—that I am committed to seeking a solution which conforms with the spirit of their project.

I want my perspective to come not only from the person who called me in, but from all the people who participate in a project. I want to make it clear from the beginning of my work with them that I am not the agent of a powerful clique or a leader of "the counselors," but am responsive to the entire group. In so doing I am helping to recall the egalitarian ideals which animated the project's formation, ideals which may have been eroded by recent stress or chronic pressure. I want to understand, and help them understand, the problem in the context of their goals as an alternative service, not as a psychiatric disorder or a deficiency of technical knowledge or a matter of adjustment to a cultural norm with which they disagree. Here are two examples of "presenting problems" and my response to them:

Hotline: The founder and coordinator of a year-old suburban "hot-line for youth," a 35-year-old social worker named Alice, asks me to consult with the young people who answer the phones. She tells me that in recent weeks increasing numbers of phone aides have spoken to her about their difficulties with callers: One aide is troubled by a youth who mastur-bates while he talks to her; another is skeptical of his abilities to deal with a suicidal call; another is upset when someone "talks crazy." The coordinator wonders if I could give some basic lectures on psychopathology and psychiatric diagnosis.

We talk for several hours about the ongoing operation of the hotline; about her desire to galvanize and educate the community to respect their children's autonomy; about the stuffiness of traditional agencies and their censorious insensitivity to the felt problems of young people. We can hear the muffled rings of the phones in the next room. Occasionally a phone aide barges into her office, excuses himself, asks questions and ducks out again.

I learn that the coordinator is terribly overworked, that she serves as unofficial confidante and therapist as well as coordinator and supervisor; that all of the details of administration—of scheduling, training, publicity and community education—must be attended to by her. She is fond of the young phone aides, feels that they are bright and sensitive, but hesi-tates to turn over much of the administrative responsibility to them: Some-times they seem so irresponsible and bewildered; and, besides, what would the Mental Health Association which sponsors the hotline say?

I suggest to Alice that neither of us really knows the best way, if indeed there is any way at all, for the hotline to use my skills; that the only way to find out is to ask the people who do the work. I suggest that I take some time to get to know how the hotline functions; to read their descriptions of training; and sit around with the young people while they answer the phones. At the next monthly training meeting, where the paid phone aides, the volunteer aides and various professional advisers will be present, we will talk about me and my interests and skills and let those present ask questions and speak with one another about my possible usefulness.

The group foster home. Several times in the course of getting acquainted with alternative services in an urban neighborhood, 17-year-old Tom is mentioned to me. He lives in a group foster home for adolescents where six teenagers stay with two counselors until they are 18. He is, according to the counselors in the runaway house and teachers at the free high school, "crazy" and "dangerous." They tell me that the counselors in the group foster home are at their wit's ends and are prepared to commit Tom to a mental hospital. They wonder aloud if I can be of help. Could I do some kind of intensive therapy with Tom? Is there a place where he could go which is less repressive and more pleasant than a traditional mental hospital?

When Fred and Ann, the group foster home counselors, get in touch with me, I arrange to visit them. In their late 20's, dressed in dungarees and tee shirts, they lean forward from a thrift shop sofa to detail their difficulties with Tom. For his first 8 months in the house Tom was shy and tractable, eager for, but wary of, affection from his counselors. In the last few months he has begun to act increasingly strange. He accuses Fred and Ann of not caring for him and of wanting to destroy him. He spends long periods of time alone in his room, screaming at unseen tormentors. He refuses to discuss his work in school or to participate in communal tasks such as dishwashing and house cleaning. When questioned, he becomes enraged and abusive; on several occasions he has pushed and punched both counselors and the young residents. He says he trusts no one in the house and resists any attempts to "help" him.

Afterwards I ask Fred and Ann about themselves and the house. He is a former seminarian, an Army veteran of 29. She is 26, taught high school and worked at the runaway house before she came to the group foster home. Both have been politically active as campaign workers for liberal politicians and as participants in the recent May Day demonstrations. To them the house is a place where they try to live and work with young people in an open and noncoercive fashion. At the house, things are not always easy. Sometimes they know that they are more "authoritarian" than they want to be. But they wonder how else the house will stay even minimally clean, and whether some of the kids wouldn't be content to watch the TV all day.

But Tom is really most on their minds. They cannot say more than half a dozen sentences without returning to some new piece of destructive or incomprehensible behavior. Just recently he has begun to come into Ann's room late at night to grab her and then swear at her when she tells him to leave. She and Fred are scared and baffled, afraid that he might hurt them physically or that they, in their efforts to be helpful, might unknowingly be destructive. The other residents, they tell me, are fed up as well as scared; they want Tom out. Would I see him in therapy or prescribe medicine to calm him? Do I know, they wonder, of another place for him to live?

I tell Ann and Fred that I would like to see and understand Tom as a member of their home, not as a psychologically ill individual. Perhaps their perspective on him is only one among many ways of understanding what is going on. They have lived together for many months. Perhaps Tom's behavior is best understood in the context of his relationships to those around him. The best way for me to understand what is going on is to see them all together—the two counselors and the six teenage residents. I suggest, if everyone in the house approves my coming and knows why I've been asked, that I come to their weekly house meeting.

The Work of Consulting

Consultation is a dialectical process. As a consultant my work includes participating in the process and understanding it. Though there are certain commonalities of attitudes and ideologies in alternative service projects, each situation is a new world. And though my own perspective is limited, I too am different in each situation. My actions and observations, questions and interpretations change the situation into which I have been called. The changed situation is reflected in and expressed by changes in the individuals in the group, in their relationships with one another, in the work of the larger group to which they belong, and in the relationships between all of these and me.

This dialectic is personal. Like the workers in the projects, I do not believe that people should be constrained by rigid, socially-defined roles; and so, like them, I try to be open to putting and understanding myself in new situations. Over 2 years I have grown closer to the people with whom I have worked. I have become more friendly, available, receptive and participative in ways I would not have imagined. These informal acts seem to arise naturally from my consultation with alternative social service groups, to complement and enrich it.

When they are going through crises I feel comfortable listening to individual young people, taking a walk with them, sharing my perceptions and feelings. If someone wants psychotherapy I will help find him a therapist; if he needs a recommendation for a job I will write one. If a group foster home resident has just moved out on her own I may visit her in her new apartment, bringing with me a housewarming gift. If people are celebrating, I will eat and drink and party with them, at their homes or at mine. The longer I work with these young people the more we become important parts of each others' worlds.

Here briefly are outlines of some of the major changes that have taken place in 2 years of consultative work.

Hotline. The meeting with the entire staff of the hotline spawned a planning meeting of 20 members. Here the phone aides decided that they would like me to be part of a group where they could talk about "whatever we feel like: problems with troublesome callers, difficulties at work, personal problems, psychological theory, whatever."

This group consisted of a dozen of the most active phone aides, half of them paid, half volunteers, all in their late teens or early 20s. For 9 months, we met 2 hours once weekly. I was an increasingly involved but almost wholly nondirective presence. At times our discussion focused on the relationship of members in the group (whether membership should be open or closed; how one or another person dominated or retreated from the discussion; one person's expression of feelings for another); at times they dealt with individual "problems" (one person's difficulties with her parents, another's impending abortion, a third's preoccupation with acid flashbacks); and at times they dealt with work-related problems (how to handle someone who is suicidal; frustration with callers who will not accept help or advice; the difficulties of going to school, holding a second job and working at hotline).

Gradually a feeling of closeness developed, an ease with being vulnerable in the group and a confidence that problems could be worked out with the help of the other members. Each of the phone aides learned that the others were equally concerned about appearing to be competent and "together" phone aides; and each discovered that, like him, the others vacillated between suspicion that they were "just as messed up as the callers" and a conviction that their problems were trivial compared to those of the people who called. They shared common problems of growing up and away from their parents and provided support for each other's efforts to do so. They tried, among them, to sort out dissatisfactions with school from anxieties about it; and debated at length and in different contexts the relative advantages of and relationships between political and personal change.

Slowly the group began to exercise more influence on the hotline. Occasionally a phone aide who was not a member would come to discuss a pressing problem with us. More often it was the style and substance of group discussions which affected the rest of the hotline. Having discovered that all the group members sometimes grew anxious on the phone, the aides could be more supportive of others who worked with them on their shifts. Feeling more comfortable about talking over their problem calls with me they could make better use of another psychiatrist who consulted with them. Accustomed to scrutinizing the power relationships in the group, they could now examine those in the hotline as a whole: If they could deal with a sometimes overwhelming member of the group, then they could begin to deal with him and with others who became overwhelming in administrative meetings. One of the group members summed up the effect: "Hotline," he said, "is supposed to be about communication and sharing. It happens in this group, so maybe we can make it happen on the phones and in our committees."

After 5 months, the 15 paid staff asked me to come as a "facilitator" to their monthly meetings with the coordinator and the executive director of the Mental Health Association. The phone aides wanted more responsibility, more active participation in making the decisions and setting the policy which governed their work. They thought I might help them assume this power and exercise it fairly.

I entered this new group—the paid staff members—trusted by six of the members who were in the previous group and with good will from most of those who had not been. From the beginning I felt comfortable taking a more active role than I had previously. I had discovered over the 4 or 5 months of "the group" an ability to be frank with the phone aides. I had a sense also of the kinds of things that troubled them; and had experienced their capacity for understanding and change and mutual supportiveness.

When, in the first meeting, some of the paid staff spoke irritably of difficulties with new volunteers, of absenteeism and lack of enthusiasm, I asked them if they had asked the volunteers why they were dissatisfied. And when they said they hadn't, I asked about their failure to do so. Quickly they began to question themselves: What was hotline about anyway? How did they expect to be useful to the callers, to help them deal openly with their problems, if they, the paid staff, didn't deal with theirs? Hotline was about communicating with and helping people to look at what was troubling them, and helping them to act on that knowledge. Maybe like the callers, they were scared to confront other peoples' criticisms. But they had to, if they wanted to improve their service. And they couldn't improve their service if they weren't more open with each other.

At this point one of the newer phone aides described her difficulties in first coming to hotline, the anxiety of training, the feeling that the more experienced staff—and especially the paid phone aides—were exclusive, cliquish and condescending. Having listened carefully, other people shared their own memories of first coming to hotline.

Then the group began to discuss concrete ways for making the experience at hotline more educational and less threatening. They began to consider reforming the hiring and training procedures as well as ways of dealing interpersonally with their self-protective cliquishness. Later that day and during the following meetings, the paid staff began to question its role.

During the next two meetings, the impatience of one staff member with another's work led to a general discussion of the difficulties the whole paid staff had in getting and receiving constructive criticism from one another. Hesitantly each phone aide talked about his work, the difficulties that he experienced with it, and the help that he would like from the others.

At the following meeting the discussion was widened to include the structure of the hotline as a whole. Alice confessed that she was reluctant to give up certain kinds of responsibility even though she would like to. The paid staff in turn said that she ought to give some up. She could not deal with all the work; and, beyond that, hotline was "about sharing responsibility." Just as they had to listen to and give responsibility to their volunteers, so Alice had to hear and to yield responsibility to them. Alice agreed.

With this shared insight as a basis, the staff over the next year changed virtually every aspect of hotline. The young paid staff took over from professional volunteers (psychologists, psychiatrists, social workers) the chairmanship of all the committees. They reformed the selection procedure and made it conform more to the felt needs of the new volunteers—mixing introspective and supportive sessions with didactic discussions about drugs, sex, and community resources. Instead of appearing occasionally and resentfully at professionals' lectures on "psychiatric problems" the phone aides themselves organized workshops on the problems they perceived. They took part in a massive program of community education; and initiated—in response once again to both the callers' needs and to their sense of their own expanding skills—a crisis-oriented "outreach" program.

Gradually, the paid staff meetings came to be of central importance to the functioning of the hotline. They provided a source of support and criticism for highly-motivated workers, an arena for discussion of hotline problems and an opportunity to make major policy decisions. In these early sessions, and in the ones that followed, I tried to point out the interconnectedness of personal change and group difficulties with organizational structure and economic and political realities. I worked to keep a perspective on all of their perspectives and as I did so tried to provide an example to the phone aides of this kind of understanding. I tried to help the aides translate individual feelings into group action; to understand the effects of group and social forces on their feelings; to appreciate the immediacy of their relationships in the group and to investigate them as reflective of more widespread hotline situations: One phone aide's anxious hustling for more paid hours might reflect an inconsiderateness toward his fellow workers; but it was also responsive to the low hourly wages. Smoking dope in the office was perhaps a form of "acting out" against the association which permitted the hotline to use it facilities; but it was also the gesture of young people who were furious at their elders' condescension. An experienced phone aide's sudden temptation to tell the police about a troublesome caller raised an intrinsically important issue; but it also reflected his anxiety about his departure from the hotline and his somewhat insulting fear that chaos would follow.

The group foster home. By the time the first house meeting was half over, Tom and Ann were at it: Ann gently, patiently, explaining and inquiring; Tom, shouting, swearing, demanding. Ann had simply wanted to know what subjects Tom was taking at the Free High School, and Tom replied that "it's none of your [*expletive*] business." When Ann said she was "interested" in him and "cared" about him, he began to shout and swear at her, accusing her of "lying" and "[*expletive*] me over." When she asked for specific examples, Tom maintained that this request for specifics was just one more example of "what you are doing to me." He insisted that Ann hated him. The more vehemently she, Fred, and the other teenagers denied this—"how about the time she sat up all night with you" or "took you on a camping trip," etc.—the more incoherently furious Tom became. "You're crazy," his best friend said to him in conclusion. "You belong in a hospital."

The next week the group opened with a discussion about cleaning the house. Almost everyone had been negligent, but Tom rapidly became the focus of anger. "I'll clean up if I feel like it," he said. "And if I don't, no amount of prodding will get me to do it. The only reason I clean up," he added, "is because if I don't you'll throw me out." When the others denied this, Tom said that they were crazy, that they were robots. At this point several house members turned to me. "You see what we mean," said one. "It's hopeless."

I suggested that they hadn't really tried to understand what Tom meant, that rather than deal with the substantive issues that he had been raising, they had decided that he was crazy. What were the issues they asked? Well, I suggested, Tom felt that he had the right to decide what he wanted to take at school, and if, indeed, he wanted to take anything at all. Ann, on the other hand, was sure that it was good for Tom to take certain courses or at least some courses; and this was not apparent to Tom. But it wasn't simply a matter of disagreement, because at one point—in fact when Tom had first come to the house—he had been told that he either had to go to school or work in order to stay there. So the velvet glove of Ann's concern for Tom's education and welfare concealed the mailed fist of banishment for disobedience to her wishes.

At the end of this meeting, I told the members of the house that I thought I could be helpful to them by continuing to come as participant-observer to their weekly meetings and asked them to decide if they wanted me. They informed me later that week that they did; and, in addition, they invited me to have dinner with them after each meeting.

Over the next 4 or 5 weeks many of the powerful but unacknowledged contradictions of the house's operation became available to the group's scrutiny. Each time the group threatened to ignore one, Tom escalated his "crazy" behavior—once he spat at Ann, another time he threw a table in Fred's direction. Often he sat rigid and trembling, his fists clenched, his eyes rolled upwards. He accused the other people in the house of being "on an ego trip," hypocritical and murderous.

As a consultant, my function was to help Tom to articulate his difficulties with the house and to help the rest of the house to understand them as criticisms rather than symptoms. "You say you care about me," Tom summarized, "but you are willing to force me to do things I don't want to because you, with your values, believe that they are good for me. It's clear to me that you care more for your values than you do for me."

Soon the counselors could see that they were attending more to bureaucratic demands—the expectations of the larger collective of which the house was a part; the welfare department which financed and supervised Tom's living situation—and cultural conventions—the belief that teenagers should be in school or gainfully employed—than to a particular young person's needs. The counselors acknowledged the disparity between their point of view and Tom's, and admitted to the contradiction between "caring about Tom" and insisting he go to school; and this in turn led them to question the attitudes which permitted them to "do things for the teenagers" whether or not the latter were capable of doing these things for themselves, or indeed wanted them to be done.

As the social pressure on Tom eased, he stopped "acting crazy" and began, without coercion, to take part in house activities.

Since the counselors had felt uncomfortable in their patronizing role, the results of this process, though anxiety-provoking, were also liberating for them. They began to feel freer to challenge the assumptions of their jobs and to divest themselves of much of their power over the teenagers. Allowing the rules and structures of the house to conform to the non-coercive ideals that they shared with the young people, they became more credible to them and more helpful.

It now became important for me to support all of the house members in their ongoing struggles to make the house more democratic: to point out at once the consequences of inequities of power and the difficulties which they experienced in giving up their roles as "counselors" and "kids."

One problem with which the house had to deal was drug use. Previously there had been a counselor and project-imposed rule against drug use in the house: Anyone caught with drugs would be kicked out. In fact, one person had been caught and allowed to stay. Generally, the "kids" had lied about drugs, claiming that there were none in the house, while hiding them from the counselors. Inevitably this drove a wedge between the counselors and the young people. The "kids" were resentful and guilty, the counselors, suspicious and self-righteously angry at the betrayal which they knew the young people were perpetrating. In addition, none of the young people felt free to talk about drug-related problems: fears of addiction, the possibility of hepatitis, a bad trip that they had or were having.

Only when serious group discussions were finally held about drugs in the house, about the real dangers of police arrests and the possible closing down of the house; and only after the young people had a real stake in and power over the house did they agree not to have drugs there. It was no longer a "counselor's rule," but a matter of common interest and of group survival.

The greater equality between counselors and teenage residents provided the basis for new and more democratic processes of decisionmaking. All decisions—regarding budgets, hiring of new counselors, rules, admission of new young people to the house, overnight guests—were made in common. The greater equality also provided a basis for greater personal frankness in the meetings. Teenage residents who were not afraid that some privilege would be taken away could criticize counselors more freely or reveal personal difficulties without fears of arbitrary reprisal. Similarly the counselors, no longer burdened with moralistic postures, could be more straightforward about their own annoyances, anxieties and concerns.

To sustain these changes, the house began to insist that the larger organization of which they were a part respect their developing autonomy. In the ensuing struggles, the group foster home began to push the entire collective to live up to the ideals of openness and freedom, of respect for young people and participatory democracy which had animated its formation. The young people and their counselors began to ask for a greater voice in overall decisionmaking, for workshop discussions on drugs and sex, and for changes in hiring procedures which would respect the autonomy of each project. As the struggle intensified, I supported the house's initiative and helped its members to articulate positions based on our common experience. Simultaneously, I became a participant in the decisionmaking of the larger collective—an advocate as well as advisor.

This change in role—as important to me as it was to the members of the house and the larger collective—was precipitated by a conflict over hiring procedure. Ann was leaving and the house wanted to hire Jeanine to replace her. Tom and Liza, another teenaged resident, had known Jeanine for a year; she had come to visit them in the house, had invited them to her own home. In the course of hours sitting at the house's kitchen table she had come to know the other young people and their counselors. With Ann about to leave she seemed a natural choice to replace her. After a week's formal interview, it was clear that all the house members wanted her as a counselor; clear also that they feared and resented the power of the larger collective to veto their decision.

When Jeanine's hiring was vetoed by a counselor from the other group foster home, a full-scale battle ensued. Alan said he thought Jeanine was irresponsible and untrustworthy, that he did not want her in his collective. The house members refused to honor his veto. They contended that his objections were based partly on his justified anger at some of the house's past actions and partly on his desire to control them. In any case they felt that his exercise of his veto was proof that he should not have one, that the structure of the collective should change to respect their autonomy. They were the ones who would be living and working with Jeanine and were capable of deciding if they wanted to. The collective should support, not oppress, them.

Gradually my involvement increased. I began by trying to mediate between the two group foster homes, helping the house to acknowledge that it had pushed through Jeanine's hiring but pointing out that the larger collectivity had long been only a constraining myth; the house's hiring of Jeanine was an assertion—perhaps hasty and inconsiderate but still accurate —of its actual independence. When the mediation was inconclusive, I found myself involved with the entire collective of projects.

In several day-long meetings at which almost all of the collective's 40 workers were present I provided support for the house members. I tried to point out that in obeying the letter of its rules the larger group was subverting the spirit of collectivity which was actually developing in the house. Jeanine was already a real member of the house. If the larger collective tried to deny the house's right to have her there, they were violating the human needs and relationships which the house—and indeed, the whole alternative service collective—had been formed to further.

As I spoke I heard myself grow angry and impassioned; it was important to me that the young people in the house had whomever they wanted there. As the struggle continued I felt close to them and they—surprised and pleased at the extent of my support—seemed to grow closer to me. Occasionally, I found myself saying "we" instead of "you" or "they" when I referred to the house.

By the time the larger collective finally allowed Jeanine to be hired, each of the individual projects was becoming more conscious of its own needs, more desirous of independence, and more sensitive to the arbitrary power which could be exercised by the collective as a whole or by its coordinators. Within 2 months a group was created to reorganize the larger collective, to make it more responsive to each project, its workers and the young people whom they served. Because the struggle over Jeanine's hiring had brought me closer to the larger collective, I felt comfortable joining the reorganization group, eager to share my experience, and help shape the larger collective.

Conclusions

The longer I work with alternative services and the young people who are involved with them, the more it seems that conclusions are actually progress reports, that clinical summaries can only be chapters in biography and autobiography. At our best, we consultants and counselors, teenage phone aides and teenage residents are engaged in a common effort to provide and receive services without simplifying or mystifying or abstracting our experience of those whom we serve or of one another. We are, as we do this, consciously trying to build communities which are at once flexible enough to sustain our differences and our growth and strong and open enough to respect, and perhaps change or include, those whom we touch.

Hotline. In the current monthly meetings there are five people from the original discussion group—eight, including Alice, from the first paid staff meetings that I attended 18 months ago. At them, the business of the hotline —scheduling, reports on committee work, planning for training and publicity —is carried on with steadily increasing ease. Everyone seems to feel responsible for a portion of the workload, eager to assume or share duties. More and more the staff seems to want to use the meeting time to offer and receive criticism, to ask for help on specific problems with callers and with their reactions to them.

The integration of new paid staff is anticipated by members who have been around, and discussed thoroughly. To avoid the discomforts of the past, the old staff plans to have extra discussions and "sensitivity training" sessions for new members.

Instead of being its recalcitrant stepchild the hotline has become a permanent part of the Mental Health Association. Its members now participate in the larger work of the Association, supporting its programs for young people, confronting those policies they disagree with, providing the association as a whole with a kind of leavening action. When recently there were complaints from the landlord about noise and litter, hotline and the Mental Health Association responded jointly, with few divisive accusations.

Hotline workers, who wanted to work face-to-face or more intensively with people and/or needed full-time jobs, have become active in other youth services in the county. One is house manager of a nearby suburban runaway house where other phone aides volunteer their time. Two of the phone aides are part of a drug counseling program in a rural area of the county. For them hotline provided "training in counseling skills"; but, more important, it was an experience in working cooperatively and intimately with others. From it they derived a conviction about the necessity for "sharing power and responsibility" that they bring to their new work. These three all continue to work at hotline; to value its services and the support of the group there; and to provide a critical perspective on a situation they know well, but now have some distance from.

Others have dropped out of hotline for a while, "burnt out," and have come back, refreshed, to work again. Their departures aroused some sadness in the other workers but were accepted with remarkable ease; everyone seemed to understand the need for time off and away. Their welcome back was sincere and unaffected. Still others have moved away, some with the intention of setting up other, similar, services in their new communities.

As the paid staff becomes more secure about its ability to work together and survive, to learn and change, the need for me seems less. Occasionally I will raise an unpleasant issue—next year's funding for instance—which has been temporarily ignored; or point out an unwanted but possible future consequence of a present action. But, increasingly, as I see my perspective emerge naturally from group discussions, I have the sense of being a reassuring presence, a valuable resource, a friend, rather than a necessary catalyst.

The group foster home. Though I stopped attending the weekly house meetings several months ago (after 20 months) I continue to keep in touch with the people who live in the house. Periodically, I hear from those who have left: An ex-counselor is asking for a recommendation or wants to stop by to say hello; a young person on his own is lonely or confused and remembers that I could listen well. In my place at weekly house meetings are a married couple who are friends of mine, a psychiatric social worker and a social psychologist. The house is pleased with them; and they, working without pay, are gratified by the mutuality and informality of their experience with the house.

For most of the young people who have lived there—who have previously spent years in mental hospitals and reformatories, in a succession of individual and group foster homes and boarding schools—the house has been a great boon. In contrast to other group foster homes (Gordon 1974) I have seen, which seem regularly to extrude one "troublemaker" or "psychotic" or "acter-out" after another, no one has been told to leave the house. It has not, as 17-year-old Ellen said, in a recent conversation "solved all my problems" but it has been "a place where you could do whatever you had to to find out what you wanted to do and who you were"; or as Liz, who has lived in the house for almost 3 years described it to a girl who was thinking about living there: "It's a place where you can learn how to live—with other people and on your own." Even for those young people who left angrily, disappointed that there wasn't "more" it was at least a "place that let you leave," one that respected a young person's right to decide. When young people leave, the house helps them get settled outside. Afterwards, it remains available for support. Young people who have left can often return to stay for a while in times of crisis or when they simply need a bed. They stop in to talk or eat or, occasionally, to go to the weekly house meeting.

Ann and Fred have gone, as has Sterling whom they hired; Jeanine remains as does Cynthia, a counselor who came 8 months ago. The feeling in the house between the young people and the counselors is generally supportive and affectionate, occasionally combative; but it is not burdened with unspoken expectations and mystified power. The counselors are firmly committed to the right of the young people to make their own decisions (and their own "mistakes"), to caring about them without coercing them. Within rules that are established in common or imposed on all by the juvenile court system, young people and counselors are free to live and grow as they want.

The lives of both counselors and young people have grown out from the house. Those who continue to live there have begun to do, on their own terms and for their own reasons, what neither parents nor reform schools nor mental institutions could force them to do. Tom has taken a full-time job which he enjoys. Ed, Ellen and Liz—all of whom had dropped out of high school—have begun to study on their own as well as to hold down jobs. And all of them have become increasingly involved in the life and work of the larger collective. I see them—Jeanine and Cynthia, Ellen and Tom—at weekly "community meetings" where the whole collective gathers or around the runaway house where they stop by to talk or just hang out.

Their experience in the house has strengthened their ability to understand the problems of the larger collective and has sustained them in recent political and financial struggles within it. Jeanine is particularly concerned with evaluating and strengthening the collective organization and with training new workers. Cynthia has been active in extending the collective's services to neighborhood people. Tom is spending some of his time studying "people in situations" and different ways of understanding families and group; after community meetings we often share our observations. Ellen is a leader in a group of alternative service workers and former "runaways" who are speaking to Congress people and Health, Education and Welfare officials about "juvenile rights" and a proposed "runaway youth act." The other day I ran into Ed delivering surplus food to Runaway House. And Liz has helped in planning the collective's "annual report."

Like the counselors and the young people my interests have also evolved. My concern with the house has enlarged to include the entire collective. My experience there has made me more knowledgeable and confident about the possibilities of creating living and working communities that can grow and change in response to the needs of the people in them and of those they serve. I want to understand how this happens; to help people who are doing it to avoid the traps that come with increasing longevity, success and size; and to be part of this process.

At the same time I have become more sensitive to the need for a larger community to support the collective efforts and to the desirability of reaching out toward young people before they become hopelessly estranged from their families.

My increased awareness of the plight of young people, of the collective's ability to work with them, and of the insufficiency and counter-productiveness of many traditional agencies and their "parent identified" individual and family therapists led me to initiate a weekly seminar in family counseling. For the last year and a half, counselors from the collective as well as graduate students and professional therapists in the Metropolitan area have come regularly to discuss each other's work with young people and their families; to generate out of our shared beliefs and experiences new ways of helping and relating to them. Slowly, these graduate students and therapists have become part of the larger community which supports the collective of projects.

Similarly, I have tried to help the reorganization group to be continually responsive to the needs of the entire collective, to make it an ongoing "internal consultation and evaluation group." There I have learned, with representatives from each of the projects, to work and to think together with a group of people. We try to be sensitive to individual needs and to show how these may reflect project and collective-wide problems. Reorganization gives the entire collective an ongoing perspective on itself; it provides a forum for new ideas and future plans; generates support "task forces" for individual projects that are in turmoil and new structures for collective-wide needs; and it provides a thoughtful, self-critical brake on precipitous action.

Consultation itself has become a collective process.

References

Bakan, David. Adolescence in America. *Daedalus*, 100(4):979–995, 1971.

Bremner, Robert H., *Children and Youth in America*. A documentary history. Volumes I and II. Cambridge: Harvard University Press, 1971.

Gordon, James. Schizophrenia. *Collier's Yearbook*, 1971a. pp. 45–53.

Gordon, James. "Who is Mad? Who is Sane?" The radical psychiatry of R.D. Laing. *Atlantic*, 230(1):50–66, January, 1971b; and Ruitenbeek, Hendrik. *Going Crazy: The Radical Therapy of R.D. Laing*. New York: Bantam Books. 1972. pp. 65–101.

Gordon, James. The Vietnamization of our children. *The Washingtonian*, November, 1972.

Gordon, James. "Group Foster Homes for Adolescents: What Makes Sense?" Unpublished paper (to be finished 1974).

Hall, Stanley G. *Adolescence: Its Psychology and Its Relations to Physiology, Anthropology, Sociology, Sex, Crime, Religion and Education*. New York: Appleton, 1904.

Handlin, Oscar, and Handlin, Mary. Facing life: Youth and the family in American history. *Atlantic*, 1971.

Mead, Margaret. *Coming of Age in Samoa*. New York: W. Morrow and Company, 1928.

Mead, Margaret. *Growing Up in New Guinea*. New York: W. Morrow and Company 1930.

6

Community Psychiatry With the Communications Media*

Stephen B. Bernstein and Beryce W. MacLennan

Investigations of the possible role of the community psychiatrist as consultant to, or collaborator with, the communications media (television, radio, newspapers, magazines) and the impact of these media as molders of mental health attitudes are notably lacking in psychiatric literature.

This paper deals with two subjects: (1) the community psychiatrist as mental health consultant to one of the media—a commercial radio station; and (2) the possible roles of the media in preventive psychiatry and in the initiation of positive action to foster community mental health. We will describe a project to explore these areas that was begun under the auspices of the National Institute of Mental Health.

Implicit in many types of mental health consultation is a multiplier effect whereby an individual consultant may influence the care of varying numbers of people, whether these be the clients of a group of social workers, the students in a specific school, or the inhabitants of a police precinct. The multiplier is a function of the number of persons with whom the consultant helps the consultee to deal. The communications media—their administrators, program planners, writers and public personalities—both reflect and mold public attitudes. Therefore they must be considered actual or potential social agencies. The potential positive effects on community mental health of consultation and collaboration with a radio station with 25,000 to 50,000 listeners, a newspaper with a million readers, or a television station with three million viewers can only be surmised.

The project described here involved consultation with a commercial radio station in the areas of intramural staff relations and organizational needs, mental health program planning, off-the-air community-oriented activities, and subsequent collaboration with the station in a community action program.

The planning of the project had certain inherent complexities different from those in most previously described consultations. This was because the proposed consultation was to a commercial, federally regulated, nonpsy-

* Reprinted from the *American Journal of Psychiatry*, Vol. 128, 1971, pp. 722–727 by permission of the publisher and the authors. Copyrighted 1971, The American Psychiatric Association.

chiatrically oriented agency. Initiation of the relationship would be by the consultant rather than by the consultee. The consultant would be involved in an area in which he had little technical knowledge. On the other hand, ameliorating factors included: (1) the presence of dynamically oriented management consultation in many industries; and (2) Federal Communication Commission regulations that require public service involvement by the media, making licensure renewal in some respects dependent upon this involvement.

Entry Phase

Since this was regarded as a pilot project, we made efforts to initiate a consultation on a small scale. An FM radio station was felt to be the most feasible because many were available in the area, their programming was thought to be quite flexible and fairly independent of large network programming requirements, and they seemed to have local autonomy. We sent letters of introduction to several area radio station program directors presenting one of us as a research psychiatrist at the National Institute of Mental Health who was interested in the role of the communications media in benefiting the community. Ongoing consultation by this psychiatrist in areas of "public service programming, liaison with medical and mental health specialists, and community service" was offered. Although consultation on intramural staff relations was thought to be an important area, we felt that the station would be more likely to accept advice in less personal areas and in general would be resistant to interpersonal intervention. This supposition proved incorrect, since replies to the letter were unsatisfactory until the subject of consultation in the area of "organizational needs" was added to subsequent letters.

Although early efforts were made to contact station program directors, it soon became evident that effective contact could only be made through the general manager of the station, since program directors do not have the authority or independence to acknowledge the need or usefulness of such consultation. Eventually we learned that since most area FM stations were owned by AM stations, consultation would be applicable to both because they were generally integrated functionally.

We received a response to the exploratory letter from the general manager of a large commercial AM-FM station whose FM program director fortunately had shown the letter to him. The station was one of the top three in a large eastern metropolitan area with a listenership at various times of between 25,000 and 60,000 persons. It was known in the community to be quite progressive and intensely interested in community service. It had had successes in public service documentaries and had even on several occasions influenced legislation through its activities.

At the initial meeting with the general manager, consultation was offered in the following areas: organizational and staff relations, medical and mental health program planning, and assistance in off-the-air community activities in which the station was involved. There was open discussion of the fact that the type of consultation proposed was new, although consultation to industry by management consultants was common. The type of relationship envisioned, although we hoped it would result in improved productivity on the part of the staff, would also be aimed at exploring the various ways a radio station could affect community medical and mental health and effect social change. It was obvious that the general manager saw a possible benefit for the station through the initial goal of increasing his ability to deal with his staff and thereby increasing their efficiency and competence. He also expressed a great deal of interest in improving community-oriented educational and action programs both on and off the air.

The consultant's own goals were to make use of the opportunity to learn about the area of public communication; to help the general manager to achieve his goals for the station; and to explore the possibility of future collaboration with the station in understanding the effect of the media on community values and various ways in which the media might further preventive and remedial mental health care. Both consultant and consultee acknowledged, however, that the exact nature of the consultation and the specific results and goals that might be expected would emerge as the consultation developed.

The Consultation

The consulting psychiatrist and the general manager agreed to meet once weekly for approximately 1 hour. In addition, the consultant would attend the monthly meetings of department heads and would also have one 1-hour session with each of the seven department heads. It was hoped that subsequently the individual department heads would call upon the consultant for private discussions of their own areas (AM programming, FM programming, news, community activities, engineering, sales, and business management).

It was decided that the consultant would be introduced to the station as a psychiatrist who was acting as a management consultant. Department heads were encouraged to meet with the consultant to discuss interpersonal or other departmental matters. It was clearly stated that the consultant would meet with the general manager once weekly but that the issues discussed between the consultant and the individual department heads would in general be kept confidential.

The expectations and concerns of both the consultant and the general manager at this point bear on the initiation of the consultation. Following

Caplan (1964), the relationship of the consultant to the general manager and the staff members was seen as relatively unstructured, open, and as not involving the seeking out of unconscious material or discussion of matters more appropriate for psychotherapy. It was felt that by merely being "in proximity," the consultant would be sought out by the staff and could become involved in the various aspects of the radio station and its functioning. The consultant believed that early signs of his acceptance by the department heads would be evidenced by requests for discussions of their areas or work. These discussions were thought vital in many ways, since the department heads worked in the areas of community involvement that were to be part of the consultation.

Initial concerns of the consultant were that discussions of the interpersonal relationships of the staff members and the general manager might bring up resistance to the consultation and that the consultant would be blamed for possible staff changes that might occur (in a displacement of anger from the general manager). He also wondered whether the consultative relationship with the general manager would make a working relationship with the department heads unfeasible, thereby closing the areas of community service to the consultant.

The general manager hoped that the consultation would help him to become a better leader and decrease some of the hostility present among the department heads. He also hoped that his department heads might learn how to deal more effectively with their staffs. He saw the consultation as innovative both for the corporation that owned the station and for the communications industry. He was, however, concerned about the initial effect of the introduction of a psychiatrist on the station personnel: whether this would be seen as a sign of difficulty or poor leadership by his superiors at the corporate level, and whether he would be thought to be weak or incompetent by his subordinates at the station.

The general manager described some of the details of the radio business, the history of his own station, and the personalities of the department heads. It was obvious to the consultant from the perceptive descriptions and characterizations of the department heads given by the general manager and from his own observations of some of the group dynamics at several staff meetings that there was a general feeling of anxiety, anger and insecurity. This was partly due to the recent loss of a charismatic general manager who had been promoted to a position in a different city. The current general manager, who had been his program director, was himself involved in the feeling of loss. These feelings were also manifested as a division between several older, more established department heads and the newer, younger ones, who were in conflict over philosophical goals in broadcasting, program orientation, and the amount of community involvement of the station. The department heads were involved in a group-dynamic situation that did not allow them to have a primary identity with the goals of the station

but forced them to deal with their own insecurity by building their departments into private empires, competing with other departments. The acting
out of these feelings took the form of inefficient interdepartmental communication, resulting in such problems as advertisements being put on the air late
and contracts being misplaced.

The initial clarification of the dynamics of this situation with the general
manager served both to orient him toward understanding his staff and also
to educate him in methods he could use to evaluate future situations. The
general manager agreed with this clarification and saw that it fit in well
with his own characterizations of his personnel and their relations.

Requests by individual department heads for consultation at first were
infrequent because of the desire of each for control and autonomy in relation to other department heads and to the general manager. Meetings were
held with the department heads at the suggestion of the general manager,
but although they would discuss difficulties in staff relations, they would
rarely discuss the needs of their own departments. However, the availability
of the consultant for meetings, and the fact that it was known that these
were handled discreetly, together with the frequent presence of the consultant at the station, tended to gradually increase the number of informal
conversations with the department heads.

During these discussions, when specific conflicts were brought up, efforts
were made to have the persons involved talk about them informally.
Objectivity was encouraged by asking that one person consider what he
would do if he were in the place of another. Emphasis was placed on the
tendency of people to "tune out" each other in conversation, especially
when they are angry with each other.

The general manager wanted to be the kind of executive who could allow
his department heads to be independent individuals; he saw himself as an
advisor rather than a controller. In private conversation with him the consultant tried to help him increase communication among various staff
members and also help him support department heads regarding their competence. A feeling of security would decrease their need for control and
foster identification with the station as a whole. Material from the current
working situation was used to point out difficulties in communication. The
most common topic of conversation was the relationship of the general
manager to his department heads and the dynamics of this group. The
general manager was able to understand and apply these concepts. After
about a month, the initial goals of the consultation became more clear;
these were to increase staff communication with the station as a whole rather
than with individual departments.

Landmarks

During the first 6 months of the consultation, a series of events occurred that showed an increase in trust and respect for the consultant by the general manager and staff and that led to an increased openness and acceptance of the consultant in different areas of the station's operation.

The first landmark occurred when one of the older (and certainly more aggressive) department heads, who was at first quite unsympathetic to the need for consultation, suggested that in addition to the once-a-month department head meeting, a second, less structured meeting be added to help "increase communication." The acknowledgement of the need for such meetings by the department heads, the successful leadership of the meetings by the general manager, and the resulting cohesion of the group brought the consultant closer to the group and made them more able to ask for his advice regarding the work of their individual departments.

The next landmark was an invitation to the consultant, who was warmly referred to by many of the staff as "the station shrink," to a station-sponsored dinner where several new station disk jockeys were to be introduced to prospective advertisers. When the consultant declined to attend, the program director who had made the suggestion replied, "I think having a station shrink is a mark of status, and we'd be proud to have you there."

Requests for aid by department heads in the content areas became more numerous. Although the consultant declined to be "on the air," he was of assistance in other ways. At a time when there were bomb scares in numerous cities across the country, the news director requested a brief formulation concerning what makes a person call in a bomb threat. On another occasion advice was asked on how to go about finding an expert to discuss the subject of prostitution on a proposed documentary series.

The final sign from the department heads of group cohesion and identification with the general aims of the station occurred approximately 4 months after the consultation began. This was signaled by the department heads encouraging the general manager to redecorate and refurbish the station. When told by him that economic circumstances would make it necessary to put off the redecoration, they banded together to work out arrangements whereby they could reduce their own department budgets sufficiently to make the redecoration of the station feasible. This was seen, both by the consultant and the consultee, as a definite sign of staff unification and identification with the station as a whole. Although at times there were reversions to previous miscommunications and hostilities, these were of short duration and were easily dealt with.

Results were readily observable after 6 months. These included increased department head and general staff communication, interdependence and identification with the station as a whole, greater understanding and ability to react to change, lessening of acting out of hostilities, and finally, the ability of the entire department head group to act in a common effort that will be described next.

Community Involvement

Four months after the beginning of the consultation, the consultant was asked by the general manager and the station news director to participate in planning and preparing an extensive documentary series on drug abuse. The invitation to participate and collaborate seemed to signal the consultant's acceptance into the program-content area, an area that was more closely protected than the staff's interpersonal relations.

A 20-part documentary series emphasizing drugs of abuse was prepared for airing in 3 minute segments, five times a day, together with editorials, public service announcements and evening talk shows. All of these encouraged citizen involvement, especially that of civic organizations such as Kiwanis, Rotary and PTAs. A 115-page source book describing the area's drug abuse and mental health facilities and alternative action programs in drug abuse prevention, education, treatment and rehabilitation was prepared by the station together with an audio-visual presentation. Both of these were presented at meetings of the civic groups that had become interested in the project by the broadcasts. Involvement of these organizations either individually or in association with the various social agencies that were interested in the project was encouraged.

The station set up a drug abuse "hot line" under the supervision of various social agencies and in cooperation with the consultant. Civic organizations were encouraged to set up community houses in local areas where information on drugs and treatment facilities could be given and discussions on drug abuse could be held between potential or current drug users and representatives of drug abuse agencies.

The first of these community houses was set up in a small building on the radio station grounds and was staffed by station personnel, local college students and other volunteers. Seven other centers are currently functioning well, and 15 more will soon open at municipal recreation facilities.

The station has thus acted as initiator, coordinator and facilitator of this community action project. Evaluation of the effort is being carried out by measures of listener response, activities of organizations involved, and results of the activities.

Conclusions

The consultation and collaboration we have described occurred under the most fortuitous circumstances. The station involved was successful, open to new ideas and already committed to extensive community service programming and activities. They were a receptive group of people, and in spite of some initial interpersonal difficulties, the consultant entered a stable situation.

Although this effort at community psychiatry with the media centered around a specific radio station, it is applicable to other radio stations, television, newspapers, and magazines. Areas in which the communications media might further community mental health are numerous. For example, "soap operas" might incorporate hints on child care in their stories; other programs might be as successful in educating parents as "Sesame Street" seems to be in educating children. General managers of television and radio stations and newspaper editors might participate on local mental health boards and thereby become increasingly responsive to local mental health needs. Through consultation to advertising councils, advertisers might come to sponsor more creative mental health programs, and advertisements might stress adaptive and coping skills. If greater mental health involvement can be shown to be beneficial to the goals of the station, newspaper, or magazine and in some way pay off in the reward system of the media, continued effort can be assured.

Consultation and collaboration as we have used the terms here signify a relationship between professionals, with the consultant or collaborator possessing certain skills useful to the consultee. Certainly a knowledge of interpersonal relations, group dynamics, liaison with mental health experts and experience in community service qualify a consultant. The independence and autonomy of both the consultant and consultee, and the nonregressive relationship fostered, assure a professional relationship. In these ways, consultation with the communications media can lead to collaboration in the area of community mental health.

Reference

Caplan, G. *Principles of Preventive Psychiatry*. New York: Basic Books, 1964.

7

Mental Health Consultation to Early Child Care

Stanley I. Greenspan, Robert A. Nover, and C. Hal Brunt

Mental health consultation to day care and other early child care settings is emerging as new and exciting work. What is valuable about early child care settings is the potential enhancing effect they can have on the developing child. We would like to view mental health consultation to day care or other early child care settings in terms of its goals regarding this potential. During the early years, more than at any other time, growth is rapidly taking place in all lines of development. The complexity of factors which contribute to the emotional development of the child and the variety of ways in which organizations, groups or individuals can facilitate the emotional development of children provide the mental health consultant with the opportunity for making his contribution in many different and imaginative ways. Because mental health consultation to early child care is not a clearly delineated field, we would like to approach our task with some important preliminary considerations before discussing our specific consultation experiences.

First we will consider aspects of the attributes and skills that the day care consultants need and the types of contributions they may make. Secondly, we will present a model which consultants may use to conceptualize how to facilitate emotional development. Thirdly, we will present three illustrations of how we as mental health consultants worked in different child care settings.

I. General Considerations on the Role of the Mental Health Consultant in Day Care

The study of children in the earliest years of life has been characterized as a new frontier for mental health. A growing body of data supports the thesis that the developing child has a high degree of plasticity and is as often limited by his environment as his genetic potential. The environment may either serve as an agent of irreversible damage or may enhance a child's potential development (Hunt 1971; Lourie 1971).

Day care programs of all types are now developing. New perspectives toward child rearing, coupled with the growing demand for early child care, require that mental health professionals examine their relevance and consider the contributions they can make.

The potential damaging effects of early separation, inconsistent early mothering figures, and a lack of consistent and early stimulation are well documented (Bowlby 1969; Ainsworth 1969; Caldwell 1970). Some investigators have suggested that the type of mother-child interaction necessary for optimal growth can only occur at home with a loving, sensitive mother. Similar conditions, they feel, are almost impossible to create artificially in a day care setting and, therefore, day care should only be used where absolutely essential or where the home is clearly noxious. Others suggest the quality of care is more relevant than issues regarding separation from the mother. There is, however, general agreement that certain types of care can enhance the development of children who otherwise would receive inadequate care, and there is a growing body of practical knowledge on how to set up growth-facilitating early child care environments (Provence 1967; Evans 1972; Elardo 1972).

While we are accumulating research, we need to know more about specific methods to stimulate emotional development. How, for example, do we integrate our knowledge of cognitive development and affective development in order to formulate programs which would facilitate both aspects of the personality? While there are some useful general ideas of what constitutes a good or facilitating environment (Joint Commission Report on the Mental Health of Children 1970), we have not yet arrived at sophisticated or differentiated descriptions of such environments. More longitudinal and comparative studies are needed to reinforce our clinical beliefs.

We must also consider how much experience mental health consultants have with preschool children. While psychiatry is only one source of trained mental health consultants, it should be noted that few training programs in child psychiatry funded in the last 5 years by the National Institute of Mental Health placed any emphasis on training psychiatrists specifically for working with children in the early years of life. In a review of 97 training programs in child psychiatry, 34% mentioned a comprehensive study of child development while only 12% emphasized work with children under the age of 5 years. The problems are thus compounded.

While there is clearly a need for more training in the area of early child care, the mental health consultant can contribute from what he already knows in terms of research, consulting, educating, developing programs to influence policy, as well as in diagnosis and treatment.

A mental health consultant to early child care settings should have direct experience with children and a clinical approach based on a thorough knowledge of childhood psychopathology as well as child development.

This approach is important because dealing with the many perspectives contributing to the field of child care demands a comprehensive view of all factors influencing the growth process. While the different points of view may complement each other, they may offer conflicting explanations for behavioral phenomena which may lead to different program and policy recommendations. For example, those with a socio-economic orientation to child care might recommend making investment opportunities available to a community to improve its financial status. Through that, they would predict that the family and the care of children would improve. Those with a child-oriented approach might recommend that limited financial resources available be given to centers which would deal immediately with the physical and mental health problems of children.

Another illustration of the implications of different orientations has to do with what approaches will be supported by our research efforts. If research on outcome is done by those with an educational orientation, with the outcome measure an assessment of intellectual development, the elements in a program which support emotional development, such as measures of self-esteem and flexibility of coping style may be ignored. This issue becomes significant where the focus on cognitive development may interfere with proper emotional development as was noted in some of the Parent Child Centers (Work 1972). The mental health consultant must recognize that if we attend to only those outcomes which we know how to measure, we may be ignoring important areas of development which we cannot measure and only barely conceptualize.

In addition to a basic clinical approach, the mental health consultant to early child care settings needs specific expertise in understanding the relationship between the constitutional endowment of a child, the facilitating environment, and subsequent manifest behavior. More specifically, at a psychological level his expertise extends to understanding the complex interplay of needs and emotions; capacities for regulation; reality testing and self-esteem maintenance; fears, and self-imposed restrictions; the capacities for forming and maintaining relationships and how all of these inter-relate to facilitate adaptation or lead to maladaption.

Through his understanding of psychopathology, the mental health consultant should also be able to delineate not only developmental deviations, but the wide variations of normality and the confusing gray area between pathology and normal functioning. As part of this orientation, many mental health consultants will be expert in the impact of the unconscious. Through clinical work the mental health consultant will have a vantage point from which to see the impact of unconscious forces on the life of the individuals, groups, and communities.

Due to his intense individual work with many different youngsters, the mental health consultant should have a unique understanding of the internal life of children. In addition to working with children directly, facilitating team efforts, and educating others about children, he can facilitate the design of environments which will assure sensitive personal contact between a child and his care-taker. The elements of quality and constancy which are essential to proper emotional development are not easily provided. For example, through accurate clinical observation, Margaret Mahler (1972) has delineated the subphases of Separation-Individuation. In the "rapproach-ment" subphase, she emphasizes that the child who has been behaving independently, with a feeling of his mother's power, realizes his separateness and needs greater maternal contact. A sensitive mother will usually respond to her child's greater need. Would a day care worker without an intimate relationship to a child recognize this greater need, or view the child's need for more contact as regressive and inappropriate? The mental health consultant needs to translate such subtle clinical observations into practical suggestions for day care workers. These would go beyond general comments about good or bad mothering and begin to delineate specific needs of children and specific growth facilitating attitudes and responses from the environment. In addition, the mental health consultant can help child care workers respect their own emotions and wishes which may interfere with proper caretaking.

The mental health consultant can also stimulate a clinical research attitude. Community-based programs which are primarily interested in services often feel research is contrary to their basic goals and see researchers as intruders. The mental health consultant can convey a clinical research attitude which is a middle position between service delivery and pure research. He can convey to the staff of a center the importance of accurate behavioral and emotional descriptions to help them understand the results of their inter-ventions. Learning to observe and report subtle emotional and behavioral change enhances the clinical ability of individual staff members, and also forms the basis of a most valuable type of research for pilot programs. Solnit, in the Joint Commission Report, emphasized that all service delivery should also serve research goals.

II. A Framework for Mental Health Consultation to Early Child Care

Having presented some aspects of the role of the mental health consul-tant in early child care settings, we have further developed a specific model within which the mental health consultant can organize his approach to the consultation. As stated earlier, our goal in mental health consultation is to facilitate the growth and development of children with emphasis on emo-tional development. In order to accomplish this, consultants have become involved with entire organizations, groups, and key personnel in a wide variety of endeavors from understanding the administrative structure of a setting to helping the caretaker and/or parents of a child understand the types of difficulties that particular child is having. With such a multitude of potential functions, the consultant must always keep in mind his advocacy for the child. The consultant may become involved with the organizational structure of an institution and the way this structure affects the staff, and the way the staff affect one another; however, the influence of these relationships on the child must remain the focus.

The assumption often is that if one works with the organization, understands the administrative structure, identifies psychopathology and educates the staff, eventually the young child will benefit. However, one must be alert to the consultant's potential for a defensive attitude about the lack of complete knowledge available in many areas concerning child development and attempt to delineate how the consultant's involvement with a setting will facilitate specific developmental processes in the child. As he studies the organization, for example, he should also be delineating the specific ways the organization's vicissitudes influence the child and his development. There are four general ways in which an early child care setting can facilitate the emotional growth of young children. In the following discussion, reference will be made to the setting or environment with the understanding that specific individuals are the representatives of the environment.

Goal 1—To Accurately Perceive What the Child Is Communicating

Accurate perception of what a child is communicating contributes to reality testing. Very young children do not communicate directly and whatever language they may use may not have the same meaning to them as it does to adults. In order to perceive accurately what a child is communicating it is imperative to understand how children at different developmental stages communicate, i.e., their particular language. Occasionally a person who spends a good deal of time with a child may come to understand his language intuitively, as an empathetic mother does. In day care settings, however, intense continual, one-to-one relating is not the rule.

Even with sufficient knowledge, a second factor often complicates the accurate perception of what a child is communicating. This factor is the caretaker's own emotional capacities. It is not uncommon for adults in an environment to distort a child's communication, not out of ignorance, but because of anxiety about what the youngster is presenting. Adults who have difficulty with aggression may tend to deny destructive behavior in a young child and instead describe the child as "playing nicely." The accurate perception of what a child is communicating depends on both the cognitive and emotional capacities of those comprising the child's environment.

Goal 2—To Empathetically Understand What a Child Is Emotionally Experiencing

Empathetic understanding of a child's emotions will help the child gain a sense of security in the expression of his emotions and, through that, a sense of trust in his world. This task also depends on the emotional and cognitive capacities of those comprising the environment. Because children do not communicate directly, an understanding of the child's inner experiences at different stages of development is important. Even with sufficient knowledge adults will often distort or be unable to empathetically understand the child because of their own emotional concerns. It is known that caretakers, including mothers, will often either over-identify with the emotional concerns of the children they care for or will be aloof and distant and unable to empathetically understand the emotional concerns of the children.

Goal 3—To Respond in a Temporally Effective Way to the Child's Communications

Temporally effective responses help the child establish a sense of internal control and eventually secure internal boundaries. A child defines himself and develops his internal control system through feedback from the environment. Not every response from the child demands an immediate response from the environment. Children also need to establish a capacity for delay and reliance on their own internal controls. Temporally effective responses by adults should take into account the child's relative need for both immediate and delayed feedback.

Goal 4—To Respond Flexibly and Differentially to the Child's Communications

Flexible and differential responses to a child's communications help the child establish a flexible coping style. Some adults tend to respond in generalized and rigid ways to all behaviors of children. Even to be rigidly positive in responding to children's communications leads to misconceptions by the child about mature interpersonal communications and to the development by him of a rigid coping style. Since the child defines his inner world in part by responses from his environment, the more differentiated or specific these responses are in relation to the child's various communications, the greater will be his capacity to form a differentiated repertoire of coping mechanisms. Adult responses should be specific to specific needs of the child in different situations. The capacity for flexible and differential responses from the environment depends on both cognitive and emotional capacities of the day care workers. For example, rigid attitudes about sexual behaviors might lead the caretaker to respond inflexibly to certain behaviors in a child, consolidating fixed attitudes in the child toward these behaviors. Different types of sexual behavior and exploration need different responses from the adult. Some sexual behavior might be stopped; other sexual behavior might be tolerated or encouraged depending upon the age, sex, and situation of the child and adult. It is important to recognize that a superficially appearing flexible response from the "enlightened" adult will not help the child establish a flexible coping style as the child will sense the adult's true anxiety and inflexibility.

To optimally accomplish the above four goals, a cognitively sophisticated and emotionally mature environment is needed. While the cognitive require- ments are often emphasized, especially in model day care programs, the requirements of emotional maturity from the setting need further emphasis. If we consider that children openly express concerns about dependency, sexuality, aggression, control, power, separation, and that all adults have some difficulties in some of these areas, it is not then unreasonable to assume that those working with children will experience conflict some of the time in some areas.

Our general model is based on the concept of a hierarchy of affective issues concerning dependency, aggression, and sexuality stemming from each developmental level of childhood. These affective issues become mani- fested in child-adult interactions due to the child's developmentally ap- propriate and/or special concerns. To the degree the adult has not resolved some of these issues, he or she experiences anxiety and puts into effect certain defenses which will interfere with facilitating the child's growth with regard to these issues. Some appreciation of these affective issues, the anxiety they generate, and the coping devices which follow, will facilitate the adult's capacity to relate to children. It should be highlighted that many consulting attempts in the mental health field focus on understanding and openness in communication. This approach is specific in that it attempts to delineate for caretakers the specific affective concerns that interfere with their understanding and responding. From the most blatant distortion of reality (denial) to more subtle and sophisticated inflexible attitudes toward certain behaviors of children, the adult conflicts will surely have their impact on the child's development.

In applying this framework, the child cannot be considered as a unitary entity. The child must be considered in the context of his family, i.e., in the context of his relationship with his mother, father, siblings, and extended family. Many children in the first 2 years of life experience themselves as a part of a parent and many parents experience themselves as a part of their infants. Caretakers in different settings may also have this experi- ence with the infants they care for. When considering a young child, we are often considering a parent-child organization which is partially dif- ferentiated and partially fused. For example, we cannot ignore the mother who brings her child to the infant center early in the morning and seems panicked at being separated from her infant. Responding to her panic is responding to the child's needs as well. We must perceive, empathetically understand, and respond in a temporally effective and flexible way to the mother's communications just as we would wish to do with the child. We also would, where indicated, want to help all family members to facilitate the child's development in these ways, thus extending the approach of the setting into the home and bringing a sense of continuity to the child's care. If this basic idea is extended a step further, we must not only take into account a child's relationship with family members, but also the history, traditions, values, and attitudes of their culture of origin and/or the culture in which they live.

The caretaker who interacts closely with infants or young children will also be influenced by family, peers, day care supervisors and administration. The supervisors and administration will in turn relate to a larger agency or a board of directors or the owners in a privately owned center, who in turn may relate to a government bureaucracy. Even in family day care where one woman is both the caretaker and the director, she relates to others in the neighborhood, her own family and often to a social service agency. What must be the focus is the way in which certain aspects of this complex network can either facilitate or interfere with the four goals outlined.

III. Illustrations of Mental Health Consultation in Three Early Child Care Settings

Early child care programs include a broad range of day care services. Infant day care primarily serves children under 2 years of age, while family day care implies care of young children by a woman in her own home. Private center-based care where children are brought to a program, usually run for a profit, is another major way of organizing day care services for children.

Infant Day Care

The infant education center where we consulted for 18 months was organized in the early 1970s to provide quality day care to a maximum of 30 black infants, 3 weeks to 2 years of age. The program was established by the local neighborhood community working administratively through a local "Model Cities" funding agency. The stated goals were to develop a program of stimulation and enrichment geared to each child's needs and abilities and to provide health and mental health services to facilitate the child's physical, emotional and cognitive development. There was a parent education program as well as ongoing inservice training of the staff members in the care of young children. Special priority for admission was given to children with physical, nutritional and emotional problems as well as infants of teenage mothers—so called "high risk" children.

Once the mental health consultant has assessed the overall administration, he can turn to the problems encountered by the individual staff in caring for the infants in their care, gearing his consultation to the ongoing staff training program. For example, several of the mothers of infants in the program where one of us (Nover) consulted were clinically depressed and a few were borderline. None had had previous contact with a mental health professional. The consultant's role in this case was one of assisting the staff in obtaining for these mothers the emotional support they needed. Many of the staff were concerned about drawing attention to the mothers' problems for fear they would alienate them from the program. This was especially true of those parents who were known drug addicts. It was, therefore, necessary to solve these issues in consultation before the staff could effectively deal with the mental health needs of the parents. Successful relations with the parents is a key to success in any day care program. This further illustrates our point that the child is part of a parent-child organization and in order to facilitate the child's development, one must attend to the needs of the parent, especially when severe clinical illness is present.

Early case finding and early intervention with infants is a potential area of expertise for the child psychiatry consultant in infant day care and one where the most rewards may be forthcoming. Also it provides an opportunity for the mental health consultant to do what he knows best. One method for assessing personality development that we developed was a bi-weekly, interdisciplinary meeting that was held at the center. The ongoing progress of several children was reviewed at each meeting. There was cooperation between the consultants, which included the pediatrician as well as a child development specialist. Others on the interdisciplinary team included a nutritionist, educational specialist, child care workers and the administrator of the program. All of these individuals played a key role in the formulation of the daily care of each child in the center and hence *all* were *necessary* participants in the meetings that reviewed each child's developmental progress. As each child's development was reviewed, a developmental prescription was formulated. A key aspect of the formulation of the prescription was the inclusion of information from staff members who provided day-to-day care of the children. The developmental prescription was intended to have an impact on all of those aspects of the life of the child both at home and at the center where the multidisciplinary group felt improvements were indicated. The prescription was then acted upon in the ensuing weeks by the staff at the center and the child's development was once again reviewed.

A child 12 months of age was reported by the staff to have great difficulty napping in his crib at the center, particularly in the first 2 or 3 days of each week. He was also reported to have a lack of interest in eating his meals while at the center. Other information brought into the meeting by the social work aide revealed that the child had slept in his mother's bed since 1 month of age (a not uncommon finding in many urban communities and one that occasionally leads to smothering of the infant). The social worker also learned that the boy, the mother's first child, was kept up late at night in order to keep the mother company. In addition, the child had an irregular eating schedule at home and was still being given baby food. The prescription formulated by the consultants recommended that the mother be encouraged to place the child in a crib of his own at home. In addition, a specific staff person was assigned to feed the child each day, and the mother was given nutritional counseling. Coordination of the sleeping pattern of the child at home on weekends and at the center was worked out. Here the child's specific needs were delineated and his environment extending into his home was altered to meet his needs.

Another key role for a mental health consultant to infant day care centers is to assist the staff in improving communication with each other and with the parents. The majority of the staff experienced difficulty understanding and being objective about the problems of those parents whom they served who were economically deprived, emotionally disturbed, or physically ill. Many of the staff came from a similar background and it was difficult for them to put distance between themselves and the needs of the children. The staff often felt thrust into roles of baby sitters and diaper changers which affected their own images as infant caretakers and stimulators. Understanding of the balance between useful empathy and over-identification was useful in helping the staff.

The staff of the day care center, in dealing with the problems presented by the parents of the child, had no previous experiences in utilizing the mental health professional as a consultant. It was necessary that the relationship develop as an outcome of mutual trust. One way to do this was by using a weekly group meeting that enabled the staff to express their concerns about individual infants. These group meetings served to build respect among the staff for each other, to make them more aware of each other's needs as well as those of the infants and parents. The staff thus learned to translate the expression of their own thoughts and observations into attempts to enhance the infant's capacity for communication in a natural and spontaneous way. A key factor in this aspect of the consultant's work in a day care center is the recognition of the fact that the staff themselves may have been inadequately mothered and raised in situations where conversation and curiosity were discouraged or squelched. Developing and furthering this capacity in the staff of an infant center is an ongoing task of a mental health consultant. Providing day care is stressful and at times exhausting. The mental health consultant needs to be aware of these stresses and to help the staff sort out their own feelings in order for them to conduct meaningful programs for the children in their care. In the group the mental health consultant attempted to convey a method by which the staff could get in touch with their own feelings and take useful distance from them (e.g., in the instances where they led to over-identification) so that they could, on their own, use introspection to enhance their skills with children.

The mental health consultant also has a role to play in the implementation of different types of programs for infants and parents with varying needs, depending on age, social and family conditions and the developmental stage of the infant. Alternatives more suitable for some children than for others such as home day care and part-time day care need to be explored, and day care providers need to be educated as to their efficacy. Infant day care for children under 2 should not replace parental care but ought to be available to those infants where economic and social forces lead to the infant being deprived of opportunities for healthy growth and development. For the consultant who is primarily interested in the child, this is perhaps the most important area to assess.

The mental health consultant in an infant day care center, furthermore, has a unique opportunity to use his clinical skills and research methods to learn about development in the first 2 years of life and to validate basic theoretical assumptions, early intervention techniques, and assessment procedures, as well as those developmental deviations assumed to lead to maladaptation and psychopathology in later life.

Family Day Care

In family day care also known as home day care, a person, often a mother, cares for a small group of other parents' children in her home. It is the oldest form of day care (Stewart 1968) and is currently being viewed not only as an efficient way of caring for children while parents are working, but as a way to facilitate child development and care for children with special needs (Foley 1966; Edwards 1968). Of the approximately 5 or 6 million children under 6 years of age who have working mothers (Keyserling 1973), approximately 37% are cared for in someone else's home (Low and Spindler 1968). Preliminary investigations have led researchers to be quite optimistic in their impressions of the quality of care currently given in family day care and of the potential for further developing this resource (Keyserling 1972; Emlen 1972; Henicke 1973; Sale 1973). The assets of family day care include physical convenience, cultural continuity, small size, similarity to the family, potential for good nurturance, new learning, and consumer control.

Certain basic questions arise concerning family day care: What transpires in the home between day care workers and the children? What programs would be useful to facilitate the potential of the family day care environment to further the development of children? To both learn about the experiences of family day care workers and enhance their skills at the same time, Greenspan organized an unstructured group training program with the Department of Social Service in a suburban county. The purpose of the training program was to learn about the workers' experiences. We expected to facilitate their capacity to cognitively and empathetically (1) understand the children in their care, (2) understand their personal reactions to the children, and (3) respond to the children in ways that would facilitate psychological growth within the framework of the four goals of the training program (outlined earlier).

Two groups of eight women were formed and met for eight sessions. The 16 women, ages 23–50, were racially mixed. The group leaders were two social service workers who were involved daily in administrating family day care in the county. The group leaders received a course in group principles and supervision from a child psychiatrist (the mental health consultant) and a psychologist. In addition to our anticipating emotional growth in the group members, we had an expectation that the experience of leading a group under supervision would facilitate the leader's psychological growth with regard to future work with family day care workers.

Some principles of group leadership that we stressed to the leaders and some of their difficulties which emerged will be described. The leaders were told that they had two roles: (1) to define the group by establishing its boundaries, (2) to facilitate the discussion of overt and covert themes that emerged naturally.

The group leaders were instructed (1) to attempt to sensitively understand what a group member was saying, (2) to facilitate discussion among the other group members by rewording and clarifying, (3) to pose questions that would further develop the theme that a member of the group was raising, (4) to highlight the group theme when it seemed to be emerging in fragments, (5) to use any acceptable means to encourage members to express their thoughts or feelings, and (6) to facilitate the development of their expressions. The leader was *not* to direct or suggest issues for discussion under any circumstances. For example, where there was a sense of nothingness, apathy, or boredom emanating from the group, the issue to be discussed or developed was apathy, nothingness, or boredom.

In order to be able to facilitate the group discussion a number of techniques were stressed. One technique was to move between process and content. For example, if the women were talking about food preparation in a competitive manner, the leader could point out their competitiveness (process) or could facilitate the discussion on food preparation (content).

A second technique was to look for affect within the group. If the group talked about food preparation and the predominant affect seemed to be one of apathy or boredom, the emotion was highlighted as an essential issue. This could develop into a discussion of apathy or boredom in general, and/or a discussion about what to do when children were bored or what to do when one was bored when taking care of children.

A third technique involved moving between the adult and child world and between relationships within and outside the group. An example of movement from the adult to child world was seen when the women in the group were competing with one another and discussion of adult competition ensued. When this discussion had been exhausted, the leader could have proposed that the group use their insights about adult competition to understand competition among children. Similarly, the leader could suggest that the adults fantasize about child situations they didn't understand in order to better understand what children may be experiencing.

In addition, it was possible to move from within the group to what happened in relationships outside the group. Using the above example of competition, the leader could ask the women to explore the theme of competition in their other relationships. Similarly, when someone mentioned a relationship problem that involved outsiders the leader could ask if the same problem existed in the group.

A fourth technique was to emphasize the differences between stereotyped and flexible ways of dealing with stressful situations. The leaders were to highlight how different response patterns could reflect different perceptions of the child's communications and different personal reactions to a child. They were to further highlight how feelings of anxiety, helplessness, or anger within the day care workers could foster stereotypic behavior which might interfere with the potential for flexible ways of responding to the children.

The basic principle for the leaders to follow was to be sensitive to issues being raised and to attempt to generalize from them. In this way, core areas of conflict or difficulty around themes of dependence, aggression, control, power, and separation would be highlighted from the specific contents and processes within the group.

In consultation with both group leaders we were sensitive to their emotional struggles while teaching them the principles of group leadership. The main issues were the leaders' initial feelings of suspicion and helplessness, their tendencies to deny or cover their own emotions stimulated by the group, and their use of specific defenses in dealing with strong emotions that arose in the group. One of their most prominent defenses was to claim boredom. It was interesting to see this defense emerge in the group leaders whenever the group interaction seemed most intense around primitive emotional issues.

The consultant used the consultation experience as a model for group leaders to use when conducting their own groups. We tried to understand the leaders' concerns in relation to the feelings the group was stimulating in them. The parallel would be for them to show the family day care workers how children stimulate certain feelings.

The group leaders both had quite interesting experiences. One group leader began her experience quite suspicious of family day care workers, calling them "noodles." She felt they were mercenary, uncaring, and "a pain in the neck." She ended the group experience feeling a part of her group and looking up to some of the family day care workers as mother figures. She expressed a sincere warm regard for them. In addition, this leader was initially quite suspicious of any approach which was focused on emotions. At the end of the experience, however, she was quite enthusiastic and suggested that in the future she should have individual interviews with the ladies to enhance their emotional exploration. Some group issues which she had some difficulties with were experiences of boredom, feelings that she was accomplishing nothing, occasional feelings that she was damaging the family day care workers, and feelings that she didn't know what she was doing.

We felt that the other group leader did not have as positive an experience. While she began the experience more optimistically, she became progressively more anxious during the group experience. She could not tolerate much emotionality and attempted to keep the group on concrete issues.

This consultation experience is unique in that the consultant implemented his goals through setting up the training groups. Some aspects of the groups' experiences should be illustrative. We will highlight a few aspects of the day care worker groups' experiences dealing with problem children and the group members' movement to become more open and cohesive.

> In a discussion of how to deal with a negativistic, passive boy who wouldn't sleep during the day, the family day care worker said she felt the boy had to conform to what the other children were doing. She had been involved in a power struggle with him where he stubbornly refused to sleep. An elucidation of the power struggle, verbalization of her angry feelings and suggestions from the group for her to be more flexible in her approach to him and to find some alternative activity for him, helped the day care worker become more flexible and the situation improved in a relatively short period of time.
>
> Two boys, 3 years old, refused to play with other children and attempted to form a symbiotic tie to the home day care worker. The home day care worker's concerns as verbalized in the group, included guilty and angry feelings as well as a general tension she felt in relation to these children. These feelings resulted in her giving them attention when they were in the symbiotic patterns. The group discussed with the mental health consultant the children's fears and dependency needs and the worker's general reactions to children's intense needs and emotions. After the home day care worker had spoken about her concerns, she noticed that her problem children began playing with the other children.

Other problems dealing with overt aggression, injuries, negativism and separation were also presented in the group. What impressed us most was the group members' desire for help and for their appreciation of beneficial changes in their children. Often, however, it was not clear what in the group experience had been helpful to the home day care workers. We felt that because of guilt, anger or feelings of helplessness about a child's behavior, the day care worker often inadvertently reinforced this behavior. Because of her continuing concerns the worker was locked into a maladaptive pattern. Verbalizing her feelings decreased her anxiety and permitted her to think and respond more flexibly. There were times when specific recommendations were helpful but these incidents were not as impressive as the nonspecific group effect. Even a seemingly minor change in a young child's environment may have a major impact on his behavior and eventual personality organization. In supervising the group leaders, the consultant stressed the mechanisms the leaders could use to facilitate this type of group process.

We were also impressed with the home day care workers' openness.

> A mother in one of the groups discussed rather calmly a 5-year-old boy whose behavior toward a younger boy indicated excessively aggressive sexual tendencies. This led to a general discussion of homosexuality, during which one lady told the group about her theories of sexual anatomy in relation to homosexuality. She confused homosexuality with hermaphroditism. This same lady equated nose bleed in boys with menstruating, and thought excessive nose bleeds could result in a boy's becoming sterile.

We felt that the verbalization and openness of the day care workers in the group, as indicated in part by the individuals volunteering their idiosyncratic explanations of sexuality, etc., highlighted the usefulness of an unstructured group setting as compared to a structured didactic setting.

The women formed rather cohesive groups quite easily and related to each other warmly. Their common concerns with children fostered an initial bond. We had anticipated more apprehension and initial resistance. Only one member left a group prior to termination. Racial issues were discussed in a displaced form in one group. While the group leader became tense, the group members used the discussion productively. As the two groups were coming to an end, the members talked quite enthusiastically about meeting on their own, exchanging equipment, and setting up outings with each other. This reflected their wish to maintain a support system for themselves after the group experience was formally terminated.

Center-Based Group Day Care

Group care in centers has become a natural life setting for many young children and all signs point to increases. To create a partnership between the fields of mental health and center-based day care is an important goal of mental health consultation. In doing so, there are two aspects of the consultation we will focus on: (1) the need for attention to the organizational system which surrounds any day care center, and (2) the direct use of our clinical knowledge of psychotherapeutic principles in training day care workers.

One of us (Brunt) established a relationship with the coordinator of child day care centers in the Public Health Department of a suburban county. The coordinator of day care was responsible for insuring high quality in day care programs provided by operators of center-based group care. The coordinator provided guidelines to newly developing centers, inspected each center for yearly licensing and enforced the State regulations. Particular attention was given staff-child ratios, the proper use of appropriate equipment, age-appropriate program planning, and the maintenance of health records. Licensing was done in collaboration with the environmental health staff who attended primarily to the sanitary and physical conditions of centers.

The day care division staff related to about 160 operating centers plus newly developing centers. Except for three, all were private, profit-making centers, serving about 7,000 children from 2 to 6 years of age. In 1970 about 2/3 of a million people were living in the county, including about 56,000 children spanning these 4 years of life. Thus, about 12% were reported to be in licensed centers. Estimates go considerably higher when unlicensed or "underground" centers are included.

From the beginning of the work it was clear that the day care coordinator and the mental health consultant shared similar goals which included: early detection of emotional or developmental problems, parent education, training of day care workers, and improvement of the relationship between the staff of the health department and day care centers. During the introductory phase visits were made to 16 proprietary day care centers with the health department staff on their routine monitoring visits. The findings were revealing of the problems faced by the private day care operators.

The day care operators had some disagreement with the State regulations. An organization of private day care operators was suing the State to block enforcement of the regulations. Many felt they were penalized by the strictness of the regulations and their efforts to comply. Some felt the strictness of the regulations encouraged "underground" operations. Major complaints concerned kitchen equipment, space requirements, and teacher-child ratios. Many of the operators repeatedly stated that the parents were very pleased and that the Government had no business interfering. This is an illustration of an organization or setting perceiving its "partial care-taker," the State regulatory organization, as rigid, arbitrary, and capricious. It corresponds to goal No. 4 in our framework of conditions leading to optimal growth and development. Not only did many of the day care centers fail to develop properly, but they behaved in a similarly rigid manner with the children in their care.

Eight programs appeared to adopt an authoritarian school model as illustrated by the grouping of 3-year-olds around a large table with one child standing in front reciting on a subject chosen by the teacher. Such practices indicated the frequent lack of recognition of the specific developmental needs of the child. The following all-too-familiar orders were common: "clean up," "don't cry," "stack the books," "straighten the chairs," "get in a circle," "toe the line." Rigid attitudes seemed to interact through the various levels of the system and finally have an impact on the children: Government administrators ←→ center directors ←→ center staff → children. Goals No. 2 and No. 4 were most prominently interfered with and the center staffs had difficulty being empathetic and flexible.

Many center staff had considerable experience (up to 15 years) in day care work, considered themselves to be doing a good job, and seemed to feel the regulations challenged their competence and threatened their self-esteem. When this observation and comments about the ramifications of rigid attitudes were made to the inspection team by the mental health consultant, it was helpful in encouraging a more tempered approach to monitoring, rather than the "strong arm of the law" approach which tended to foster rebellion or encourage rigidity.

There were several obvious problems that showed no improvement despite the efforts of the day care inspection team. The unannounced site visits by the Day Care Coordinator and Sanitarian of about 2 hours, once or twice a year, seemed helpful for approving the facilities, counting children and staff, checking the equipment list and reviewing health records, but rarely was it possible to focus on the emotional environment or child-adult interactions—a factor deserving a high priority.

Many centers seemed to be competitive with each other which tended to encourage higher quality, but unfortunately the competition most often focused on the appearance of the building and equipment rather than program content. Parent participation seemed minimal. Very few centers had attempted regular parent meetings; some required appointments for parents to visit. Attitudes by the operators toward parents were variable: some reported parent abuse of children; some felt parents abused the operators by coming late to pick up their children and withholding payments; others felt parents called on them for guidance as part of the extended family.

Within the Health Department, the day care staff, the environmental health staff, and primarily early childhood educators and sanitarians were often in disagreement about priorities in the regulations and who would have most influence in issuing the license. Isolated at the top of the organizational structure was the Director of the Health Department, a medical doctor, who was caught in the middle with complaints from his staff about priorities as well as complaints from the private operators about delays in licensing.

The problems which interfered with the functioning of the centers lay in three major lines of communication stemming from (1) interpersonal relationships between providers and monitors of day care, (2) the relationships among the providers of day care, and (3) the relationships between the various levels of administration within the monitoring agency (the Health Department).

All of these human problems in working together directed away from the primary task of the centers and had an impact on the development of the children. An extreme example occurred in the sudden closing of a center by the Health Department without adequately preparing the children or arranging for another placement. At times it seemed the interference was stemming from personality problems, but most often it was role confusion and inappropriate administrative practices which encouraged the interpersonal problems to mount. Using the principles and techniques of mental health program consultation and communication facilitation, suggestions were made for improving these working relationships. A few of the suggestions included the following: regular jointly planned meetings between providers and monitors to help develop a trusting alliance; regular meetings of the Health Department personnel, referred to above as monitors, to better clarify their roles and priorities (these meetings included the Director of the Health Department, the Day Care Division staff and the Environmental Health staff); separate visits to centers by the Day Care staff and Environmental Health staff to separate the consideration of such issues as costly kitchen equipment and program content; meetings of private day care operators with resource persons to discuss such issues as better accounting skills and cooperative buying of supplies. Much of the general anxiety and resistance to change by private day care operators stemmed from their anticipated loss of financial security, which was marginal at best.

The need to change organizational structure and to intervene in systems has been widely reported and acknowledged as important in carrying out the primary task. However, many mental health consultants are not trained in this area. Mental health consultants are often asked to provide case-oriented consultation when organizational change might be the most compelling need. One of the tasks for the consultant is to clarify with the center the kind of consultation they need and decide what part of the consultative role he is equipped to, or wishes to, provide. We have emphasized here the need for an organizational perspective and the use of these consultation techniques when a mental health professional is consulting in day care. However, as mentioned earlier, this organizational perspective must always be viewed in specific instances of its relationship to facilitating the child's development.

Another contribution unique to the mental health consultant is to address troublesome child-adult interactions and parent-staff interactions. On the basis of research studies and clinical experience, we believe that optimizing the development of children necessitates close attention to their relationships with others; therefore this emphasis is a natural one for the mental health professional. In this particular setting, the most feasible approach to influencing these relationships is to participate in training programs for providers of day care.

To aid in meeting the training requirements for group day care workers in Maryland, courses were sponsored by the State and funded through the Federal Manpower Development Training Act. State guidelines were provided for the courses, but the responsibility for implementing the course regarding specific content and staff was with each training facility. In this county the courses were organized by the Coordinator of Child Day Care in the Health Department. Three courses of 64 clock hours each were offered during the time of our participation, including about 20 day care workers in each course. Most of the workers where white women between 20 and 30 years of age. The teachers were early childhood educators who had previously taught similar courses. The mental health consultant and the teachers worked together in conceptualizing and planning the courses. The consultant was defined primarily as a resource person.

For most of the day care workers, this was their first contact with a child psychiatrist. In introducing himself to the classes, the consultant told them he would try to be helpful from the point of view of someone who had specialized training in a child's emotional development. Much of the course was devoted to planning for such subjects as the age-appropriate use of blocks, music, books, science, outdoor equipment, or meals. Other subjects included interpersonal relations of children in groups, understanding play and the physical problems of children. Certain other topics were of special interest to the consultant, such as the training in observations of children at 2, 3, and 4 years of age. These included both age-appropriate behavior and problem behavior. The majority of the group found the observations anxiety-provoking but the discussions very helpful. It seemed paradoxical that these people who observed children daily and knew a great deal about them became fearful and uncertain when asked to organize their observations. It was hoped that the observations would help the workers clarify the basis for program planning as well as recognition of problems. It became clear that most of the workers in these sessions were well aware of a child's problem but were reluctant to formally acknowledge it and to deal with it. Their reluctance seemed to stem from uncertainty about the reactions of parents and senior staff to the identification of a problem and uncertainty about the most appropriate action to take. The mental health consultant attempted (1) to help expand their repertory of responses to children and (2) to help them learn how to talk to a parent about a child whose behavior suggested a developmental or emotional problem. Skills translated from training and experience in interviewing techniques are useful to the worker in talking with parents, especially about problem areas. One of the methods used with the hope of facilitating helpful child-adult interactions was to present a number of situations from the Child-Adult Situational Index (Greenspan, Silver, Brunt 1974). The situations are structured similarly to this one:

The worker discovers a 3–1/2-year-old girl and a 4–1/2-year-old boy sitting in a corner behind the blocks with their pants down. Each worker was asked to respond with a brief statement about what the children and worker might be thinking and feeling and what action the worker might take. Some workers denied this had ever happened in their centers. Several felt the boy was too old for the girl and should be stopped from seducing her.

These situations provided an excellent stimulation to begin a discussion and an opportunity for the workers to organize their responses. We tended to organize the discussion around the four goals outlined earlier and especially looked for and commented on problems the workers would have with accurate perception, empathetic understanding and temporally and flexibly effective responses.

At the end of the courses most workers felt it had been a helpful experience which had motivated them for some continuing education. Throughout the course they pointed out how often parents ask them for counseling about child rearing. To fulfill these requests they wanted to learn a more organized method of understanding a child's development and assessing his needs for specific intervention. We felt that many workers and operators of private profit-making centers would welcome and can be positively influenced by mental health consultation and training.

Of course there were a number of familiar problems in the work. In the training sessions the workers would often present the behavior of children in their own families as disguised case consultation. Special care had to be taken to prevent the group from labeling any behavior as related to pathology. Religion and politics were frequently presented as issues. Some centers and workers were associated with various religious beliefs which influenced their child-rearing attitudes and program design. Opposing political ideologies were apparent between those who tended to favor public day care centers and those who obviously had an investment in private day care. The mental health consultant found working with early childhood educators an excellent experience and one good way to gain some continuing education about young children and particularly the behavior of children in groups. Of course, our competitiveness had to be recognized. However, the interdependency of those who work in early child care was more obvious, which no doubt stems from the nature of the young child whose physical, emotional, social, and cognitive components of development are so intricately interdependent.

Assessment of Consultation Experience

An important aspect of the consultation experience is an assessment of the differential impact of the consultant. We (Greenspan, Brunt) attempted to design ways to assess the characteristics of child care workers and the behavioral changes that occur as a result of training. To these ends, we developed a number of instruments which were aimed at reflecting our basic orientation of assessing emotional growth, emotional interaction, and level of psychological change that occurs as a result of training and consultation.

One of the instruments developed to measure outcome in the training program was the Child-Adult Situational Index. A projective test, it presents verbal descriptions of situations between adults and children. These situations were created to stimulate feelings around core conflict areas that occur between adults and children such as those around dependency, passivity, aggression, sex and separation.

For each situation the child care worker was asked to describe what she imagines the child is thinking and feeling, what she imagines the adult might be thinking and feeling, and how she imagines the adult should respond to the child. The responses were then scored for accuracy of perception, balanced empathetic understanding of emotion, temporally effective responsiveness, and flexibility and quality of response. The index scores assess the ability of the child care worker to perceive overt action and subtle emotion, integrate these perceptions and respond in a flexible, sensitive manner.

Looking at the individual situations, each one of which tapped a different conflict area, it was interesting to observe that the biggest differential between the pregroup and postgroup experience in favor of positive change was evident from a situation which read: "A 3-year-old girl walks over to the day care mother and hits her on the leg, she runs away and then come back and spits at the day care mother." This situation was intended to tap aggression toward the authority figure. Similar results occurred with regard to a description of a disruptive hyperactive child. The two items with the least differential between pre and post deal with dependency and sex. One read: "A 2-1/2-year-old boy begins crying and saying he wants Mommy. The day care mother tries to comfort him, but he cries even harder." The other read: "A 4-1/2-year-old boy hangs on the day care mother's shoulders. As he slides down off her, he rubs his hands against her breast. He does this a few times during the morning." This description was often ignored. The questions dealing with peer and authority aggression and being out of control seemed to discriminate change well, while questions that dealt with separation and sex did not. It is interesting to note that these results corresponded to the issues with which the day care workers and their leaders had the most difficulty.

Conclusion

We have attempted to describe some possible aspects of mental health consultation to early child care programs. The mental health consultant is in a position to use his dynamic understanding of human interaction to enhance the skills of caretakers, facilitate the growth and development of young children and to develop outcome measures for training of day care workers.

Many factors impinge on a child's growth and development both from within the child and from his environment. These include the child's physical, social, intellectual and emotional state as well as his own family setting. All of the factors may either enhance or impair the child's development. It is the function of the mental health consultant to assess these factors in order that he may contribute positively to the child's development both in the early child care setting and in his own family.

In the rush to organize and provide child care services, caution is necessary. Well organized settings, well trained staff and adequate services are only a few of the necessary ingredients for an early child care program to operate optimally. The mental health consultant has a unique opportunity to both participate in and contribute to the development of early child care services. However, he also has an obligation to be sure that the services offered match the needs of the child and his family.

References

Ainsworth, Mary O. Object Relations, Dependency and Attachment: A Theoretical Review of the Infant-Mother Relationship. *Child Development*, 40(4):969–1025, 1969.

Bowlby, J. *Attachment and Loss, I*, New York: Basic Books, 1969.

Caldwell, Bettye; Wright, Charlene; Honig, A.; and Tannenbaum, J. Infant day care and attachment. *American Journal of Orthopsychiatry*, 40:397–412, Apr. 1970.

Edwards, E. Family day care in a community action program. *Children*, 15(2):55–58, 1968.

Elardo, Richard, and Pagan, Betty. *Perspectives on Infant Day Care*. Orangeburg, S.C.: Southern Association on Children Under Six, 1972.

Emlen, A.C., and Watson, E.L. *Matchmaking in Neighborhood Day Care: A Descriptive Study of the Day Care Neighbor Service*. Portland, Oregon: Children's Bureau, OCD, DHEW.

Emlen, A.C. Slogans, slots and slander: The myth of day care. (brief review) *American Journal of Orthopsychiatry*, 42(2):250–251, 1972.

Evans, E. Belle, and Saia, G. *Day Care for Infants*. Boston, Mass.: Beacon Press, 1972.

Foley, F.A. Family day care for children. *Children*, 13(4):141–144, 1966.

Greenspan, S.I.; Silver, B.J.; and Brunt, C.H. "An Interaction Assessment Instrument: The Child-Adult Situational Index." Unpublished paper. Mental Health Study Center, Adelphi, Maryland, 1974.

Henicke, C.M.; Friedman, D.; Prescott, E.; Puncel, C. and Sale, J.S. The organization of day care: Considerations relating to the mental health of child and family. *American Journal of Orthopsychiatry*, 43(1):8–22, 1973.

Hunt, V. McV. Parent and child centers: Their basis in the behavioral and educational sciences. *American Journal of Orthopsychiatry,* 41(1):13–35, Jan. 1971.

Joint Commission on Mental Health of Children. *Crisis in Child Mental Health: Challenge for the 1970's.* New York: Harper and Row, 1970.

Keyserling, M.E. Our children are our future: Early childhood development and the need for services. *American Journal of Orthopsychiatry,* 43(1):4–7, 1973.

Keyserling, M.E. *Windows on Day Care.* New York: National Council of Jewish Women, 1972.

Lourie, Reginald. The first three years of life: An overview of a new frontier of psychiatry. *American Journal of Psychiatry,* 127:1957–1963, May 1971.

Low, S., and Spindler, P. *Child Care Arrangements of Working Mothers in the United States.* Children's Bureau Publication Number 46–1968. Washington, D.C.: Children's Bureau, Office of Child Development, D.H.E.W., 1968.

Mahler, Margaret S. On the first three subphases of separation individuation. *International Journal of Psychoanalysis,* 53:332–338, 1972.

Provence, Sally. *Guide for the Care of Infants in Groups.* Child Welfare League of America, 1967.

Sale, J.S. Family day care: One alternative in the delivery of developmental services. *American Journal of Orthopsychiatry,* 42(2):261–262, 1972.

Sale, J.S. Family day care: One alternative in the delivery of developmental services in early childhood. *American Journal of Orthopsychiatry,* 43(1):37–45, 1973.

Stewart, G.J. Day care: An under-used resource in child welfare. *Child Welfare,* 47(4):207–211, 1968.

Work, Henry H. Parent child centers: A working reappraisal. *American Journal of Orthopsychiatry,* 42(4):583–595, July 1972.

Training Mental Health Consultants: Some Illustrations, Problems, and Issues

8

Experiences in the Training of Mental Health Consultants

William J. Polk and Beryce W. MacLennan

Training in mental health consultation has paralleled the practice of consultation. Scope and methods have evolved from early case-oriented psychiatric evaluation (Abrahamson 1968; Aldrich 1968; Mendel 1966), to more sophisticated client- and consultee-oriented consultation undertaken with individuals or groups of consultees (Berlin 1964; Caplan 1959), with a gradual broadening of scope to include human relations, administrative, and program consultation (Caplan 1959; Newman 1967; MacLennan et al. 1970). A new dimension is added in community mental health center consultation programs when consultation is utilized by community mental health center staff as a tool in meeting the mental health needs of their catchment area (MacLennan, Quinn, and Schroeder 1970).

Each increase in scope has made new demands on mental health professionals and required them to learn additional skills.

Many writers have commented on the role and identity crisis which clinicians undergo when they move from direct treatment to consultation. Signell and Scott (1972) give a detailed description of this process as observed by them in a year-long seminar. They comment on the anxiety engendered in gaining access to and acceptance by consultees, in learning to understand situations at second-hand and at multidimensional levels and in being more definite and assertive than many therapists are trained to be.

Rogawski (1968) points out that while consultants require the clinical skills of "listening with the third ear" and of understanding psychodynamics and their management, the consultant must also be able to develop a nontherapeutic relationship based on mutual respect for competence. Caplan (1959) also emphasizes the danger of treating the consultee as a patient, and stresses that the consultant must be willing to relinquish decisionmaking and final responsibility for action to the consultee. Most beginning consultants and inexperienced consultees find the provision of direct mental health service very seductive. Caplan (1959) comments that it is sometimes harder for fully trained professionals than for students to make this change. As can be seen from our examples, problems can be experienced in both situations.

Rogawski (1968) points out that consultants must know and be able to use their own competence in the consultant relationships. In case consultation with groups of consultees, consultants must be able to assist the consultees in formulating and diagnosing problems, advise them on individual, family and group management, and understand the individual and group dynamics of the consultees. They must be able to discuss the problems in the language of the consultee and to understand the institutional and community background (Scheidlinger 1969; Newman 1967). In program consultation, consultants must also be competent to deal with management, institutional and interagency problems and to advise on planning and evaluation. They have to, at least, be able to analyze the structure and functioning of the institutions in which they are to work. Community mental health consultants must also acquire the habit of thinking strategically about the needs and resources of their catchment area when they make choices about initiating new consultations. They must make the shift from thinking primarily about the individual, to also considering the needs of groups of people and the major problems in the community with which they are working. This requires competence in conceptualizations, planning and community organization in which most mental health workers have not been trained (Libo 1966; Wolberg and Lawson 1962). It also implies a consideration of how other services need to reorganize and whether community values require change if mental health problems are to be solved. Therapists tend to be uncomfortable with adopting positions implying value judgments and have mixed feelings about the extent of their function in examining interpersonal components of other agencies. They feel uneasy about reaching out into the community and extending their services to other institutions. They experience the normal anxieties of relinquishing direct control, of understanding the situation at second-hand and of coping with these complex demands.

The training experiences reported here did not attempt to address the full spectrum of consultation training, but only to respond to certain perceived needs. The first experience, supervision of second-year psychiatry residents learning about consultation for the first time, highlighted a number of practical issues. The second experience was with an interdisciplinary group of professionals who had completed training in their core mental health fields, and who were now learning consultation theory. The third experience was a training program for the staff of a community mental health center, already familiar with many issues of consultation, but who were encountering difficulty in initiating and developing a relevant consultation program. The fourth conference was a workshop for professionally sophisticated State and regional mental health officials who were engaged in consultation on community mental health center development and in assisting centers to provide consultation and educational services.

Training in Consultation
for Psychiatric Residents

The first program to be described consisted of supervision of second-year psychiatry residents who were conducting consultations with agencies or groups in the community. This program extended over several years, at times consisting of one or two residents supervised individually, at other times consisting of four residents seen together as a group. The trainee's autonomy in the consultation experiences varied greatly, ranging from accompanying an experienced consultant regularly and occasionally filling in for him, through taking over an established consultation that had been ongoing with an agency for years, to fulfilling a specific request from an agency for mental health consultation, or to seeking in the community groups which might be interested in a consultation arrangement. Over this period of time a number of issues emerged which are pertinent to the field training of consultants.

One basic concern is the selection of a consultation training experience appropriate to the time scale of the trainee. Many student consultants have a 1-year exposure to consultation, which comes somewhere during the process of learning their core discipline. This year of exposure usually amounts to about 10 months. It is advisable to avoid the temptation to provide a naturalistic "beginning to end" experience for the trainee, in which he makes initial contacts with an agency, assesses and discusses needs, negotiates a contract, does the actual consultation and terminates. This complete package usually will require more than 10 months for an inexperienced consultant to carry out. It is preferable either to assign trainees to the same ongoing consultations from year to year, with only minimal renegotiations each time, or to have them select quite circumscribed projects.

Another matter of importance is choosing a consultation situation appropriate to the particular abilities of the trainees. A number of factors, such as level of professional development, quality of life experiences so far, and specialized information acquired in the past, go into this assessment. A particular kind of problem can arise when the trainees are still learning their core discipline. It is not until one has finished training that one has smooth and clearheaded access to his knowledge; the kind of access that facilitates hearing a case presented and then putting ideas together effectively for teaching. In this regard the residents sometimes were handicapped, going forth as mental health experts prematurely; they did not have the smooth access to their knowledge yet, and could not provide enough useful help to the consultees. The older, more mature person, can often cope with this situation by drawing on his broad life experiences to provide interventions that will be useful to the consultees. If he is experienced in group process or human relations, these skills too can provide a reserve to draw upon. Thus a lack of a specific expertise will not leave him with as little to offer the consultees as the young resident in the same situation. In the authors' experience, this extra reserve of general skills in seasoned professionals more than made up for problems they encountered, as described by Caplan, in changing from therapy to a consultation mode.

At the other end of the scale of expertise, the nonprofessional possesses another sort of reserve to make up for deficiency in specific skills. In this case the reserve usually consists of detailed first-hand knowledge of the setting about which he is consulting. Thus, it would seem to be the young professional, part way through his training, who has the narrowest selection of interventions to offer his consultees and is most vulnerable to disappointing them.

A related issue arises from the problem-finding capacity of consultation itself. For example, a competent young resident helped his consultee group to see that their most important problems were not mental health issues, but community/social issues. The discussions subsequently began to drift away from the resident's expertise, until it became apparent that he had no greater knowledge than the consultees about those issues. He was out of his field now, but in his role as consultant was still looked to for expert guidance. When he could not provide this guidance the group became disillusioned with the whole notion of consultation. As described above, this unfortunate result is more common with the trainee-consultant with a narrow band of skills; the more experienced consultant, even if he were not an expert in the new area, might still offer help as a mediator, resource person, or discussion leader, or feel comfortable in pointing out his lack of experience in this new area.

When a trainee's consultation does change its focus, there are a variety of options open to the organization providing the training. The trainee may terminate his work with the consultees, directing them to someone better qualified for their new needs. At this point, however, the trainee is without a field experience. He has indeed learned a vitally important aspect of consultation, but he may still need training in other specific skills. If there exists a large pool of ongoing consultations, he might be attached to one of them, or he might take over a brief circumscribed consultation with another agency, or he may be encouraged to stay with the original group of consultees, following them into the new area. This too could be immensely educative for him, although not in the originally defined skills. He would, of course, need additional supervisory help with this option.

It does appear that in order to provide the flexibility needed to respond to problems like the above, an organization providing a formal, time-limited training must maintain a significant number of ongoing consultations, or have access to consultations in a number of affiliated agencies. In the case of the smaller community mental health center training its own staff, the education process may more easily extend over enough time to provide the necessary breadth of experience.

Another issue is the consultant's failure to recognize ambivalence. The usual approach to consultation focuses more on reality needs, overt and covert, than it does on deeper feelings of hostility, love, envy, etc. The new consultant is less ready to look for such emotions in the consultees. This is in marked contrast to the usual experience in learning psychotherapy where it is readily acknowledged that the patient will feel ambivalence about the therapist. Consultation has more of the politeness of a social relationship, in which hostility is hidden. Some consultees who in fact are terribly ambivalent are enthusiastic and welcoming on the surface. Students all too often accept this facade as the reality with the result that they fail to understand difficulties that develop in the relationship. There are multitudinous vehicles available to consultees for the covert expression of ambivalence: the hapless trainee who is constantly kept waiting; promises made that there would be someone prepared to present a case, which don't materialize; being asked to wait in a room in the middle of winter, without the heat on; a receptionist who doesn't know the consultant's name after several visits; consultees who are tied up with "important" phone calls.

A final issue related to training consultants is that personality differences tend to be disregarded, as though consultation were so procedurized that one person was interchangeable with another. This seems to be a result of an overemphasis on cognitive factors. In supervising clinical psychotherapy the instructor takes into consideration the therapist's personality. However, this appears to be less common when teaching consultation.

In addition to the issues described above which focus mainly on the consultant, there are also a number of concerns which relate to the consultees. First, of great importance in a training situation, is the atmosphere of the agency. When an agency is in turmoil, with frequent turnover of staff and administrators, or with strains or conflicts in the organization at every level, there are so many multilevel problems that it is foolish to assign a fledgling consultant to the agency. To be sure, this type of agency may well need all the outside help it can get, and a skillful consultant may have a great deal to offer, particularly in the area of human relations, but a novice will only be swallowed up in the chaos. He probably will underestimate, initially, the amount of organizational conflict, and set up a consultation geared more to mental health case-oriented issues. Only as time goes on will it become apparent that there is little interest in discussing cases, as the consultees use the relative freedom of the consultation time to complain more and more about the agency. By this time it may be too late to set up regular visits with the higher levels in the administration and in essence completely restructure and renegotiate the consultation. (It is also somewhat more difficult for a young, inexperienced consultant to convince high level administrators to meet with him. Besides their greater age and sense of stature in the community, they already have a wealth of detailed knowledge of the agency that the consultant knows nothing about. Such arrangements can indeed be made, but it involves the charisma and force of personality of the consultant to a much greater degree.)

A related issue is the agency with built-in problems, such as a teenage hotline with inevitable adolescent anti-authority issues. A psychiatrist must spend a great amount of time initially overcoming resistance, convincing the staff composed primarily of youths that he is not an authoritarian establishment figure. Not infrequently the young psychiatrist, eager to ingratiate himself with the youths, focuses too much in going along with their wishes, and is unable to define what arrangements are reasonable and what are not.

One reason consultee agencies often are not selected for trainees as carefully as psychotherapy patients are, has to do with safety, and the generally conservative stance of any clinical undertaking. When one selects patients for students to treat, the sicker ones are either diverted to other settings, or, if chosen, the student's work with them is monitored by a whole host of built-in safeguards. This is done primarily, of course, to protect the patient, but as a secondary benefit it protects the therapist from cases he is not equipped to handle. In the selection of agencies with which to consult, this overriding concern for clinical safety is not present. An agency may have turmoil or chaos; people may leave or be fired; work may not get done at a high level; but no one is going to take an overdose of pills, or wind up psychotic in a hospital ward. Of course, one is concerned about the welfare of the agency and the student, but the powerful motivation to be careful, so characteristic of the clinical setting, is not present. As a result, the process of selecting agencies for students is looser than it should be; students find themselves in over their heads more often than they should.

A final problem related to the consultees occurs when the consultees are not the ones who originally sought out the consultation. When all the negotiations are carried out with the administrator who wants the consultation for his agency, to the neglect of the line level people who will actually be meeting with the consultant, there arise problems of low motivation, ambivalence, or outright hostility. This unfortunate situation parallels the therapist trying to treat an unmotivated patient. It is a losing battle from the start. Negotiations must include the actual consultees, so they do not experience the consultation as an imposition from their superiors. If they do, the anger, or more typically passive aggression, really aimed at the superiors will fall onto the consultant. A variation of this problem, which is seen more in some agencies than others, has to do with the rapid turnover of staff. For example, the hotline youths that one negotiates an elaborate "contract" with may drop out and others wander in and wander out over the course of the year. Discussions held at the beginning were with people who are not there anymore. Short of avoiding this type of organization entirely, it becomes necessary to repeatedly re-clarify the goals of the consultation.

Introduction to Consultation
for Mental Health Professionals

The second experience to be described was a series of four seminars intended to be a survey of the consultation literature. It was part of an overall program that included classes 2 hours a week for 2 years, with a concurrent community experience, usually a consultation.

The course content included Community Psychiatry, Social Psychiatry, Consultation, Program Administration and other subjects, with the seminars on consultation occurring in the first year. The initial intent was to present writings representing the development of consultation and its later elaboration, with a conceptual framework to hang the material on. The students included psychiatrists, nurses, social workers, psychologists, and hospital chaplains.

About 2 months before the seminars were to begin the teacher was made aware that the students were expressing dissatisfaction with the program. This was unusual, since the program had typically been well received in past years. Classes filled each year, and graduates spoke of the program's value in quite positive terms. The specific complaints were that the students had too small a role in the selection of curriculum, and that the faculty did not show enough interest in their particular work experiences. They felt powerless, groping in the dark, and isolated from each other. The faculty, in fact, was seriously concerned with these problems, yet somehow the distress of the class was persisting.

It became apparent that human relations consultation for the teaching program itself would be as important as the didactic work, and the faculty was open to whatever seemed reasonable. Two goals were set: to help the class develop a sense of cohesion, and to show that the faculty was genuinely interested in the students' work. The initial plan was to have advanced students in the program come to class and present their consultations. The reasoning went that since these consultations would have been ongoing for at least a year, they would be well thought through and lend themselves to analysis. However, this plan was never implemented.

At the first seminar the students' desire to discuss their *own* material was expressed. The teacher realized this would be a tailor-made vehicle for attaining both goals, i.e., increasing cohesiveness and convincing the students of the faculty's interest in their work. It was also realized that the first-year-students, as a rule, were just in the process of beginning their consultation projects. Hence, there would be a price to pay of having less elaborate experiences to analyze.

A plan was set up as follows: Each student was attached to two classmates, to be "discussants" for his presentation. Before the scheduled class meeting these three people were to meet privately, for the student to give his entire presentation to the "discussants." The three of them would then discuss the material until the discussants felt they knew it well enough to present it themselves. From that point on, the student who had done the consultation would have no more involvement in the presentation. At the scheduled class time, the first discussant would present a 2-minute descriptive capsule, summarizing the consultation, after which the second discussant would present an 8-minute analysis. Then the class would be invited to question and discuss for another 5 minutes.

Naturally, these times were not rigidly adhered to, but the presentations did tend to take only about 15 minutes each, of which most of the time was spent in analysis and interaction. In addition, the three classmates involved had an opportunity to interact intensively as a small group themselves. A list of various parameters of consultation was given to the students, to use if they wished, to conceptualize the analysis. It included aspects such as the contract, the agency's background, the initial plan, the model, specific examples of typical sessions, the time scale and any accomplishments to date.

The first goal, that of developing cohesion, was attained successfully. The threesomes did meet, with an immediate and striking increased familiarity among the students. The opportunity to collaborate around a work problem served as an excellent vehicle for personal ties. In the class discussions there was a tone of friendly goodwill, with constructive criticism and little defensiveness. Where before the students had not known what each other was doing, now everyone had a clear idea of where the others were in their projects, how they shared problems, and how they could be mutually helpful.

The second goal, to demonstrate genuine faculty interest, was attained as well. The class spontaneously began negotiations in a constructive way with the faculty around their grievances, with an optimistic expectation that the faculty would listen and that things could be worked out. These negotiations did take place, with what seemed to be quite satisfactory results. The class's suggestions for the curriculum were implemented to everyone's satisfaction. A year later, the class was working well, with good cohesion and high morale.

Although it was not a major goal, another result of the "discussant" plan was livelier, more analytical presentations. The restriction of 2 minutes for the first "discussant" to give the basic facts of the consultation forced the selection of only the most essential aspects to present, thus eliminating a great deal of unnecessary detail. Furthermore, since the "discussants" were not presenting their own program they were less defensive in presenting the material. Problems were described with less anxiety, and the class reacted in the discussion in a more objective manner. The "discussants" added distance which seems to have been quite helpful.

The reading part of the unit, which had originally been its central feature, was slightly anticlimactic after the events discussed above.

A Seminar in Consultation
for a Community Mental Health Center Staff

The administrators of a community mental health center requested a consultant to provide a seminar on consultation for their staff. The staff consisted of 14 mental health professionals of varying experience ranging from 2 to 15 years in their profession. Four members had prior training in consultation and 10 were conducting some consultation at the time the seminar started. Although a fair amount of consultation was in process, the administrators reported that staff seemed to encounter difficulty in making consultation contracts and in conducting consultation through the initial phases. The administrators also considered that the objectives and strategy for the consultation program were not adequately planned. Consequently the seminar was designed to refresh the staff's knowledge of the basic concepts of community mental health consultation; to identify and work out problems they were experiencing in their day-to-day practice; and to study how the particular needs and resources of the catchment area affected their choices in developing consultation. Objectives were to improve the quality of consultation and to enable the center to conduct a more active and more relevant program.

In a preliminary meeting with the staff it was decided that the first two sessions would be concerned with a discussion of the various theories of community mental health consultation. Readings were provided. Following this introduction, 15 sessions would be held in which the seminar would be conducted as a model group consultation. Members would present problems from their ongoing consultations and seminar participants would react as consultants to each other.

The first problems presented concerned the initiation of consultation, discussions with administration about the problem, and the establishment of a contract with the consultee regarding the purpose of the consultation and how it would be conducted. One situation illustrated for seminar members the importance of selecting an effective sponsor: The Office of Education in the local diocese had designated a particular school principal to act as liaison between other principals and the community mental health center. The liaison principal subsequently introduced the center's consultant to two other principals who, she felt, could use consultation. They, however, interpreted this act as indicating their lack of competence, and as a result were angry and resisted contact. One made and cancelled several appointments. The other saw the consultant once but made no further arrangements. The consultant did not know what to do. After discussing the situation in the seminar, he again telephoned the principals and was able to learn of their reactions and to clarify the misunderstanding. The seminar members discussed the problems in assessing the relationship between sponsors and consultees and became more aware of the need to be alert to differing perceptions of the meaning of behavior.

Two sessions were focused on problems concerned with the dynamics of consultee groups. In one of these, a teacher who was extremely anxious insisted on monopolizing the meetings to the annoyance and boredom of the other consultees. The seminar group examined how they might help the teacher and thereby prevent the disintegration of the group or a verbal attack on the monopolizer. They also considered the possibility of generalizing from this experience in terms of dealing with monopolization in other groups, and how teachers should handle monopolizers in their own classrooms.

Feelings which consultees might have in exposing themselves and their problems in the consultation were also experienced in similar fashion by the consultants in the seminar. In one problem brought to the seminar, it became clear that the consultant's reaction to a consultee was due to countertransference; the consultant was thus helped to identify the source of the difficulty and to respond in terms of reality. In another situation, an elderly woman became bedridden and dependent on her retired husband. He, in turn, became depressed. This situation aroused many feelings in the consultee nurse and the consultant about helplessness and aging. As a result, they found themselves immobilized and unable to solve the problem. The exploration of these feelings in the seminar enabled the consultants to perform a similar service for the consultee and thus free her to work with her patients.

Two sessions were held on program development consultation with the staff studying data characterizing two catchment areas and designing a consultation program for each of these areas. In the first of these sessions, the consultant provided data for a theoretical area and in the second the staff brought the data for their own area. Emphasis was placed on identifying the critical mental health problems in the area: which caretakers were most involved with the problems; what resources were available; and how the consultants could most effectively gain access to provide indirect services. These planning sessions were particularly interesting in that they uncovered the resistance of some of the staff to outreach and consultation. Several members felt free to acknowledge how much more comfortable they were working in their offices, treating patients directly as they had been trained and responding only when they were requested to intervene. These conflicts took a long time to resolve partly because the leadership of the center also had some mixed feelings about developing a truly comprehensive community mental health program. The reluctance to take on new responsibilities and to learn new skills was not only explored as a problem for members of the seminar but also was recognized as a common problem for many of their consultees who were taking on new responsibilities.

The last session was concerned with procedures and dynamics of terminating or transferring consultation programs, and with a discussion of the seminar model.

The participants were asked whether the seminar had been useful to them and, if so, how; whether it had affected their practice; and what changes they would like to suggest in the seminar if it were to be given again. Several members reported some changes in attitude. They had increased confidence; were able to be more understanding and tolerant of the consultees; were more willing to involve the consultee in the planning and evaluation of the consultation. One consultant recognized and came to terms with his reluctance to leave his office. Others reported they knew more about how to set up and start consultation; others that they understood better the role of administration in regard to consultation. Most of the consultants stated that they had a better appreciation of what needed to be considered when two or more consultants worked together.

Several consultants found it hard to attend both to what was being discussed at the content level and to what was going on in the consultation group in regard to its leadership and dynamics. However, this comprehensiveness of attention is what is necessary in both group therapy and group consultation and is a skill which must be acquired.

A Workshop for Government Officials on Program Development Consultation

The last training effort to be described was an 8-hour workshop offered to State and regional officials who were engaged in providing program consultation to community mental health center staffs in the development of their centers and of the consultation and education component. The first 2 hours were consumed by an overview of consultation theory and a presentation of a model for a consultation and education component in a community mental health center. The other 6 hours were concentrated on the discussion of problems which the officials were encountering in the course of their work. Aims were to clarify the nature of the problems and to identify skills and knowledge which the officials would require in order to be effective.

A major problem for State and regional officials was the multiple roles which they were compelled to adopt. They were not only expected to provide technical assistance to the centers but they also had to monitor and evaluate the quality of the services which the centers offered and were frequently responsible for influencing decisions in regard to the funds which the centers received.

The workshop members identified three different categories of what they called "vested interest" consultation. The first of these was when a community mental health center offers consultation to a collaborative agency such as a school and can also offer or withhold treatment services. The second was consultation offered within a program development or monitoring role where the consultant's agency had power to recommend withholding or granting money, continuing or eliminating a program, reappointing or not reappointing staff. A third was when the consultant himself held such veto power over the funding of a center's program.

Problems for discussion thus centered around how to clarify one's role, how to gain the trust of the consultee, how to define the degrees of authority and power, and the extent of confidentiality which could be offered. The State and regional consultants had also to be concerned with where their allegiances lay. If they were paid by the State to whom did they belong, their employer or the consultee? Was there sometimes a conflict of interest? How could they function effectively, restrain themselves so that they did not try to take over the consultee program and yet ensure that the services, which the State wanted, were in fact developed?

These discussions led into the holding of further workshops which were concerned with the processes of planning community mental health services. These workshops included the study of intergroup relations theory, particularly the interface problems which occur when two agencies interact; the application of Bion's Basic Assumptions and Lewinian field force theories to program consultation; and techniques for undertaking institutional and situational analyses.

Conclusion

The four experiences in teaching consultation, which are described above, illustrate the wide diversity of needs which are encountered in training consultants. This diversity has to do with the level of sophistication of the trainees and the situations in which they find themselves. In order to respond effectively, programs had to be individually designed to meet the specific needs of the students. However, these experiences also raise questions about the point at which mental health workers are ready to become consultants and about the sequential development of training as it relates to the tasks which consultants may be required to assume. In many ways the principles involved in training consultants are similar to those involved in the training of any kind of human caregiver. However, problems are compounded by the broadness of scope in community mental health consultation and in the confusion about its definition. There is a need to experiment with models of training in different facets of the work and in the selection of suitable candidates.

References

Abrahamson, Stephen. Methods of teaching. In: Mendel, Werner, and Solomon, Philip, eds. *Psychiatric Consultation.* New York: Grune & Stratton, 1968. pp. 41–48.

Aldrich, C.K. A specialized teaching program for residents in psychiatry. In: Mendel, Werner, and Solomon, Philip, eds. *Psychiatric Consultation.* New York: Grune & Stratton, 1968. pp. 26–32.

Berlin, I.N. Learning mental health consultation: History and problems. *Mental Hygiene,* 48:257–266. Apr. 1964.

Caplan, Gerald. An approach to the education of community mental health specialists. *Mental Hygiene,* 43:268–280, 1959.

Libo, Lester M. Multiple functions for psychologists in community consultation. *American Psychologist,* 21(6):530–534, June 1966.

MacLennan, Beryce; Quinn, Robert; and Schroeder, Dorothy. *The Scope of Community Mental Health Consultation and Education.* Rockville, Md.: National Institute of Mental Health, 1970.

Mendel, Werner. Psychiatric consultation education. *American Journal of Psychiatry,* 123(2):150–155, Aug. 1966.

Newman, Ruth. *Psychological Consultation in the Schools.* New York: Basic Books, 1967.

Rogawski, Alex. Teaching consultation techniques in a community agency. In: Mendel, Werner, and Solomon, Philip, eds. *Psychiatric Consultation.* New York: Grune & Stratton, 1968. pp. 65–85.

Scheidlinger, S., and Sarcka, A. A mental health consultation: Education program with group service agencies in a disadvantaged community. *Community Mental Health Journal,* 5:164–171, Apr. 1969.

Signell, K.A., and Scott, P.A. Training in consultation: A crisis of role transition. *Community Mental Health Journal,* 8(2):149–160, 1972.

Wolberg, A., and Lawson, E.P. The training of mental health consultants at the postgraduate center for psychotherapy. *Int. Mental Health Research Newsletter,* Vol. 4, No. 3, 1962.

9

Some Problems in Consultation

Beryce W. MacLennan

This chapter describes some typical problems in consultation and how consultants have worked with them. The material is arranged so that readers can discuss how they would tackle each problem before reading about the progress of the consultation. In this manner the reader can consider alternative courses of action and then compare and discuss those alternatives with the approach which was actually used. There is no suggestion that the actions taken are necessarily better than those which the reader might propose, but it is hoped that they will stimulate thought of how typical problems may be handled.

The problems are explored sequentially as follows:

1. Assessing a Catchment Area's Need for Consultation
2. Gaining Access for Consultation
3. Consultation on Developing a Group Therapy Program
4. An Inadequately Negotiated Consultation Contract
5. A Rural Emergency—Consultation to a Rural Community Action Program
6. A Problem in Transferring a Consultation
7. A Case Consultation Uncovers a Systemic Problem

1. Assessing a Catchment Area's Need for Consultation

Statement of the problem. A community mental health center was formed to serve the mental health needs of a catchment area of 100,000 people, part of a county of 600,000. The Center's staff and budget were necessarily limited; hence it was essential to have as clear an understanding of the characteristics and needs of the catchment area as possible so as to plan programs intelligently.

How should they go about this task?

Action taken. The staff first looked at the overall census figures for their area. They learned there were 40,000 children under 18 years of age, 10,000 people over 65 of whom 7,000 were living alone, and 8,000 were women. Of the 50,000 people between the ages of 18 and 65 years of age, 10,000 were female heads of households and 5,000 were living on their own. Thirty thousand of these adults were married. They found 20,000 people were living in poverty. Of the adults, 7,000 were unemployed, 10,000 were managers or professionals and 30,000 were in blue collar or lower-middle-income white collar jobs. Many families had two wage earners. The mean family income was in the high average range.

When they looked at the 10 census tracts within their area, they found that the population varied. The poor were clustered in two tracts. One tract had many elderly people. One was obviously affluent. Several had high percentages of young families with young children; others with teenagers. One tract showed a large number of unattached people and a high rate of transience. Two other tracts also showed a high rate of transience and in comparison with previous census figures seemed to be in transition. The census data also showed that there were 20% black people and 5% foreign born in the area and that these were also clustered in certain tracts.

The staff then read the annual report of the county which described the nature of the county as metropolitan, largely residential, with some commercial, a small amount of light industry, an expanding population, a high rate of land development. This report also showed the political and governmental structure in the county and, in brief, the service resources. The State and county jointly shared responsibility for health and social services, community development, correctional services and law enforcement. Employment and rehabilitation were exclusively State services, and the Board of Education was an elected body independent of the county and responsible to the State. County taxes were raised by real estate assessments only. Recreation services were dependent on local interest but the county provided staff if local groups could provide matching funds, a facility and supplies. One neighborhood in the catchment area was incorporated and had its own police force.

The staff also read the reports of the human service agencies. They learned the organization, staffing and budget of these agencies, their responsibilities and those they served. They found out what resources were lodged in their own area. They learned that the area was served by one police precinct, that there were two public health clinics offering prenatal, well baby and family planning services and that public health nurses offered outreach services from one nursing district. Five public health nurses and a supervisor provided this service. Infant and maternal mortality were low except in census tracts with high poverty rates. In these tracts, attendance at clinics was also low. A local nonprofit hospital was situated in the catchment area and provided a range of inpatient and outpatient services available on an 'ability to pay' basis. The center had arranged for 10 psychiatric beds in this hospital which also provided detoxification services. The staff learned that approximately 20 patients a month were sent to the State hospital 30 miles away. Emergency ambulance service was provided by the four volunteer fire stations in the area. Two private nursing homes with 150 beds also offered some care.

From the *Yellow Pages,* staff discovered that there were five general practitioners, two pediatricians, two private psychiatrists and a private psychologist in the area itself and a group practice just outside the area. From discussions with major insurance carriers it seemed as if approximately 40% of the population carried private insurance and 20% were eligible for Medicare or Medicaid. The remainder were uncovered. A family service agency, a mental health hotline and a youth rap center also served the area.

From the annual reports of the agencies, staff learned that three juvenile and two adult parole and probation officers served the area from the county courts. Their caseloads ran about 60 persons each. Two correctional training centers operated by the State provided residential care for children and youth. The county jail and a nearby State prison provided custodial care for adults. Twelve thousand persons were on some form of relief and these were served by a unit with a supervisor and seven workers. The social service department also licensed 50 children's day care homes serving 250 children. They also licensed 10 foster homes for 50 dependent and neglected children. There were 10,000 preschool children in the area, about a thousand of whom attended licensed preschool and day care centers. An unknown number were cared for by substitute parents while mothers or fathers worked.

In studying the annual report and budget of the school system, staff found that the schools in the area formed part of a larger school district which served one-third of the county. Eight thousand secondary school children were served by two high schools and six junior high schools. In addition, 2,000 teenagers who had not continued in high school were either working or unemployed. Twenty thousand children were attending 24 elementary schools. Secondary and elementary schools were arranged in clusters and each had their own pupil service and special education programs. Two clusters served the area. These two together had a staff of four psychologists, six pupil personnel and social workers and 20 guidance counselors. There was one special school for handicapped children, and special education resource teams in each senior high school, two junior high schools and six elementary schools. Five visiting teachers provided services to children who could not attend school.

The staff studied maps of the area and the *Yellow Pages* to discover that there were three recreation centers in the area but these seemed to be placed in more affluent districts. There were also two public parks with swimming pools. Three large shopping centers served the area as well as neighborhood stores. Each shopping center had a movie house, at least one restaurant, and a bowling alley. One had an indoor skating rink. Transportation was very inadequate. There were only three lines in the area so that most people were dependent on cars or local neighborhood resources. There were 20 churches and two synagogues in the area serving approximately 30,000 people.

Staff contacted the local planning agencies and learned that a recent house-to-house survey had been made of their area. This enabled them to see where the housing was in good shape and where it had deteriorated. A map had been made which indicated the type and cost of housing. The survey also described the social resources and needs of the neighborhoods. They saw that the high transient tract was deteriorating and had many bars. They predicted that alcoholism would be high in that district.

The members of the staff then moved out to talk with the various care-givers they had identified. They met with the superintendent of their school district and learned which schools seemed to have most problems and what staff seemed to need. They talked with the nurses and heard about health and mental health problems, where these were most acute and what difficulties the nurses had. The probation officers and judges at the courts told them where crime and delinquency was prevalent and the social service staff informed them where their caseloads were primarily located and what their problems were. They met with the clergy from each denomination and learned about their congregations. They found that the Cooperative Extension Service ran two homemakers groups of about 20 women each and three groups for boys.

They also talked with the county Mental Health Association's director who informed them about the active volunteers and interested citizens' groups in their area. They found that there was an association of parents with exceptional children, a 4-Cs organization, a senior citizens association, and an association for returning prisoners in their area.

In order to obtain a different perspective they met with the above groups and with neighborhood citizens associations. Thus informed, the community mental health center staff were able to pinpoint the high-risk neighborhoods in their catchment area. They had a reasonably clear picture of the needs of the area and could begin making choices in regard to the development of their limited consultation time.

Use of the data. Very frequently, in order to obtain State or Federal money community mental health centers describe their catchment areas in considerable detail but then do not use the information in planning their program. In this case, the community mental health center staff differentiated their program in accordance with the data. For instance, in the tract containing large numbers of elderly people, team members made contact with the local program for the aging, encouraged the establishment of a day center for senior citizens, provided crisis and group counseling for the bereaved, initiated a program of consultation to the local nursing homes and the managers of apartment buildings where many of the aged lived. In the transient tract, counseling and crisis management were linked to a local coffeehouse, a hangout for many of the young unattached. Alcoholism was high in this tract, so that close cooperation was developed with the county alcohol coordinator, the hospital detoxification unit, and the AA group in the catchment area. In the tracts with very young children and their families the community mental health center team worked closely with the preventive health clinics, the day care centers, the kindergarten and headstart programs and the local general practitioners and pediatricians. A child guidance agency, which provided outpatient and day treatment was encouraged to extend its range to serve the preschool population and a specialist in early child care and development provided consultation and training for staff.

2. Gaining Access for Consultation

Statement of the problem. When the Mental Health Study Center staff began to develop a community mental health center demonstration, the team members decided that it was most important to work with the schools in their areas. After sanction had been obtained from the central office for the three teams (each had responsibility for a sub-area in the catchment) to approach the educators at the local level, members reviewed the organization of the schools and what they knew about them individually. Each team met with the pupil service personnel—psychologists and pupil personnel workers—who were important informants about the schools in their subareas. One team decided to start by concentrating on three schools, a senior, junior and elementary school, which would give them contact with all the school-age children and their families in one community. They met with the principals of these schools. A second team decided to meet with the area supervisor and all the secondary and elementary school principals at their monthly meetings. The third team, located in the most rural part of the catchment area served only one junior-senior high school and nine elementary schools. The team decided to meet with each principal separately in an attempt to make arrangements to provide direct treatment services, and to establish regular consultation with each school. The team did not have an office in the subarea but conducted treatment in other community agencies such as schools, public health nursing offices, churches, and in one apartment and town house development office.

In most of the schools, members of the team were able to establish a regular meeting time with the principal during which they exchanged information about the school and the community and the principal discussed problems and plans for that particular school. As a result of these meetings, consultants also began to attend school "building conferences" to which teachers brought their problems with individual children and to

develop special programs such as teacher training workshops, or parent interview demonstrations.

In one elementary school, although the pupil services staff reported considerable stress because of the relationship between the school principal
and his faculty and below-average performance of the children, the principal decided that he did not wish a regular relationship with the mental
health consultant. He did allow the consultant to attend building conferences
once a month and provided space for him to treat any children who were
referred. The consultant came to the school 4 hours a week to undertake
evaluation and therapy with children and their parents individually or in
groups.

The consultant, however, was not satisfied with this arrangement. He
wished to be able to get to know the principal better and to be able to
help him with the problems he saw in the school.

How could he go about this?

Action taken. The consultant set out to gain the confidence of the principal.
Each time he came to the school he visited the principal's office and spent
a few minutes with him informally. He began to lunch at the school getting
to know the teachers in a casual way as well as on a more formal basis. After
about a month he asked the principal to lunch with him at which time he
discussed his progress. This became a regular monthly arrangement and
after five or six such meetings the principal began to discuss some of his
problems with the consultant. They were now on a friendly basis and the
meetings increased to twice a month. This frequency was sustained over
the next year and resulted in the principal using the consultant to help him
work out his conflicts with some of his staff, to develop special programs for
emotionally disturbed children and to study the effect on the children of
making the transition from a rural family into a modern school environment.

3. Consultation on Developing a Group Therapy Program

Statement of the problem. Family and children's agency requested consultation in starting a group therapy program. The agency had an executive
director and a program director. The former made the contact although
both were present at the first meeting. The agency consisted of five social
workers who worked with parents and adolescents, an intake worker and
two child therapists, who treated children under 12 years of age. The social
workers wished to learn how to run groups with parents and teenagers; there
was no interest in children's groups. There was sufficient homogeneity to

predicate that group therapy could easily become established as an agency program without undue casefinding. Several members of the staff were already interested including the chief social worker.

A small work group was established with the chief social worker, the intake worker, and the three workers who would lead groups. An orientation of five meetings was held with the rest of the staff. A group for older adolescents, who had or were about to separate from their parents, was established easily without problems. However, although a number of parents whose children were to be in treatment were selected for a parent's guidance group, no group was started. Although preparation for the group seemed adequate, the parents remained anxious, several refused treatment, others avoided interviews and it seemed impossible to obtain enough members for a group. Everyone seemed in favor of the program and to understand it, yet the program did not go. Subtle messages had to be coming from somewhere through the staff to the patients that groups were not good or else they would have been accepted. No one seemed to understand the difficulty.

How could this problem be solved?

Action taken. The problem was solved perhaps by chance. The consultant had joined the Technical Advisory Council to the agency Board. At a Board meeting she learned that the Board members had been urging that a group therapy program should start and were disappointed that it was not going well. Perhaps the directors were not so eager for the program because they had not initiated it.

The consultant went back to study the agency functioning and realized for the first time that as most children's cases included treatment of parents along with treatment of the child, a group therapy program for parents would throw the caseload out of balance if the agency did not either hire another child therapist, fire a caseworker or train a child therapist to run groups. When she brought this finding to the executive director, the consultant learned for the first time that the program director, a child therapist, was against the group program and determined not to run children's groups. The staff were aware of the conflict between the two directors and anxious about the possibility of a backlog of untreated children. They felt caught in the middle and did not feel free to discuss the problem. The directors then faced the problem and after 6 months or so were able to resolve it in favor of a group therapy program. The consultant returned and groups were developed successfully.

If a more careful analysis had been undertaken initially of the nature of the caseload, the structure and functioning of the agency, and the anticipated impact of the group therapy program on the agency, this problem might have been averted.

4. An Inadequately Negotiated Consultation Contract

Statement of the problem. As representative of his center, a psychologist was consulting with the local public health nursing agency. At the request of some of the nurses and with the agreement and support of the director of nursing, the mental health nursing coordinator had set up a group consultation arrangement in which the consultant was to help a nursing unit understand the mental health problems the nurses encountered in the course of their work and to extend their role in their management. These would include chronic mental health problems such as depression and sta-bilized chronic schizophrenia, developmental problems such as those encountered by girls entering puberty, and the mental health implications of serious, long-term illness and death. The consultant and the mental health nursing coordinator had met with the nursing supervisor prior to the start of the arrangement and understood that she was in support of the program. However, after the consultant had conducted several sessions, he noted that all the cases discussed were suitable for referral rather than case management so that the purposes of the arrangement to extend the role of the nurses and to increase their competence in the area of mental health were not being realized. He discussed the matter with the coordinator who agreed that she had noticed this difficulty also but did not understand why it should exist.

How could the consultant handle this problem?

Action taken. In considering where the misunderstanding or resistance lay, the consultant asked the coordinator who actually selected the cases and learned that the supervisor made the final choice. It seemed that she might have some reservations about the program. The consultant and co-ordinator met with the supervisor, presented their observations to her and asked her if she could share her feelings about the consultation with them. The supervisor angrily expressed her view that she had not been included in the decisionmaking. She considered that she had been bypassed by the coordinator in setting up the program and that her authority as a supervisor was likely to be eroded by the consultant's advice with which she might not agree. The consultant and the coordinator first accepted her feeling that she should have been included in the initial discussions of the program. The consultant then asked if she supported the extension of the nurse's roles and their need for additional training. When she agreed, he asked how they might work more effectively together and it was arranged that the three would meet regularly between sessions to discuss how to use most effectively the supervisor's choice of problems and appropriate ways of managing cases. The purpose of the consultation was then taken up again at the next regular session and the interest of the nurses in the program was reaffirmed.

5. A Rural Emergency—Consultation to a Rural Community Action Program

Statement of the problem. A consultant from a newly established community mental health center made a first visit to the director of the local Community Action Program (CAP). The area is tobacco country with over 70% of the population living in leaky, poorly insulated shacks on minimal incomes. There is no main sewage or piped water and almost no public transportation. The rich farmers control the conditions under which the farm laborers and sharecroppers live.

The CAP director immediately presented a problem. Over the weekend a woman in her late 20s, who was married to a farm laborer known as a chronic and excessive drinker, had become violent and started throwing furniture through the window. Her husband called the police and had her put in jail. Her parents had her removed from jail and took her home with them. They lived on another farm and had just sought help from the director. The woman was still very upset, crying and unable to do anything. Her husband was threatening to commit her to the State hospital. There were two small children who had been taken in by the woman's brother and his wife. The director had visited the woman and her family. She felt the woman needed treatment immediately but the husband was resistant to being involved. He did not wish to have his wife return home or to get treatment for himself. The director commented that this was not an unusual case, that the poor people felt trapped and frequently became depressed, violent or alcoholic.

What action should be taken?

Action taken. The consultant went immediately with the director to see the woman, prescribed medication and agreed to arrange for referral to the center. A social worker was assigned to the family. She was able to bring the family back together again, persuade the husband to seek treatment for his alcoholism in collaboration with the CAP, and to arrange for occasional baby-sitting and transportation so that the wife could get away from the home occasionally. She was unable to assist in improving the living quarters for this family or to help the husband increase his cash income, major sources of discontent and depression.

Having completed this case, the consultant and the CAP director then began to establish a local council of citizens and agency representatives to assess the human service and socio-economic needs of the area and to work together to develop programs to meet those needs and to bring pressure to bear on the county government to improve the lot of the agricultural laborer.

6. A Problem in Transferring a Consultation

Statement of the problem. A consultant, who was taking over a school consultation program with a group of six pupil personnel workers, ran into trouble. The previous consultant had spent 6 hours a week seeing each of the workers individually for 1 hour and also was available to them by phone if any crisis occurred. His primary focus was consultation on case management and referral. The new consultant could provide only 2 hours a week, and was concerned with how to make the best use of this time. The problem was how to cope with this reduction in time, which was bound to arouse feelings in the consultees and possibly jeopardize the consultation program.

How could the consultant handle this situation?

Action taken. The consultant met with the six workers and explained that he would only be able to provide 2 hours a week. He suggested that perhaps the most useful arrangement would be for them to meet as a group so they could all learn from each other's problems. If there were crises he would still be available by telephone. Without too much discussion the consultees agreed with this proposal and the meetings were started. However, they did not go smoothly. Attendance was sporadic. With the exception of two workers who came to all meetings, the others came only once or twice a month. There were rarely more than four workers at a meeting. The workers complained that too much was being required of them, that they were overworked, and that the teachers were always asking them to do more than they could manage. They also tended to bring up many problems between sessions individually by telephone or by detaining the consultant after the session.

After 3 months the consultant contacted all six consultees and asked them to come to a meeting to review progress. When they arrived, he informed them that he did not feel they were satisfied with the consultations and that he was not happy either. The workers angrily complained that he was not helping them sufficiently. They had too much to do, and meeting in a group did not help. Each wanted his undivided attention. The consultant replied that while they felt too many demands were being placed on them, he felt the same way. Since he had only limited time, it was necessary that they decide how best to use the time. They would like more, he would like to give more, but the time was not there.

The workers then decided that they would like to meet twice a month, during which time they would address common problems and use cases as a seminar. During the remaining 2 weeks they would share the 2 hours to schedule individual case conferences as they did not always like to expose their problems in front of each other or waste time listening to problems which did not concern them. After a time, however, the workers began to gain much more confidence and trust in each other and to come together to present their problems. They began to realize that they shared many difficulties. By the end of the year they had changed back to four group meetings a month.

7. A Case Consultation Uncovers a Systemic Problem

Statement of the problem. A child psychiatrist from the local community mental health center regularly attended monthly building conferences in a catchment area junior high school as mental health consultant to the school. Others present at the conference were the principal, assistant principal, school special service staff (i.e., school psychologist, nurse and counsellors) and teachers. All were white. (He also met weekly with the principal to discuss school problems with staff and students.) At one of these conferences a counsellor presented the problem of a 14-year-old, middle-class, black girl who was always getting into fights and creating disturbances in the classroom, the halls, and the cafeteria. The staff were unable to control this behavior although the girl was bright, did well academically and came from an intact, socially and economically stable family. She had come to the school in the eighth grade. Fighting had started when she entered the ninth grade and had become increasingly frequent during the year. The staff saw the girl as a behavior problem, angry and defiant and unable to control her impulsive, aggressive behavior. The ninth grade counsellor and the assistant principal had both seen the girl regularly and the counsellor had talked with the parents. These actions had not helped the situation and they were now considering her permanent suspension as a "disruptive child."

The consultant asked what the fights were about. He learned that there had been four fights during the semester so far. In each situation, the black girl seemed to be defending another black student against verbal attack by white students. There were clear racial overtones. The consultant remarked on this and then asked about the general tenor of race relations in the school. The principal admitted that, although only 10% of the student body was black, there were some problems. The school had been desegregated the year before and most of the staff agreed that having black students in the school made the atmosphere tense. The principal continued that during the fall he had found black students dancing outside the building before school started. He had suggested they use the gym and the phonograph there. White students then also started to dance there and friction developed between the two groups with some fighting usually over the type of music to be played. This conflict had spread and the two groups did not mix.

The consultant questioned whether this one girl's problem could be an outgrowth of the racial conflict. Was racial conflict really a central problem in the school? How did the school council deal with it? Were black students represented on the council? The school council was drawn from the academic honor roll. Although there were three black honor roll students, they were not on the council. Other cliques, such as a group of non-intellectual, more aggressive, white students known as "the greasers" were also not represented. No one at the building conference knew how the students as a whole felt about race relations.

What action should be taken?

Action taken. The principal decided to establish a task force to study student inter-group relationships. Student members were elected by all the different groups within the school and sat with staff and the consultant to explore the problem. With the establishment of the task force as a place where all groups could obtain a hearing and where specific problems could be solved, the students began to relax and the atmosphere became less tense. The black girl, who had been a problem, was elected as a black student representative. She took a leadership position on the task force and her aggressive fighting ceased. The need to deal with her as a special behavior problem was obviated when effective communication between staff and students was established. Her protest had been heeded.

A Reference Guide to the Consultation Literature

Fortune V. Mannino and Shirley E. Robinson

INTRODUCTION TO REFERENCE GUIDE

This bibliography is a completely updated revision of the bibliography published in 1969 under the title: *Consultation in Mental Health and Related Fields: A Reference Guide.* This revised version contains all of the references included in the first issue plus 490 additional references to books and articles published during the period from 1968 to 1973, bringing the total number of references to 1,136. Although every effort has been made to keep the bibliography as comprehensive as possible, the coverage may not be entirely exhaustive.

The classification scheme developed in the original version has been maintained as follows:

1. Consultation by Fields of Practice
2. Use of Consultation in Various Settings
3. Forms of Consultation
4. Professional Roles in Consultation
5. The Process of Consultation
6. Planning Consultation Programs
7. Consultation Training and Education
8. Research, Evaluations, Surveys and Reviews
9. Films and Tapes Related to Consultation Practice

To the best of our knowledge this continues to be the only bibliography on consultation which attempts to classify the entries into categories. However, as was true in the original version, many of the articles were not actually seen and had to be categorized solely by the title. This is a limitation which might have led to misclassification of articles in some instances or to failure to cross-classify in others.

A major change in this revision has been the numbering of the entries. All items have been numbered consecutively. This procedure facilitates cross referencing and avoids having to repeat entries. The numbers following authors' names in the Author Index correspond to numbered entries in the text, making it easy to locate any particular item quickly.

Most of the items listed may be found in large libraries. Those items cited having the initials (EDRS) may be purchased in microfiche or hard copy from the ERIC Document Reproduction Service (EDRS) P.O. Drawer O, Bethesda, Maryland 20014.

For those readers who are unfamiliar with consultation and who would like a general overview to orient them to the field, the following numbered references are suggested: 170, 173, 175, 201, 340, 359. Also see, Beisser, A. R., and Green, R. *Mental Health Consultation and Education,* Palo Alto, Calif.: National, 1972.

REFERENCE GUIDE CONTENTS

CONSULTATION BY
FIELDS OF PRACTICE

Consultation as a professional activity seems to be increasing in importance and in frequency of usage. Although there is probably no single definition which adequately covers the multitude of services and activities which are included under the consultation label, it basically refers to a helping process whereby an expert or specialist (consultant) attempts to assist a consultee (person, group, system) with some problem usually related to the consultee's work situation.

Consultation is practiced by a variety of professional disciplines, each having concerns directly related to professional background, training, and experience. Thus, the social work consultant is primarily involved with social work concerns such as psychosocial aspects of illness and public welfare practices; the psychiatric consultant with psychiatric concerns such as psychodynamics and psychopathology; and the educational consultant with such educational concerns as curriculum development and special subject content areas. Then there are the interdisciplinary approaches represented by the mental health consultant, drawn from the core mental health disciplines of clinical psychology, psychiatric social work, psychiatry and mental health-psychiatric nursing; and the behavioral science consultant, drawn primarily from the fields of sociology, social psychology, and anthropology. The former is mainly involved with mental health concerns on a generic level, and the latter with broad sociological and social psychological concerns.

In the section there are 369 references which are intended to give a picture of the consultation practices of professionals from the following fields: social work, psychiatry, nursing, psychology, education, mental health, behavioral sciences, medicine, and business and management. It is believed that these represent the major professional groups engaged in the use of consultation skills to solve problems in the area of human relations.

BEHAVIORAL SCIENCE

Books

1. DUBRIN, ANDREW J. *The Practice of Managerial Psychology*. New York: Pergamon Press, 1971.

161

2. Lippitt, R.; Watson, J.; and Westley, B. *The Dynamics of Planned Change.* New York: Harcourt Brace and Co., 1958.

3. Sofer, C. *The Organization from Within.* London: Tavistock, 1961.

Articles and Periodicals

4. Barrett, Richard. Comments on the preceding article: Interpersonal confrontations and basic third party function. *Journal of Applied Behavioral Science*, 4(3):345–348, 1968.

5. Bennis, Warren G. A new role for the behavioral sciences: Effecting organizational change. *Administrative Science Quarterly*, 8:125–165, 1963.

6. Bennis, Warren G. Theory and method in applying behavioral science to planned organizational change. *Journal of Applied Behavioral Science*, 1(4):337–360, 1965.

7. Bryson, Lyman. Notes on a theory of advice. *Political Science Quarterly*, 66(3):321–329, 1951.

8. Chesler, Mark, and Crowfoot, James E. Partisans as work. *Journal of Applied Behavioral Science*, 8(3):346–350, May-June 1972.

9. Dexter, Lewis Anthony. Impressions about utility and wastefulness in applied social science studies. *American Behavioral Scientist*, 9(6):9–10, 1966.

10. Dillon, George S. Comments on article below: A laboratory-consultation model for organization change. *Journal of Applied Behavioral Science*, 6(2):228, April-May-June 1970.

11. Erikson, E.G. An American consultant faces a foreign social environment. *Journal of Educational Sociology*, 29(4):184–190, 1955.

12. Gilboa, Eytan; Pines, Ayala; and Solomon, Leonard. The wizardry of change agents. *Journal of Applied Behavioral Science*, 8(3):351–360, May-June 1972.

13. Goodstein, Leonard D. Organizational development as a model for community consultation. *Hospital and Community Psychiatry*, 23(6):165–168, 1972.

14. Gouldner, Alvin W. Engineering and clinical approaches to consulting. In: Bennis, W.G.; Benne, K.D., and Chin, R., eds. *The Planning of Change.* New York: Holt, Rinehart and Winston, 1961, pp. 643–652.

15. Juarez, Leo J. The Technical Advisor as a Cross-Cultural Change Agent. Occasional Paper No. 7. Lexington, Kentucky: The University of Kentucky, 1969. (EDRS).

16. Kellner, Harold N. A consultation plan for the social system of the United States of America. *Journal of Applied Behavioral Science*, 8(3):376–381, May-June 1972.

17. Kimball, Solon T.; Pearsall, M.; and Bliss, Jane A. Consultants and citizens: A research relationship. *Human Organization*, 13(1):5–8, 1954.

18. Lippitt, Gordon L. Consulting with a national organization: A case study. *Journal of Social Issues*, 15(2):20–27, 1959.

19. Miel, Allice. How to use experts and consultants. In: Benne, K.D., and

Muntyan, B., eds. *Human Relations in Curriculum Change.* New York: Dryden, 1951. pp. 208–210.

20. MILLER, WARREN B. Psychiatric consultation: Part 1. A general systems approach. *International Journal of Psychiatry in Medicine,* 4(3):135–145, Spring 1973.

21. MORRIS, ROBERT. New concepts in community organization. *The Social Welfare Forum.* New York: Columbia University Press, 128–145, 1961.

22. MOSES, JOSEPH L. Utilization of the behavioral scientists in industry. *Professional Psychology,* 1(4):367–370, 1970.

23. PEABODY, GEORGE L. Power strategies. *Journal of Applied Behavioral Science,* 8(3):341, May-June 1972.

24. RICHARD, JAMES. Comments on article below: A laboratory-consultation model for organization change. *Journal of Applied Behavioral Science,* 6(2):229–31, April-May-June 1970.

25. ROGERS, KENN. Notes on organizational consulting to mental hospitals. *Bulletin of the Menninger Clinic,* 37(3):211–231, May 1973.

26. RUSH, HAROLD M.F. A case for behavioral science: the Raymond Corporation credits new growth and profits to a new style of management. *Conference Board Record,* 5(9):45–52, 1968.

27. SCHEIN, EDGAR H. Score one for process consultation. *Journal of Applied Behavioral Science,* 4(3):348–350, 1968.

28. TORCZYNER, JIMMY. The political context of social change: A case study of innovation in adversity in Jerusalem. *Journal of Applied Behavioral Science,* 8(13):287–317, May-June 1972.

29. WALTON, RICHARD E. Interpersonal confrontation and basic third party functions: A case study. *Journal of Applied Behavioral Science,* 4(3):327–344, July-August-September 1968.

30. WALTON, RICHARD E. Third party roles in interdepartmental conflict. *Industrial Relations,* 7(1):29–43, October 1967.

31. WOODY, ROBERT H., and WOODY, JANE D. Behavioral science consultation. *Personnel Journal,* 50(5):382–391, 1971.

See also: 454, 610, 611, 616, 646, 670, 672, 680, 686, 687, 696, 698, 703, 723, 724, 725, 730, 735, 744, 752, 772, 781, 821, 822, 1028, 1035, 1050, 1054, 1095.

BUSINESS AND MANAGEMENT

Books

32. Consulting Engineers Council. *The Practice of Consulting Engineering: A Manual of Principles and Performance.* 2nd ed. Springfield, Illinois: Consulting Engineers Council, 1961.

33. SHAY, PHILIP W. *How to Get the Best Results from Management Consultants.* New York: Association of Consulting Management Engineers, Inc., 1965.

34. STANLEY, C. MAXWELL. *The Consulting Engineer.* New York: John Wiley and Sons, Inc., 1961.

Dissertations

35. LYNCH, RICHARD M. "Professional Standards for Management Consulting in the United States." Unpublished doctoral dissertation. Graduate School of Business Administration, Harvard University, 1959.

36. SAMARAS, JOHN. "The Use of Management Consultants in Small Manufacturing Firms." Unpublished doctoral dissertation. Harvard University, 1961.

Articles and Periodicals

37. ADAMSON, CAMPBELL. The role of the industrial adviser. *Public Administration*, 46:185–190, Summer 1968.

38. ALLEN, HENRY. The consultants' world. *The Washington Post*, 264:16–30, August 26, 1973.

39. BAILEY, R. Consultants and overseas development. *The Banker*, 510:693–699, August 1968.

40. BROWN, HARRY G. Management counseling for small business firms. *The Journal of Accountancy*, 100(1):36–41, July 1955.

41. BROWN, THEODORE H. The business consultant. *Harvard Business Review*, 21:183–189, 1944.

42. CAIRNCROSS, ALEE. The work of an economic adviser. *Public Administration*, 46:1–11, Spring 1968.

43. DEAN, JOEL. The place of management counsel in business. *Harvard Business Review*, 16(4):451–465, Summer 1938.

44. DEYHLE, ALBRECHT. Management consulting or management training? *Advanced Management Journal*, 30(1):5–12, January 1965.

45. DONHAM, RICHARD. Management consultants deal with people. *Harvard Business Review*, 19(1):33–41, Autumn 1940.

46. DOWNS, A. Some thoughts on giving people economic advice. *American Behavioral Scientist*, 9(1):30–32, September 1965.

47. EATON, MARQUIS G. Advisory service; new frontier. *The Journal of Accountancy*, 100(5):56–61, November 1955.

48. Economist, The. The super consultants. *The Economist*, 221(6424):175–176, October 8, 1966.

49. FERGUSON, LAWRENCE. Social scientists in the plant. *Harvard Business Review*, 42(3):133–143, May-June 1964.

50. Fortune. Doctors of management. *Fortune*, 30(1):142–146, July 1944.

51. GLASER, EDWARD M. Organizational arteriosclerosis: Its diagnosis and treatment. *Advanced Management Journal*, 30(1):21–28, January 1965.

52. GRADY, PAUL. Management advisory services in the field of accounting. *The Controller*, 24(8):370–371, August 1956.

53. GREEN, H.L. Choosing and using retailing consultants. *Journal of Retailing*, 4:7–17, Winter 1962–1963.

54. GREEN, HOWARD L. Management consultants: How to know what you're

getting and what you pay for. *The Management Review*, 52(12):4–16, December 1963.

55. GREENBERG, D.S. Consulting: U.S. firms thrive on jobs for European clients. *Science*, 162(3857):986–987, November 29, 1968.

56. GREENHOUSE, SAMUEL M. Management consultants: Analysts or counselors? *Advanced Management Journal*, 30(1):52–54, January 1965.

57. HENDERSON, C.M. Working with planning consultants. *Public Management*, 43:77–80, April 1961.

58. HESS, DONALD P. The management consultant as a tool for executive development. *Advanced Management*, 18(1):30–31, January 1953.

59. HOLT, HERBERT. An application of psychoanalytic group techniques to the management consultant field. *Advanced Management Journal*, 30(1):37–43, January 1965.

60. JONES, DIOGENES. Confessions of a consultant. *The Management Review*, 42–44, June 1973.

61. KRENTZMAN, HARVEY C., and SAMARAS, JOHN N. Can small business use consultants? *Harvard Business Review*, 38(3):126–136, May-June 1960.

62. LAWRENCE, CHARLES. Management services and the accounting profession. *The New York Certified Public Accountant*, 27(10):671–676, October 1957.

63. McGARRAH, ROBERT E. Should the university become a management consultant? *Educational Record*, 50(3):245–254, Summer 1969.

64. MACE, MYLES L. Management assistance for small business. *Harvard Business Review*, 25(4A):587–594, Autumn 1947.

65. Management Review, The. Getting maximum results from management consulting services. *The Management Review*, 39(3):122–123, March 1950.

66. MASON, PERRY. Management services by local practitioners. *The New York Certified Public Accountant*, 28(10):707–712, October 1958.

67. MILLOTT, ROBERT F. Employment counseling consultant. *Journal of Employment Counseling*, 6(4):147–154, December 1969.

68. ROBBINS, I.D. Management services for small business through trade associations. *Harvard Business Review*, 26(5):627–640, September 1948.

69. SHAY, PHILIP W. Ethics and professional practices in management consulting. *Advanced Management Journal*, 30(1):13–20, January 1965.

70. SINGER, HENRY A. Management consulting: An introduction. *Advanced Management Journal*, 30(1):3–4, January 1965.

71. SMITH, ROBERT A., III. Consultation without revelation. *Advanced Management Journal*, 30(1):29–31, January 1965.

72. STRYKER, PERRIN. The ambitious consultants. *Fortune*, 49(5):82–85+, May 1954.

73. TILLES, SEYMOUR. Some propositions concerning the relationship between business consultants and their clients. *Management International*, 5:55–74, 1962.

See also: 7, 629, 652, 741, 939, 940, 984, 991, 997.

EDUCATION

Books

74. FAUST, VERNE. *The Counselor-Consultant in the Elementary School.* New York: Houghton-Mifflin, 1968.

75. FULLMER, D.W., and BERNARD, H.W. *The School Counselor-Consultant.* Boston: Houghton-Mifflin, 1972.

76. LAWLER, MARCELLA R. *Curriculum Consultants at Work.* New York: Teachers College, Columbia University, 1958.

77. SAVAGE, W.W., ed. *Improving Consultative Service to Schools.* Chicago: The Midwest Administrative Center, The University of Chicago, 1953.

Dissertations

78. WHITLEY, ALTON D. "Counselor-teacher consultations including video analysis to reduce undesirable student responses." Unpublished doctoral dissertation. Southern Illinois University, 1970.

Articles and Periodicals

79. ANADAM, KAMALA, and WILLIAMS, ROBERT L. A model for consultation with classroom teachers on behavior management. *School Counselor,* 18(4): 253–259, March 1971.

80. ANDERSON, V.E. Human side of curriculum development. *Educational Leadership,* 4(4):218–221, 1947.

81. BLACK, B.J. The consultant: A developing aspect of professional practice. *Journal of Home Economics,* 49(1):17–19, 1957.

82. BLACK, M.H. Problems of big city consultants. *The Reading Teacher,* 20: 500–504, 1967.

83. BLUMBERG, A. The consulting function of leadership. *Adult Leadership,* 8(9):265–266, 1960.

84. BORDIN, E.; EDWARD, S.; McKEEVER, N.; TIPTON, J.; CHARTERS, W.; and KOUNIN, J. Effective consultation. *Adult Leadership,* 3(10):13–26, 1955.

85. BRAUCHT, P. Program and services of an educational consultant or supervisor in a school for the deaf. *American Annals of the Deaf,* 112:60–63, 1967.

86. BUTT, D.E. Specialists and consultants. *Pennsylvania School Journal,* 116: 440–441, April 1968.

87. COOK, DAVID R. The change agent counselor: A conceptual context. *School Counselor,* 20(1):9–15, September 1972.

88. COSTANZA, VICTOR, and KLAPMAN, HOWARD. Developing direct classroom consultation. *Journal of Learning Disabilities,* 3(7):351–4, July 1970.

89. CURTIS, H.A. Improving consultant services. *Educational Administration and Supervision,* 39:279–292, 1953.

90. DINKMEYER, DON. A developmental model for counseling-consulting. *Elementary School Guidance and Counseling,* 6(2):81–85, 1971.

91. ENGELHARDT, LEAH et al. The counselor as a consultant in eliminating out of seat behavior. *Elementary School Guidance and Counseling,* 5(3): 196–204, March 1971.

92. ENGLISH, M.E. Preparing music consultants. *Music Educators Journal,* 50: 104–105, 1964.

93. FAUST, VERNE. Consulting: What is it all about? *Facility: The Journal of the Professional Counselors Association,* 3(4):17–18, September 1971.

94. FERNEAU, E.F. Which consultant? *Administrator's Notebook,* 2(8):1–4, April 1954.

95. GINTHER, J.R. Achievement in sixth grade science associated with two instructional roles of science consultants. *Journal of Educational Research,* 57:28–33, 1963.

96. HALL, HARRY O. South Florida School Desegregation Consulting Center. Annual Report Covering the Period from August 1, 1965 to June 30, 1966. Florida: Miami University. (EDRS).

97. HARRIS, N.C. On being a consultant. *Junior College Journal,* 37:9–13, 1967.

98. Hawaii State Department of Education. Child Study and Consultation Services in the Hawaii State Department of Education: A Summary and Progress Report. Honolulu, Hawaii: Hawaii State Department of Education. (EDRS).

99. HENDERSON, R.L. Conditions for seeking consultative help. *National Elementary Principal,* 36:256–261, September 1956.

100. HOPKINS, T.A. Pennsylvania's speech consultant system. *The Speech Teacher,* 17:64–67, 1968.

101. HUG, WILLIAM E. Some guidelines for hiring curriculum consultants. *Science Education,* 54(2):119–121, April-June 1970.

102. HULL, J.H. Value of continuing professional consultant service. *School Executive,* 71:44, 1952.

103. IRVING, J.R. School science consultant's relationship to industry. *Science Teacher,* 34:29+, February 1967.

104. JAN-TAUSCH, J. Team approach to in-service education; learning disability teacher-consultant. *Reading Teacher,* 19:418–423, 1966.

105. JONES, A.L. Role of the college consultant in curriculum planning. *The High School Journal,* 47:274–279, 1964.

106. KINTZER, FREDERICK C., and CHASE, STANLEY M. The consultant as a change agent. *Junior College Journal,* 39(7):54, 56, 58, 60, April 1969.

107. KLEINMAN, G.S. Needed: Elementary school science consultants. *School Science and Mathematics,* 65:738–746, 1965.

108. KOUNIN, JACOBS. The personal touch. *Adult Leadership,* 3(10):23–24, April 1955.

109. LAWLER, MARCELLA R. Role of the consultant in curriculum improvement. *Educational Leadership,* 8:219–225, 1951.

110. LAWLER, MARCELLA R. Raising the level of consultant service. *Educational Leadership,* 5:445–450, 1948.

111. LONG, M.A. Action vs. advice: Conflict in consulting. *ALA Bulletin*, 60(4): 357–361, 1966.

112. LUNDQUIST, GERALD W., and CHAMLEY, JOHN C. Counselor consultant: A move toward effectiveness. *School Counselor*, 18(5):362–366, May 1971.

113. McCoy, GEORGIA. Case analysis: Consultation and counseling. *Elementary School Guidance and Counseling*, 5(3):221–225, March 1971.

114. McKEEVER, NELL. How to use a consultant. *Adult Leadership*, 3(10):16, 1955.

115. McMAHAN, J. Can your district afford curriculum consultants? *School Management*, 9:90–91, 1965.

116. MAHAN, JAMES M. Regional action network of professor-consultants: A replicable curriculum change mechanism. *Educational Technology*, 12(4): 58–60, April 1972.

117. MAHAN, J.M. Using teacher questions to look at science consultant performance. *Science Education*, 56(3):329–336, July-September 1972.

118. MARCHANT, WILLIAM C. Counseling and/or consultation: A test of the education model in the elementary school. *Elementary School Guidance and Counseling*, 7(1):4–8, October 1972.

119. MARSHALL, J.E. Where consultants can help. *American School and University*, 35:33–36, 1963.

120. MIEL, ALLICE. How to use experts and consultants. In: Benne, K.D., and Muntyan, B., eds. *Human Relations in Curriculum Change*. New York: The Dryden Press, 1967. pp. 505–508.

121. MILLER, M.D. Reading consultant in a private school. *The Reading Teacher*, 20:505–508, 1967.

122. MINGOIA, E. Librarian: An effective reading consultant. *Clearing House*, 38:220–223, 1963.

123. MOBURG, L.G. New consultant gets started. *The Reading Teacher*, 20:520–524, 1967.

124. MORPHET, EDGAR L. What is a consultant? *School Executive*, 72:9, 1952.

125. MYRICK, ROBERT D. The challenge of communication for the elementary school counselor-consultant. *National Catholic Guidance Conference Journal*, 15(2):114–119, Winter 1971.

126. MYRICK, ROBERT D. The counselor-consultant and the effeminate boy. *Personnel Guidance Journal*, 48(5):355–361, January 1970.

127. OKSENHOLT, S. Foreign language education, a new key or a new consultant? *Montana Education*, 41:10–11, 1965.

128. PALMO, ARTIS J., and KUZNIAR, JOSEPH. Modification of behavior through group counseling and consultation. *Elementary School Guidance and Counseling*, 6(4):258–262, May 1972.

129. PAYNE, A. Achievement in sixth grade science associated with two instructional roles of science consultants. *Journal of Educational Research*, 57: 350–354, 1964.

130. PETERSON, S.D., and WILKEN, C.W. Industrial arts consultant: Do the States need one? *Industrial Arts and Vocational Education*, 54:24–25, 1965.

131. PHILLIPS, L.M. What a consultant hopes to accomplish. *Instructor,* 66:19–20, 1957.

132. RANDOLPH, DANIEL L. Behavioral consultation as a means of improving the quality of a counseling program. *School Counselor,* 20(1):30–35, September 1972.

133. RASMUSSEN, GERALD R. The educational consultant and educational planning. *American School Board Journal,* 147:15–16, 1963.

134. REAVIS, W.C. The place of the consultant: The school administrator needs the expert for special problems. *Nations Schools,* 41:24–25, 1948.

135. REHAGE, K.J., and HEYWOOD, S.J. Consultant services to administrators. *Elementary School Journal,* 53:131–133, 1952.

136. REINISCH, B. Need for science consultants. *Science Education,* 50:52–54, 1966.

137. ROBINSON, H.A. Reading consultant of the past, present, and possible future. *The Reading Teacher,* 20:475–482, 1967.

138. SAVAGE, W.W. State consultative services in education. *Phi Delta Kappa,* 37:291–294, 1956.

139. SAVAGE, W.W. The value of State consultative service. *Administrator's Notebook,* 4(3), November 1955.

140. SAVAGE, W.W. Making the most of the consultant. *Administrator's Notebook,* 1:1–4, October 1952.

141. SAVAGE, W.W. Local school systems and the consultants. *Administrator's Notebook,* 4(2), October 1955.

142. SCHIFFMAN, G.B. Role of a state reading consultant. *Reading Teacher,* 20:487–493, 1967.

143. SEAGULL, ARTHUR A., and JOHNSON, JOHN L. Second stage intervention: Reality based consultation for teachers of the emotionally disturbed. In: Knoblock, Peter, ed. *Intervention Approaches in Educating Emotionally Disturbed Children.* Syracuse, New York: Division of Special Education and Rehabilitation, Syracuse University, 1966. pp. 99–111.

144. SEIDMAN, ERIC. The child development consultant: An experiment. *Personnel Guidance Journal,* 49(1):29–34, September 1970.

145. SEMROW, J.J. Activities of NCA consultant-examiner corps. *North Central Association Quarterly,* 41:213–215, 1966.

146. SIMONS, HAL, and DAVIES, DON. The Counsellor and Consultant in the Development of the Teacher-Advisor Concept in Guidance. Presented at the Canadian Guidance and Counseling Association Convention, Toronto, Ontario, June 1971. (EDRS).

147. STANFORD, GENE. Psychological education in the classroom. *Personnel Guidance Journal,* 50(7):585–592, 1972.

148. THOMAS, E.L. Reading consultant at the secondary level. *The Reading Teacher,* 20:509–514, 1967.

149. TIPTON, JAMES H. Consulting under fire. *Adult Leadership,* 3(10):17–20, April 1955.

150. TRILLINGHAM, C.C. The Case for Change—in the Functions of the Inter-

mediate Unit. Paper presented to the 16th Annual Conference of County and Rural Area Superintendents. Pittsburgh, Pa.: October 20, 1961. (EDRS).

151. UMANS, S. Responsibility of the reading consultant. *Reading Teacher*, 17: 16–24, 1963.

152. WEAR, P.W. Supervisor: Coordinator of multiple consultations. *Educational Leadership*, 23:652–655, 1966.

153. WELTY, S. The county consultant. *The Reading Teacher*, 20:494,499, 1967.

154. WILLIAMS, L. Consultant-teacher transaction. *Educational Leadership*, 23: 541–544, 1966.

155. WITTMER, JOE. Microcounseling and microcounseling consultation via video-tape. *Counselor Education and Supervision*, 11(3):238–240, March 1972.

See also: 78, 126, 315, 472, 613, 682, 692, 708, 710, 715, 728, 865, 937, 938, 942, 943, 944, 945, 947, 948, 951, 952, 953, 958, 960, 964, 965, 966, 970, 982, 983, 985, 986, 988, 990, 993, 998, 999.

MEDICINE

Articles and Periodicals

156. ANSTEL, NORMAN I. What I don't want from a consultant. *Medical Economics*, 45(17):92–97, August 19, 1968.

157. BATES, RICHARD C. The art of managing a medical triangle. *Medical Economics*, 46(18):135–148, September 2, 1969.

158. BOVERMAN, HAROLD, and MENDELSOHN, ROBERT. Pediatric consultation in a State hospital. *Hospital and Community Psychiatry*, 20(3):70–73, March 1969.

159. CAMPBELL, A.D. Consultations then and now. *Canadian Medical Association Journal*, 39:1030–1032, November 1963.

160. DANTES, D.A. Medical consultation requests in a psychiatric hospital. *Hospital and Community Psychiatry*, 18(6):180–181, June 1967.

161. FELTON, J.S. Educational functions of the medical consultant in vocational rehabilitation. II. Community Relationships. *Rehabilitation Literature*, 28: 73–75, March 1967.

162. FINELTAIN, LUDWIG, and POULET, J. Examination and treatment of suicidal behavior observed in general medical service: Indications for individual and group consultation. *Semaine des Hopitaux*. 48(24):1735–1738, 1972.

163. NOLEN, WILLIAM A. When it's smart to consult by phone. *Medical Economics*, 44(1):137–144, January 9, 1967.

164. READ, HILTON S. My most unforgiveable consultants. *Medical Economics*, 44(12):165–169, June 12, 1967.

165. SCHWAB, JOHN J. Psychosomatics and consultation. *Psychosomatics*, 13(1): 9–12, 1972.

166. SIMON, ELIZABETH L. Medical consultation in a county welfare department. *Public Welfare*, 24(4):274–277, 1966.

167. SMITH, DONALD C. Pediatric consultation in adoption practice. *Pediatrics,* 41(2):519–523, 1968.

168. WARREN, M.D. The medical officer of health as a consultant in preventive and social medicine. *Public Health,* 79(2):62–69, January 1965.

169. WEBB, JEAN F. The specialist consultant in a public health agency. *Canadian Journal of Public Health,* 59(4):155–158, April 1968.

See also: 281, 740, 813, 901, 912, 1041, 1115.

MENTAL HEALTH

Books

170. CAPLAN, G. *Concepts of Mental Health and Consultation.* Washington: U.S. Children's Bureau, Publication No. 373, U.S. Government Printing Office, 1959.

171. CAPLAN, G. *Mental Health Aspects of Social Work in Public Health.* Based on Proceedings of an Institute given by School of Social Welfare, Berkeley: University of California, 1956.

172. CAPLAN, G. *Principles of Preventive Psychiatry.* New York: Basic Books, 1964.

173. CAPLAN, GERALD. *The theory and practice of mental health consultation.* New York: Basic Books, 1970.

174. CAPLAN, RUTH B. *Helping the Helpers to Help: The Development and Evaluation of Mental Health Consultation to Aid Clergymen in Pastoral Work.* Seabury Press, New Jersey, 1972.

175. KAZANJIAN, V.; STEIN, SHERRY; and WEINBERG, W. *An Introduction to Mental Health Consultation.* Public Health Monograph No. 69, 1962. pp. 1–13.

176. Milbank Memorial Fund. *The Elements of a Community Mental Health Program.* The 1955 Annual Conference of the Milbank Memorial Fund. New York: The Fund, 1956.

177. National Institute of Mental Health. *Proceedings of the Ninth Annual Conference of Chief Social Workers from State Mental Health Programs.* Philadelphia: May 16–18, 1957.

178. National Institute of Mental Health, Office of Public Information. *Consultation and Education.* Public Health Service Publication No. 1478. Washington, D.C.: U.S. Government Printing Office, 1966.

179. WELSH, G., ed. *Conference of Community Mental Health Clinics.* Harrisburg: Pennsylvania Department of Welfare, 1957.

Articles and Periodicals

180. ADLER, PETER T. The community as a mental health system. *Mental Hygiene,* 56(4):28–32, Fall 1972.

181. BILL, AYDIN A., and SAMPLE, CHARLES E. The first psychiatric emergency,

community consultation and education in Delaware. *Delaware Medical Journal,* 40(4):115–118, April 1968.

182. BINDMAN, ARTHUR J. Mental health consultation: Theory and practice. *Journal of Consulting Psychology,* 23:473–482, 1959.

183. BOONE, DOROTHY, and MANNINO, F.V. Cooperative community efforts in mental health. *Public Health Reports,* 80(3):189–193, March 1965.

184. BURGESS, CAROLINE B.; MCDONALD, ELIZABETH; and ROBERTS, MARY B. More effective mental health by activation of community potentials. *Journal of Psychiatric Social Work,* 24(4):250–255, September 1955.

185. CAPLAN, G. Types of mental health consultation. *American Journal of Orthopsychiatry,* 33:470–481, 1963.

186. DALLE, B; RETANA, C.; and BITTAN, M.T. Possibilities and limitations of a regional mental hygiene consultation. *Information Psychiatrique,* 41(88): 687–697, 1966.

187. EKSTEIN, RUDOLF; MOTTO, ROCCO L.; ROSENFELD, HERBERT; HEINECKE, CHRISTOPH; and GILMAN, LEONARD. Issues in consultation: The mental health worker and educator. *American Journal of Orthopsychiatry,* 41(2):312–314, 1971.

188. ELIZUR, A. Mental health consultation of a team in Dr. Martin Luther King Center. In: Miller, L., ed. *4th International Congress of Social Psychiatry: Abstract of papers.* Jerusalem: AHVA Cooperative, 1972.

189. FORSTENZER, H.M. Consultation and mental health programs. *American Journal of Public Health,* 51(9):1280–1285, 1961.

190. GREENBERG, IRVIN. Mental health consultation. *Canada's Mental Health,* 16(1–2):14–17, 1968.

191. HARRIS, M. ROBERT. Community mental health and mental health consultation. *Psychosomatics,* 8(5):255–258, 1967.

192. HARTOG, JOSEPH. Nonprofessionals as mental health consultants. *Hospital and Community Psychiatry,* 18(8):223–225, 1967.

193. HASSOL, LEONARD, and COOPER, SAUL. Mental health consultation in a preventive context. In: Grunebaum, Henry, ed. *The Practice of Community Mental Health.* Boston: Little, Brown and Company, 1970. pp. 703–733.

194. HAYLETT, C.H., and RAPOPORT, L. Mental health consultation. In: Bellak, L., ed. *Handbook of Community Psychiatry and Community Mental Health.* New York: Grune and Stratton, 1964. pp. 319–339.

195. KELLY, JAMES G. The mental health agent in the urban community. Group for the advancement of psychiatry. In: *Urban America and the Planning of Mental Health Service Symposium, Number 10.* Philadelphia, pp. 474–494, 1964.

196. KHAJAVI, F., and MEHRYAR, A. Some implications of a community mental health model for developing countries. In: Miller, L., ed. *4th International Congress of Social Psychiatry: Abstract of papers.* Jerusalem: AHVA Cooperative, 1972.

197. KNIGHT, JAMES A., and DAVIS, WINBORN E. Consultation. In: Knight, J.A., and Davis, W.E., eds. *Manual for the Comprehensive Community Mental Health Clinic.* Springfield: Charles C. Thomas, 1964. pp. 103–112.

198. LEVEN, S. The Nassau County psychiatric consultation clinic: A new dimension in community mental health. *Journal of Hillside Hospital*, 13: 114–116, April 1964.

199. LOCKE, NORMAN. The mental health profile—a consultation technique. *Gerontologist*, 5(4):250–251, 1965.

200. LOEB, MARTIN B. Concerns and methods of mental health consultation. *Hospital and Community Psychiatry*, 19(4):111–113, 1968.

201. MACLENNAN, B.W.; QUINN, R.D.; and SCHROEDER, D. *The scope of community mental health consultation and education.* National Institute of Mental Health, PHS Publication 2169, 1971.

202. MERCER, M.E. Mental health consultation to child health protecting agencies. In: *The Elements of a Community Mental Health Program*. New York: Milbank Memorial Fund, 1956. pp. 47–56.

203. NARETA, TOSHIAKI. Mental health consultation for students. *Kyoiku to Igaku*, 17(3):18–26, 1969.

204. NORMAN, EDWARD C. Mental health consultation in nutrition. *Journal of The American Dietetic Association*, 63:30–34, July 1973.

205. ROBERTSON, BRUCE. Primary prevention: A pilot project. *Canada's Mental Health*, 16(6):20–22, 1968.

206. ROONEY, H.L. Consultant responsibilities of mental health clinics. In: *Proceedings of a Conference on Hospital-Community Coordination for Total Patient Care*. Blackwater Falls, Davis, West Virginia: Department of Mental Health, June 12–14, 1961. pp. 32–35.

207. SIGNELL, KAREN A. Mental health consultation in the field of illegitimacy. *Social Work*, 14(2):67–74, 1969.

208. STANTON, DUNCAN, and VETTER, HAROLD J. The mental health specialist as consultant in a chronic disease hospital. *Psychiatric Quarterly*, supplement 42:282–296, 1968.

209. WHITTINGTON, H.G. The consultation program. In: Whittington, H.G., ed. *Psychiatry in the American Community*. New York: International Universities Press, 1966. pp. 115–126.

See also: 309, 320, 350, 367, 380, 383, 385, 399, 411, 416, 422, 432, 434, 439, 441, 442, 447, 459, 467, 468, 469, 477, 478, 479, 480, 481, 490, 502, 504, 505, 512, 516, 518, 519, 524, 535, 555, 557, 558, 559, 562, 564, 569, 570, 572, 573, 583, 584, 591, 601, 612, 623, 625, 628, 642, 664, 669, 674, 697, 699, 734, 749, 755, 756, 759, 765, 780, 785, 786, 790, 793, 794, 795, 803, 806, 807, 818, 819, 829, 834, 838, 849, 850, 860, 862, 864, 895, 907, 930, 931, 946, 957, 963, 1004, 1022.

NURSING

Books

210. NATIONAL LEAGUE FOR NURSES. *Some Papers on Consultation, League Exchange No. 44*. New York: The League, Department of Hospital Nursing, 1959.

Articles and Periodicals

211. AMERICAN NURSING ASSOCIATION. Functions, standards and qualifications for practice for consultants. *American Journal of Nursing*, 58:1281–1282, 1958.

212. BLUMBERG, ARTHUR. A nurse consultant's responsibility and problems, *American Journal of Nursing*, 56:606–608, 1956.

213. BRASS, MATTY. A plan for nursing consultation. *Nursing Outlook*, 3(8): 438–440, 1955.

214. CADY, LOUISE L. The tuberculosis nursing consultant. *Public Health Nursing*, 38(7):394–398, 1946.

215. DAVIDSON, SHIRLEE, and NOYES, RUSSELL, JR. Psychiatric nursing consultation on a burn unit. *American Journal of Nursing*, 73(10):1715–1718, October 1973.

216. DELOUGHERY, GRACE W.; GEBBIE, KRISTINE M.; and NEUMAN, BETTY M. *Consultation and Community Organization in Community Mental Health Nursing*. Baltimore: Williams and Wilkins, 1971. p. 219.

217. DONNER, GAIL J. Parenthood as a crisis: A role for the psychiatric nurse. *Perspectives in Psychiatric Care*, 10(2):84–87, 1972.

218. FLORENTINE, HELEN G. Assets unlimited. *Nursing Outlook*, 6(1):48–50, 1958.

219. FRANK, SISTER CHARLES MARIE. Consultation in retrospect. *Nursing Outlook*, 10(11):750–752, 1962.

220. FULCHER, ELIZABETH, and BEASLEY, FLORENCE. Consultant nurses can help staff nurses. *Nursing Outlook*, 1:208–212, 1953.

221. GEORGE, SISTER MARY. Psychiatric unit offers nurse-to-nurse consultation. *Hospital and Community Psychiatry*, 17(1):18–20, 1966.

222. GORDON, JOHN. Consultation to psychiatric nursing services. *Nursing Outlook*, 6(7):409–411, 1958.

223. HANKOFF, L.D.; BERNARD, L.G.; and OMURA, J. Visiting nurse consultation in a community psychiatry program. *Journal of Psychiatric Nursing*, 5(3): 217–232, 1967.

224. HOLSTEIN, SHIRLEY, and SCHWAB, JOHN J. A coordinated consultation program for nurses and psychiatrists. *Journal of American Medical Association*, 194:491–493, November 1, 1965.

225. JOHNSON, BETTY S. Psychiatric nurse consultant in a general hospital. *Nursing Outlook*, 11(10):728–729, October 1963.

226. KAHL, F. RUTH, and BRASS, MATTY. Cancer nursing consultation. *Nursing Outlook*, 7:145–147, 1959.

227. KLAES, MARY M. Consultant service for school nurses. *Public Health Nursing*, 40:195–198, 1948.

228. LOSTY, MARGARET A.; WALLACE, HELEN; and ABRAMSON, HAROLD. What the hospital nursing consultant does. *American Journal of Nursing*, 48:158–160, March 1948.

229. Mental Hygiene Committee of the National Organization of Public Health Nursing. Nurse mental health consultant: Functions and qualifications. *Public Health Nursing*, 42:507–509, 1950.

230. MILLER, MARY A. The hospital nursing consultant goes consulting. *American Journal of Nursing*, 52:1486–1488, 1952.

231. OETTINGER, KATHERINE B. Why a nurse mental health consultant in public health? *Journal of Psychiatric Social Work*, 19(4):162–168, 1950.

232. POORMAN, ANN. The hospital nurse consultant. *Nursing Outlook*, 3(7): 382–385, 1955.

233. PORTER, WINIFRED H. The specialized public health nursing consultant in state health departments. *American Journal of Public Health*, 41(1): 13–19, 1951.

234. RAFFERTY, RITA, and CARNER, JEAN. Nursing Consultants, Inc.: A corporation. *Nursing Outlook*, 21(4):232–235, April 1973.

235. ROBINSON, LISA. A psychiatric nursing liaison program. *Nursing Outlook*, 29(7):454–457, 1972.

236. ROBINSON, LISA. Liaison psychiatric nursing. *Perspectives in Psychiatric Care*, 6:87–91, March-April 1968.

237. RUMRIL, MARY S. The supervisor and the consultant. *Nursing Outlook*, 5(3):164–165, 1957.

238. SCOTT, RUTH. State consultants serve industrial nurses. *Public Health Nursing*, 34:271–274, May 1942.

239. SHORTAL, HAZEL. Consultation in the public health environment. *American Journal of Public Health*, 51(9):1274–1279, 1961.

240. STOKES, JOHN H. What is a consultant, with special reference to the venereal disease field. *Public Health Nursing*, 39(5):239–245, 1947.

241. TUCKER, ELIZABETH. Training, consultation, and supervision of staff in nursing homes and hospitals. In: *Mental health aspects of nursing home care. Proceedings of a conference sponsored by the Massachusetts Department of Public Health and of Mental Health and the National Institute of Mental Health*, Chatham, Mass.: June 1–3, 1964. pp. 54–72.

See also: 255, 435, 441, 552, 630, 631, 702, 704, 706, 843, 1026, 1036, 1039, 1064.

PSYCHIATRY

Books

242. MENDEL, WERNER M., and SOLOMON, PHILIP, eds. *The Psychiatric Consultation*. New York: Grune and Stratton, 1968.

243. SCHWAB, JOHN J. *Handbook of Psychiatric Consultation*. New York: Appleton-Century-Crofts, 1968.

244. WINNICOTT, D.W. *Therapeutic consultations in child psychiatry*. New York: Basic Books, 1971.

Articles and Periodicals

245. ADLAND, MARVIN. Psychiatric consultation in residential treatment: Discussion. *American Journal of Orthopsychiatry*, 28:289–290, 1958.

246. ALDRICH, C. KNIGHT. British and American psychiatry: Demand, supply and consultation in outpatient care. *Journal of the Kansas Medical Society,* 66(1):11–15, January 1965.

247. ALDRICH, C. KNIGHT. Psychiatric consultation in general practice. *The Lancet,* 1(7389):805–808, April 10, 1965.

248. BABCOCK, CHARLOTTE G. On psychiatric consultation. *Highlights,* 13(10): 145–150, December 1952.

249. BARCAI, AVNER. Increasing the use of psychiatric consultation. *Hospital and Community Psychiatry,* 19(5):134–135, 1968.

250. BAUDRY, FRANK; WIENER, A.; and HURWITT, E.S. Indications for psychiatric consultation on a surgical service. *Surgery,* 60(5):993–1000, November 1966.

251. BERG, LEIDA, and GREENWALD, ALBERT. Integration of psychiatric consultation into the counseling process. In: *Diagnosis and process in family counseling.* New York: Family Service Association of America, 1951. pp. 129–149.

252. BETTELHEIM, B. Psychiatric consultation in residential treatment: The director's view. *American Journal of Orthopsychiatry,* 28(2):256–265, 1958.

253. BIBRING, G.L. Psychiatry and medical practice in a general hospital. *New England Journal of Medicine,* 154(8):366–372, 1956.

254. BRODSKY, C.M. A social view of the psychiatric consultation. *Psychosomatics,* 8:61–68, 1967.

255. BURSTEN, B. The psychiatric consultant and the nurse. *Nursing Forum,* 2(4):7–23, 1963.

256. CAPLAN, GERALD. Practical steps for the family physician in the prevention of emotional disorder. In: Bindman, Arthur J., and Spiegel, Allen D., eds. *Perspectives in Community Mental Health.* Chicago: Aldine Publishing Company, 1969. pp. 615–619.

257. CASSEM, N.H., and HACKETT, THOMAS P. Psychiatric consultation in a coronary care unit. *Annals of Internal Medicine,* 75(1):9–14, 1971.

258. COLEMAN, JULES V. Contributions of the psychiatrist to the social worker and to the client. *Mental Hygiene,* 37:249–258, April 1953.

259. DAVIS, W.E. Psychiatric consultation—the agency viewpoint. *Child Welfare,* 36(9):4–9, 1957.

260. DEWALD, PAUL A., and HARLE, MARJORIE. Utilization of the psychiatric caseworker as consultant during the psychoanalytically oriented therapy of a patient. *American Journal of Orthopsychiatry,* 23(4):785–794, 1953.

261. DWYER, THOMAS F. Telepsychiatry: Psychiatric consultation by interactive television. *American Journal of Psychiatry,* 130(8):865–869, August 1973.

262. FRANKEL, FRED H. Psychiatric consultation for nursing homes. *Hospital and Community Psychiatry,* 18(11):331–334, 1967.

263. GARRETT, ANNETTE. Psychiatric consultation. *American Journal of Orthopsychiatry,* 26(2):234–240, 1956.

264. GOLDBERG, HAROLD L.; LATIF, JANET; and ABRAMS, SEENA. Psychiatric consultation: A strategic service to nursing home staffs. *Gerontologist,* 10(3):221–224, 1970.

265. GREENBERG, H.A. Psychiatric consultation in residential treatment; workshop, 1957. *American Journal of Orthopsychiatry*, 28:256–290, 1958.

266. GROTJAHN, MARTIN. The aim and techniques of psychiatric family consultations. In: Mendel, W.M. and Solomon, P., eds. *The Psychiatric Consultation*. New York: Grune and Stratton, 1968. pp. 181–186.

267. HADER, M. The psychiatrist as consultant to the social worker in a home for the aged. *Journal of the American Geriatric Society*, 14:407–413, 1966.

268. HALLECK, S.L., and MILLER, M.H. The psychiatric consultation: Questionable social precedents of some current practices. *American Journal of Psychiatry*, 120:164–169, 1963.

269. HICKS, WILLIAM, and DANIELS, ROBERT S. The dying patient, his physician and the psychiatric consultant. *Psychosomatics*, 9(1):47–52, 1968.

270. HIRSCH, STEVEN J.; KINZEL, AUGUSTUS F.; and SKELTON, W. The correctional psychiatrist and the legal process. In: *U.S. Bureau of Prisons, a Handbook of Correctional Psychiatry*, Washington: U.S. Bureau of Prisons, 1968. pp. 31–37.

271. JACKSON, BASIL. Referral for psychiatric consultation and treatment. *Senn Journal*, 3(1):1–3, August 1973.

272. KAMPMEIER, R.H. The psychiatric consultation in the general hospital. *Southern Medical Journal*, 59:979–980, August 1966.

273. KIMBALL, CHASE P. Liaison psychiatry in the university medical center. *Comprehensive Psychiatry*, 14(3):241–249, May-June 1973.

274. KLAGSBRUN, SAMUEL C. Cancer, emotions, and nurses. *American Journal of Psychiatry*, 126(9):1237–1244, 1970.

275. KOUMANS, A.J.R. Psychiatric consultation in an intensive care unit. *Journal of the American Medical Association*, 194:633–637, 1965.

276. LEIGH, HOYLE. Psychiatric liaison on a neoplastic inpatient service. *International Journal of Psychiatry in Medicine*, 4(2):147, Spring 1973.

277. LEPAGE, ANTOINE; AIRD, GEORGES; BRIONES, LUIS; and VILLARD, HENRI-PAUL. Reasons for psychiatric consultation in the general hospital. *Canadian Psychiatric Association Journal*, 14:253–258, June 1969.

278. LIDDON, SIM C. The referring physician and the psychiatric consultant. *Postgraduate Medicine*, 51(2):179–183, 1972.

279. LIPOWSKI, Z.J. Consultation-liaison services in the general hospitals. *Psychotherapy and Psychosomatics*, 21(1–6):232–234, 1972–73.

280. LITIN, E.M. Preoperative psychiatric consultation. *Journal of the American Medical Association*, 170:1369–1372, 1959.

281. MENDEL, W.M. The psychosomatic consultation. In: Mendel, W.M., and Solomon, P., eds. *The Psychiatric Consultation*. New York: Grune and Stratton, 1968. pp. 187–195.

282. MENDEL, W.M. The psychiatric consultation. *Medical Times*, 94:984–986, August 1966.

283. MENOLASCINO, FRANK J. Psychiatric long distance consultation for the mentally retarded. *Mental Retardation*, 9(1):23–25, 1971.

284. MEYER, E., and MENDELSON, M. Psychiatric consultation with patients on

medical and surgical wards; patterns and processes. *Psychiatry,* 24(3): 197–220, 1961.

285. Mozes, R.; Noy, P.; Dinoor-Kaplan, A.; and Wollstein, S. Psychiatric consultations—the consultant and his reactions. *Harefuah,* 68:18–20, 1965.

286. Nicolle, F.I. Psychiatric problems in general practice liaison between psychiatry and general practice: When and how to refer. *Southern Medical Journal,* 58:23–25, January 1965.

287. Papanek, G.O. An exploratory model of community psychiatry. *Hospital and Community Psychiatry,* 17(4):91–95, 1966.

288. Perkins, G.L. Psychiatric consultation in residential treatment; the consultant's view. *American Journal of Orthopsychiatry,* 28(2):266–282, 1958.

289. Prince, G. Stewart. Psychiatric consultation. *Sociological Review Monograph,* 6:85–92, December 1962.

290. Proctor, R.C. Consultative psychiatry. *Medical Times,* 86:1043, 1958.

291. Rabiner, Charles J., and Nichtern, Sol. Psychiatric service to community: Pilot program for its extension. *New York State Journal of Medicine,* 69(5):713–716, 1969.

292. Riley, Mary Jean. Psychiatric consultation in residential treatment: The child care worker's view. *American Journal of Orthopsychiatry,* 282(2): 283–288, 1958.

293. Schiff, S.K., and Pilot, M.L. An approach to psychiatric consultation in the general hospital. *American Medical Association Archives of General Psychiatry,* 1(4):349–357, 1959.

294. Schwab, John J. The psychiatric consultation: Problems with referral. *Diseases of the Nervous System,* 32(7):447–452, 1971.

295. Schwab, John J., and Kuch, Helga. The psychiatric consultation patient. *Psychiatry in Medicine,* 1(3):251–257, 1970.

296. Schwartz, L.A. Application of psychosomatic concepts by a liaison psychiatrist on a medical service. *Journal of Michigan State Medical Society,* 57(11):1547–1552, 1958.

297. Senseman, L.A. Psychiatric referrals: Tact and understanding necessary to induce patient to accept psychiatric consultation. *Rhode Island Medical Journal,* 47:588–589, December 1964.

298. Solomon, P. An overview, summary and conclusion. In: Mendel, W.M., and Solomon, P., eds. *The Psychiatric Consultation.* New York: Grune and Stratton, 1968. pp. 196–215.

299. Stein, H.D. Use of the consultant, discussion. *American Journal of Orthopsychiatry,* 26(2):249–251, 1956.

300. Treusch, J.V., and Grotjahn, M. Psychiatric family consultations. *Annals of Internal Medicine,* 66:295–300, 1967.

301. Van Ophuijsen, J.H.W. The psychiatric consultation. *American Journal of Orthopsychiatry,* 19:397–403, July 1940.

302. Wouters, F.W. The use of the psychiatric consultant. *Journal of the Medical Association of Georgia,* 50:597–598, December 1961.

303. WRIGHT, BENJAMIN. Psychiatric consultation in residential treatment: The psychologist's view. *American Journal of Orthopsychiatry*, 28:276–282, 1958.

See also: 270, 374, 376, 377, 388, 389, 393, 395, 396, 401, 402, 403, 407, 409, 410, 418, 423, 427, 429, 430, 433, 437, 440, 444, 446, 448, 450, 455, 457, 462, 465, 466, 475, 484, 493, 495, 496, 501, 514, 517, 521, 527, 528, 529, 531, 532, 533, 536, 537, 538, 539, 540, 541, 542, 543, 544, 545, 546, 547, 549, 556, 560, 565, 566, 571, 577, 578, 585, 586, 589, 594, 598, 603, 604, 605, 606, 607, 622, 627, 647, 651, 657, 705, 718, 732, 743, 750, 753, 758, 760, 777, 799, 803, 815, 824, 843, 846, 854, 878, 888, 893, 897, 914, 923, 928, 935, 941, 1002, 1009, 1012, 1014, 1040, 1046, 1047, 1061, 1065, 1066, 1067, 1081, 1082, 1094.

PSYCHOLOGY

Books

304. JACOBSON, STANLEY. *School Project on Consultation Skills.* Washington, D.C.: D.C. Public Schools and Washington School of Psychiatry, 1966.

Articles and Periodicals

305. ABIDIN, RICHARD R. A psychosocial look at consultation and behavior modification. *Psychology in the Schools*, 9(4):358–364, October 1972.

306. BARD, MORTON, and BERKOWITZ, BERNARD. A community psychology consultation program in police family crisis intervention: Preliminary impressions. *International Journal of Social Psychiatry*, 15(3):209–215, 1969.

307. BENYAMINI, KALMAN. Some trials facing the psychologist away from the clinic. *Professional Psychology*, 2(3):255–258, Summer 1971.

308. BERKOWITZ, HERSCHEL. The child clinical psychologist in the schools: Consultation. *Psychology in the Schools*, 5(2):118–124, 1968.

309. BINDMAN, ARTHUR J. The clinical psychologist as a mental health consultant. In: Abt, L.E., and Riess, B.F., eds. *Progress in Clinical Psychology*. New York: Grune and Stratton, 1966. pp. 78–106.

310. BINDMAN, ARTHUR J. The psychologist as a mental health consultant. *Journal of Psychiatric Nursing*, 2(4):367–379, July-August 1964.

311. BIRNBAUM, MORTON P. The State hospital psychologist as a consultant in the public school. *Hospital and Community Psychiatry*, 22(9):269–271, September 1971.

312. BONKOWSKI, ROBERT J. Mental health consultation and Operation Head Start. *American Psychologist*, 23(10):769–773, October 1968.

313. CONANT, JAMES C. The psychologist and occupational mental health. In: Collins, Ralph T., ed. *Occupational Psychiatry*. Boston: Little, Brown and Company, 1969. pp. 69–79.

314. CRARY, WILLIAM G., and STEGER, HERBERT G. Prescriptive and consultative approaches to psychological evaluation. *Professional Psychology*, 3(2): 105–109, 1972.

315. CUSTER, G.E. A look at the personnel consulting business. *Personnel Administration*, 22(5):24–30, 1959.

316. DINKMEYER, DON. The "C" group: Integrating knowledge and experience to change behavior, an Adlerian approach to consultation. *Counseling Psychologist*, 3(1):63–72, 1971.

317. FINE, MARVIN J., and TYLER, MILTON M. Concerns and directions in teacher consultation. *Journal of School Psychology*, 9(4):436–444, 1971.

318. GALLESSICH, JUNE. Organizational factors influencing consultation in schools. *Journal of School Psychology*, 11(1):57, March 1973.

319. GLASSER, E.M. Relationships of the psychological consultant in business and industry. *Journal of Counseling Psychology*, 8(1):116–120, 1961.

320. GLUCK, M.R. School organization and the mental health consultation process. *Psychological Reports*, 12(3):671–676, 1963.

321. KATKIN, EDWARD S. Psychological consultation in a maximum security prison: A history and some comments. In: Golann, Stuart E., and Eisdorfer, Carl, eds. *Handbook of Community Mental Health*. New York: Appleton-Century-Crofts, 1972. pp. 641–658.

322. KLEIN, DONALD. Consultation processes as a method for improving teaching. In: Bower, E.M., and Hollister, W.G., eds. *Behavioral Science Frontiers of Education*. New York: John Wiley and Sons, 1967. pp. 401–419.

323. LIBO, LESTER M. Multiple functions for psychologists in community consultation. In: Adelson, Daniel, and Kalis, Betty L., eds. *Community Psychology and Mental Health: Perspectives and Challenges*. Scranton, Pa.: Chandler Publishing Company, 1970. pp. 308–319.

324. McDANIEL, L.J., and AHR, A.E. The school psychologist as a resource person initiating and conducting in-service teacher education. *Psychology in the Schools*, 2(2):220–224, 1965.

325. MEACHAM, MERLE L. The School Psychologist: Classroom Consultant in Behavioral Techniques. Paper presented at Annual Meeting of American Psychological Association, Washington, D.C., September 3–7, 1971. (EDRS).

326. MEYERS, JOEL. A consultation model for school psychological services. *Journal of School Psychology*, 11(1):5, March 1973.

327. MURPHY, L.B. The consultant in a day-care center for deprived children. *Children*, 15(3):97–102, 1968.

328. RON, KATRIT. The school psychologist and mental hygiene. *Mental Hygiene*, 52(3):395–399, 1968.

329. STEPHENS, THOMAS M. Psychological consultation to teachers of learning and behaviorally handicapped children using a behavioral model. *Journal of School Psychology*, 8(1):13–18, 1970.

330. WATERS, LINDA G. School psychologists as perceived by school personnel: Support for a consultant model. *Journal of School Psychology*, 11(1):40, March 1973.

331. WAXER, PETER, and WHITE, RONALD. Introducing psychological consultation to a university community. *Canadian Psychologist*, 14(3):256–265, July 1973.

332. WEINBERGER, GERALD; LEVENTHAL, THEODORE; and BECKMAN, GEORGE. The

management of a chronic school phobia through the use of consultation with school personnel. *Psychology in the Schools,* 10(1):83–88, January 1973.

333. WEISS, S.W. Role of the psychological consultant in a school setting. *Delaware Medical Journal,* 37(6):136–139, June 1965.

334. WILLIAMS, DONALD L. Consultation: A broad, flexible role for school psychologists. *Psychology in the Schools,* 9(1):16–21, January 1972.

335. WINICKI, SIDNEY A. The case conference as a consultation strategy. *Psychology in the Schools,* 9(1):21–24, January 1972.

336. WYMAN, CHERRY. Psychologists help solve learning problems. *Momentum,* 3(2):8–13, May 1972.

See also: 397, 412, 453, 473, 474, 590, 641, 722, 737, 746, 765, 768, 797, 857, 859, 877, 994, 1010, 1037, 1090, 1110, 1113.

SOCIAL WORK

Books

337. American Association of Medical Social Workers. *Consultation.* Two papers given at the Meeting of the American Association of Medical Social Workers, New Orleans, May 12, 1942. Menasha, Wisconsin: George Banta Publishing Company.

338. National Conference of Social Work. *Administration, Supervision, and Consultation.* Papers from the 1954 Social Welfare Forum. New York: Family Service Association of America, 1955.

339. RADER, M.T., and WHIDDEN, A.G. *The Case Work Consultant and Visiting Nurses.* Austin: The Hogg Foundation for Mental Health, 1960.

340. RAPOPORT, LYDIA, ed. *Consultation in Social Work Practice.* New York: National Association of Social Workers, 1963.

Articles and Periodicals

341. U.S. Department of Health, Education, and Welfare, Children's Bureau. *Selected papers from a workshop on consultation.* Washington: Superintendent of Documents, U.S. Government Printing Office, 1965.

342. ALT, EDITH S. Social work consultation in prepayment medical care plan. *American Journal of Public Health,* 49(3):350–354, March 1959.

343. ARNOLD, MILDRED. The specialized consultant in child welfare services. In: *Proceedings of the National Conference of Social Work, 1941.* New York: Columbia University Press, 1941. pp. 426–439.

344. BARTLETT, HARRIET M. Consultation regarding the medical social program in a hospital. In: *Two Papers Given at the Meeting of the American Association of Medical Social Workers.* Menasha, Wisconsin: George Banta Publishing Company, 1942.

345. DECKER, J.H., and ITZIN, F. An experience in consultation in public assistance. *Social Casework,* 37:327–334, 1956.

346. DRAKE, RUSSELL. The use of consultants in a state agency. *Public Welfare,* 4(4):88–90, 1946.

347. FELDMAN, FRED. The tripartite session: A new approach in psychiatric social work consultation. *Psychiatric Quarterly*, 42(1):48–61, 1968.

348. FOSTERLING, CHARLES, and McNAMARA, FRANK P. *Child Welfare*, 49(7): 379–385, July 1970.

349. GALLANT, CLAIRE, and MACDONALD, BARBARA. Partners in change. In: Sarri, Rosemary, and Maple, Frank F., eds. *The School in the Community*. Washington, D.C.: 1972. National Association of Social Workers, Inc. pp. 275–283.

350. GALLEGOS, REUBEN A. The social worker as a mental health consultant. In: *Collected Papers from a Short Course on Current Trends in Army Social Work*. Washington: Walter Reed Army Institute of Research, 1962.

351. GILMORE, MARY H. Consultation as a social work activity. In: Rapoport, Lydia, ed. *Consultation in Social Work Practice*. New York: National Association of Social Workers, 1963. pp. 33–50.

352. GOLDMEIER, JOHN. Applying a general systems approach to consultation in public welfare. *Public Welfare*, 29(3):316–319, Summer 1971.

353. HAGEE, FLORENCE. The social worker: Consultant on the firing line. In: Berlin, I.N., and Szurek, S.A., eds. *Learning and Its Disorders*. Palo Alto: Science and Behavior Books, 1965. pp. 181–191.

354. INSLEY, V. Social work consultation in public health. In: Caplan, G., ed. *Concepts of Mental Health and Consultation*. Washington: U.S. Department of Health, Education, and Welfare, Children's Bureau, 1959. pp. 215–232.

355. JACOBSON, SYLVIA R. The psychiatric social worker as visiting case consultant to community social agencies. *Journal of Psychiatric Social Work*, 22: 98–104, 1953.

356. KANE, RAYMOND. Social work consultation to the priest. *Catholic Charities Review*, 50(8):4–10, 1966.

357. MONTALVO, FRANK F. Casework consultation in overseas adoption. *Social Casework*, 40(3):129–136, 1959.

358. O'KEEFE, DANIEL. The psychiatric social worker as team member and consultant. In: *Proceedings, The Annual Work Conference on Psychiatric Social Work*. Baton Rouge: Louisiana State University, School of Social Work, 1958.

359. RAPOPORT, LYDIA. Consultation. In: Lurie, Harry L., ed. *Encyclopedia of Social Work*. New York: National Association of Social Workers, 1965. pp. 214–218.

360. RASHID, RIFAT. Use of international consultants. *International Social Work*, 2(3):5–7, 1959.

361. RIEMAN, DWIGHT W. Midway: A case story of community organization consultation. In: Shore, M.F., and Mannino, F.V., eds. *Mental Health and the Community: Problems, Programs and Strategies*. New York: Behavioral Publications, 1969.

362. RIEMAN, DWIGHT W. Issues and principles of consultation in relation to other professional people. In: *Proceedings of the Ninth Annual Conference of State Chief Social Workers, May 1957*. Bethesda, Maryland: National Institute of Mental Health.

363. ROWEN, ROBERT B. Model for service delivery in school social work. *Journal of International Association of Pupil Personnel Workers*, 14(4):173–180, September 1970.

364. SIKKEMA, MILDRED. The school social worker serves as consultant. In: *Casework Papers, 1955*. New York: Family Service Association of America, 1955. pp. 75–82.

365. SILVERIO, J.S. Learning through consultation abroad. *International Social Work*, 3:23–27, 1960.

366. SLOANE, P. The use of a consultation method in casework therapy. *American Journal of Orthopsychiatry*, 6(2):355–361, 1936.

367. TASCHMAN, H.A., and MANNINO, F.V. Some comments on consultation in social work and mental health. In: *Collected Papers From a Short Course on Current Trends in Army Social Work*. Washington: Walter Reed Army Institute of Research, 1962.

368. VAN DRIEL, AGNES. Consultation in relation to the administration of social service programs. In: *Consultation: Two papers given at the Meeting of the American Association of Medical Social Workers*. Menasha, Wisconsin: George Banta Publishing Company, 1942.

369. WARRINER, ALICE. The psychiatric social worker as consultant. *Public Health Nursing*, 41:392–397, 1949.

See also: 392, 426, 436, 522, 529, 553, 570, 576, 593, 618, 626, 639, 658, 660, 662, 663, 674, 678, 711, 726, 739, 748, 783, 784, 810, 817, 823, 887, 896, 968.

USE OF CONSULTATION IN VARIOUS SETTINGS

The 213 items in this section deal with the application of consultation techniques to problem situations within specific settings, such as schools, social agencies, hospitals, correctional institutions, etc. These do not necessarily represent the only settings in which consultation is applicable, but do appear to be the major settings written about by practitioners who record their experiences in the literature. Since publication of the first Reference Guide in 1969 there has been a marked increase in the number of articles focusing on consultation to the clergy and to early child care settings such as day care, head start, etc. This increase has necessitated adding several new subcategories. One new subcategory, "Specialized Settings," includes articles on consultation to such groups as the blind, minorities, camps and the media.

To avoid unnecessary cross-referencing, the items in this section reflect the experiences of consultants who come into the setting from outside, usually from different professional disciplines and backgrounds. Articles by consultants who characteristically work within certain settings, such as the educational consultant in the school system, are not cross-referenced here.

CLERGY

Books

370. ALDRICH, C. KNIGHT, and NIGHSWONGER, CARL. *A Pastoral Counselling Casebook.* Philadelphia: The Westminister Press, 1968.

Dissertations

371. FORRESTER, ARTHUR W. "Relationships Between Ego Strength and Certain Expectations of Mental Health Consultation, with Special Reference to Conservative Baptist Clergymen of New England." Unpublished doctoral dissertation. Boston University Graduate School, 1971.

372. HOMMEN, DONOVAN L. "An Assessment of the Effects of a Community Mental Health Center Laboratory Training-Education-Consultation Program

in Bereavement Ministry for Parish Clergymen." Unpublished doctoral dissertation. Boston University Graduate School, 1972.

373. STEWART, JOHN T. "Some Factors Associated with Clergymen's Projected Responses to Mental Health Consultation with a Focus on Patterns of Dependency." Unpublished doctoral dissertation. Boston University School of Theology, 1971.

Articles and Periodicals

374. DRAPER, EDGAR. Psychiatric consultation to clergymen. In: Pattison, E., ed. *Clinical Psychiatry and Religion*. Boston: Little, Brown, and Co., 1969. pp. 269–278.

375. HILTNER, SEWARD, Theological consultants in hospitals and mental health centers. *American Journal of Psychiatry*, 128(8):965–969, 1972.

376. McWHIRTER, DAVID P. Consultation with the clergy. *The Psychiatric Consultation*. New York: Grune and Stratton, 1968. pp. 119–131.

377. ROCKLAND, LAWRENCE H. Psychiatric consultation to the clergy: A report on a group experience. *Mental Hygiene*, 53(2):205–207, 1969.

378. THOMAS, PAUL R. Pastoral counselor program. In: Williams, H., ed. *314(D) —A Force For Service*. Topeka, Kansas: Department of Social Welfare, 1970. pp. 61–65.

379. TRACHTMAN, DAVID L. Consultation services to the clergy. *Bulletin of the Rochester Mental Health Center*, 3(2):48–51,1971.

See also: 1106, 1109.

CORRECTIONAL AGENCIES

Articles and Periodicals

380. ABRAMSON, MARC F. Participant observation and attempted mental health consultation in a public defender agency. *American Journal of Psychiatry*, 127(7):964–969, 1971.

381. BAYER, CHRISTOPHER A., and BRODSKY, MARVIN J. Prison programming and psychological consultation. *Canadian Journal of Criminology and Corrections*, 14(4):325–334, 1972.

382. BERLIN, IRVING N. Psychiatric consultation on the antidelinquency project. *California Journal of Secondary Education*, 35:198–202, March 1960.

383. BERLIN, IRVING N. Mental health consultation with a juvenile probation department. *Crime and Delinquency*, 67–73, January 1964.

384. BIXBY, F. LOVELL. New Jersey's consultation system for improved probation services. *State Government*, 38(2):96–99, 1965.

385. CHWAST, J. Mental health consultation with street gang workers. In: Reckless, W.C., and Newman, C.L., eds. *Interdisciplinary Problems in Criminology: Papers of the American Society of Criminology*. Columbus, Ohio: Ohio State University, 1965. pp. 13–21.

386. CORE, HARRY M., and LIMA, DAVID R. Mental health services to juvenile

courts: Consultation and education for court personnel. *Hospital and Community Psychiatry,* 23(6):174–178, 1972.

387. ELKINS, ALAN, and PAPANEK, GEORGE. Consultation with the police: An example of community psychiatry practice. *American Journal of Psychiatry,* 123(5):531–535, 1966.

388. FRIED, FREDERICK. Psychiatric consultation and adult probation case management. *Federal Probation,* VII(2):12–14, June 1973.

389. GIBSON, ROBERT. The psychiatric consultant and the juvenile court. *Mental Hygiene,* 38(3):462–467, 1954.

390. GOLDIN, GURSTON D. The psychiatrist as court consultant: A challenge to community psychiatry. *Community Mental Health Journal,* 3(4):396–398, 1967.

391. HUFF, FREDERICK W., and PORTER, HARRY JR. Mental health consultation in juvenile court. *Juvenile Justice,* 23(3):32–36, 1972.

392. KINDELSPERGER, KENNETH W. Consultation and consultative technique in providing consultation at the State level for delinquency control. In: *Selected Papers from a Workshop on Consultation.* Washington: Children's Bureau, U.S. Department of Health, Education, and Welfare, 1965, pp. 9–27.

393. LOOMIS, S. DALE. Psychiatric consultation in a delinquent population. *American Journal of Psychiatry,* 123(1):66–70, July 1966.

394. McDONOUGH, LEAH B., and ANDERSON, THEODORE I. Consultation to courts and corrections. In: Lamb, H. Richard; Heath, Don; and Downing, Joseph J., eds. *Handbook of Community Mental Health Practice.* San Francisco: Jossey-Bass, 1969. pp. 322–346.

395. POLLACK, SEYMOUR. Psychiatric consultation for the courts. In: Mendel, Werner M. and Solomon, Philip, eds. *The Psychiatric Consultation.* New York: Grune and Stratton, 1968. pp. 132–158.

396. RABINER, CHARLES J., and COHEN, RICHARD. Psychiatric consultation with a police youth-aid unit. *Hospital and Community Psychiatry,* 24(5):326–329, May 1973.

397. REISER, MARTIN. The police psychologist as consultant. *Police,* 15(3):58–60, 1971.

398. RESNER, GERALD. Psychiatric consultation to the public defender's office. *Hospital and Community Psychiatry,* 22(5):133–139, May 1971.

399. SABOT, THEODORE J. Mental health consultation concerning the competency of the criminal defendant. *Community Mental Health Journal.* 7(4):323–330, 1971.

400. SADOFF, ROBERT L. Civil law and psychiatry: New dimensions. *American Bar Association Journal,* 56:165–168, 1970.

401. SHOOR, MERVYN, and SPEED, MARY HELEN. Seven years of psychiatric consultation in a juvenile probation department. *Annual Progress in Child Psychiatry and Child Development,* 3:570–585, 1970.

402. SUSSELMAN, SAM. The role of the psychiatrist in a probation agency. *Focus,* 29(2):33–37+, 1950.

403. WILKERSON, WALLACE W. Psychiatric consultation with probationers and parolees. *Federal Probation*, 33(2):45–50, 1969.

See also: 270, 287, 306, 321, 400, 551, 600, 621, 844, 848, 1118.

EARLY CHILD CARE AGENCIES

Dissertations

404. KNISELY, S. "Consultant Services to Community Nursery Schools." Unpublished doctoral dissertation. Columbia University Teachers College, New York, 1964.

405. NORTON, WILLIAM J. "The Effects of Certain Counselling and Consultation Techniques on the Developmental Progress of Disadvantaged Children in a Preschool." Unpublished doctoral dissertation. Kansas City: University of Missouri, 1971.

Articles and Periodicals

406. ARNOLD, R.; PERLMAN, M.; McQUEENEY, D.; and GORDON, D. Nature of mental health consultation to pre-school programs. *American Journal of Orthopsychiatry*, 43(2):220, March 1973.

407. BROWN, SAUL L. Psychiatric consultation for Project Head Start. *Community Mental Health Journal*, 2(4):301–306, Winter 1966.

408. CORE, HARRY M. Mental health consultation in a Head Start program. *Hospital and Community Psychiatry*, 21(6):183–185, June 1970.

409. FABIAN, ALICE E. The disturbed child in the ghetto day care center: The role of the psychiatric consultant. *Journal of the American Academy of Child Psychiatry*, 11(3):467-491, 1972.

410. FABIAN, ALICE E., and TANNOR, HERMAN. The role of the psychiatric consultant to day care centers in ghetto communities. *American Journal of Orthopsychiatry*, 41(2):280, 1971.

411. FARLEY, GORDON K. Mental health consultation with a Head Start Center. *Journal of the American Academy of Child Psychiatry*, 10(3):555–571, 1971.

412. GOLDBERG, HERBERT. The psychologist in Head Start: New aspects of the role. *American Psychologist*, 23(10):773–774, October 1968.

413. GOODMAN, NATALIE, and HALLENBECK, JANE. The development and effectiveness of a teacher-to-teacher nursery school consultation service by a community mental health center. *Massachusetts Journal of Mental Health*, 2(4):41–42, 1972.

414. GREEN, MELINDA, and VALENSTEIN, THELMA. The educational day care consultation program. Ann Arbor, Michigan: University of Michigan School of Education, 1971. (EDRS).

415. KAWIN, MARJORIE R. A mental health consultation program for Project Head Start. Washington, D.C.: American Psychological Association Convention, September 1–5, 1967. (EDRS).

416. LEMBERG, ROSE; MANNIE, ROSEMARY; SELSBY, LISA; and SPITZER, ESTHER.

Mental health consultation to day care centers in a period of transition. *Psychosocial Process*, 2(2):119–127, 1973.

417. MODARRESSI, TAGHI. Working with 4-year-olds in the classroom. *American Journal of Public Health*, 62(7):985–987, 1972.

418. PARKER, BEULAH. Some observations on psychiatric consultation with nursery school teachers. *Mental Hygiene*, 46:559–566, 1962.

419. RADIN, NORMA. Evaluation of the Daycare Consultation program, 1969–1970. Ann Arbor, Michigan: University of Michigan School of Social Work, September 23, 1970. (EDRS).

420. RAPPAPORT, JULIAN, and O'CONNOR, ROBERT D. Advocacy and accountability in consultation to the poor: A case study. *American Journal of Orthopsychiatry*, 41(2):252, 1971.

421. REID, H.; BROWN, S.; HANSEN, Y.; and SPERBER, Z. Preventive interventions for the very young: An infant consultation service, interweaves service, training, and research. *American Journal of Orthopsychiatry*, 43(2):246–247, March 1973.

422. SCHWARTZBERG, B., and WEINER, R. Mental health consultation and the nursery school. *Young Children*, 21:329–334, 1966.

423. SHRIER, DIANE K., and LORMAN, STEFFI. Psychiatric consultation at a day care center. *American Journal of Orthopsychiatry*, 43(3):394–400, April 1973.

424. SMITH, ADRIENNE J. Using group methods in consultation with preschool teachers. *Hospital and Community Psychiatry*, 22(9):271–273, September 19, 1971.

425. WOHLFORD, PAUL. An opportunity in community psychology: Psychological services in Project Head Start. *Professional Psychology*, 3(2):120–128, 1972.

See also: 292, 312, 1032.

HOSPITALS AND HEALTH AGENCIES

Articles and Periodicals

426. ALBINI, JOSEPH L. The role of the social worker in an experimental community mental health clinic: Experiences and future implications. *Community Mental Health Journal*, 4(2):111–119, 1968.

427. ALBORNOZ-RUIZ, JOSE M. Psychiatric consultations in the emergency room. *Maryland State Medical Journal*, 21(9):53–60, 1972.

428. BERLATSKY, M., and LAUGA, A. Examination of psychiatric consultations on acute medical wards in terms of their usefulness for comprehensive care. *American Journal of Orthopsychiatry*, 43(2):198–199, March 1973.

429. BONSTEDT, THEODOR. Psychiatrist as consultant: Experience in community mental health centers. *Attitude*, 1(6):3–11, 1970.

430. BUIE, LOYCE C.; GOLDFEDER, J.; and SABA, T.H. A psychiatrist participates in a county health program. *Children*, 9(6):227–231, 1962.

431. DEMENT, JOHN C. Field consultation in a State health department. *California's Health*, 12(8):57–61, October 15, 1954.

432. FARLEY, BERNICE C. Individual mental health consultation with public health nurses. In: Rapoport, L., ed. *Consultation in Social Work Practice*. New York: National Association of Social Workers, 1963. pp. 99–116.

433. FOX, HENRY M. Psychiatric consultation in general medical clinics: An experiment in postgraduate education. *Journal of the American Medical Association*, 185:999–1003, 1963.

434. HOWELL, ROGER W. Mental health consultation to public health nurses. In: *The Elements of a Community Mental Health Program*. New York: Milbank Memorial Fund, 1956, pp. 57–68.

435. ISSACHAROFF, AMMON; GODDUHN, JEANETTE; SCHNEIDER, DIANE; MAYSONETT, JEANNE; and SMITH, BARBARA. Psychiatric nurses as consultants in a general hospital. *Hospital and Community Psychiatry*, 21(11):361–367, 1970.

436. JANSEN, PATRICIA W. The social worker on the public health agency team. *Nursing Outlook*, 16(10):42–44, 1968.

437. KAUFMAN, M. RALPH. A psychiatric unit in a general hospital. *Journal of Mount Sinai Hospital*, 24(5):572–579, 1957.

438. KRIS, ANTON O. An adolescent consultation service in a State mental hospital. *Massachusetts Journal of Mental Health*, 1(1):32, Fall 1970.

439. MADDUX, JAMES F. Consultation in public health. *American Journal of Public Health*, 45:1424–1430, 1955.

440. MENZIES, M. ALBERT. Preventive psychiatry: The psychiatric team as consultant to the public health nurse. *Canada Medical Association Journal*, 93(14):743–747, October 1962.

441. MOUW, MILDRED, and HAYLETT, CLARICE H. Mental health consultation in a public health nursing service. *American Journal of Nursing*, 67:1447–1450, 1967.

442. RIEMAN, DWIGHT W. Group mental health consultation with public health nurses. In: Rapoport, L., ed. *Consultation in Social Work Practice*. New York: National Association of Social Workers, 1953. pp. 85–98.

443. SALK, LEE. Psychologist in a pediatric setting. *Professional Psychology*, 1(4):395–396, 1970.

444. SOLOMON, PHILIP. The psychiatric consultation in private practice. *Medical Annals of the District of Columbia*, 37(6):322–323, June 1968.

445. STAGE, THOMAS B. Theological consultation in mental hospitals. *Hospital and Community Psychiatry*, 22(7):210–211, July 1971.

446. STRATAS, NICHOLAS E., and CATHELL, JAMES L. Psychiatric consultation with community physicians. *Hospital and Community Psychiatry*, 17:202–204, 1966.

447. WHITTINGTON, HORACE G. Consultation with health agencies. In: Whittington, Horace G., ed. *Psychiatry in the American Community*. New York: International Universities Press, 1966. pp. 127–143.

448. WHITTINGTON, HORACE G. Private psychiatric practice, evaluation of psychiatric consultation in private practice—and implications for achieving continuity of psychiatric care. *Journal of Kansas Medical Society*, 66:21–22, January 1965.

449. WILLIAMS, CORRINE R.; WOODWARD, N.; MARSHALL, BARBARA; and OLIVER, JOAN. Four approaches to dietary consultation for nursing homes. *Hospitals*, 41(5):92–100, March 1, 1967.

450. WODINSKY, ABRAHAM. Psychiatric consultation with nurses on leukemia service. *Mental Hygiene*, 48(2):282–287, 1964.

See also: 20, 158, 160, 208, 222, 225, 250, 252, 257, 262, 264, 265, 267, 272, 274, 276, 277, 278, 279, 283, 284, 287, 288, 293, 295, 303, 327, 344, 443, 594, 608, 615, 617, 630, 640, 718, 736, 750, 785, 843, 870, 897, 914, 981, 1002, 1014, 1023, 1040, 1046, 1061, 1077, 1082, 1116, 1117.

INDUSTRY

Articles and Periodicals

451. BALINSKY, BENJAMIN. Outside consultants to industry: Strengths, problems, and pitfalls (symposium): II. Some experiences and problems in appraising executive personnel. *Personnel Psychology*, 17(2):107–114, 1964.

452. BARRETT, RICHARD. Outside consultants to industry: Strengths, problems, and pitfalls (symposium): VI. Comments on the symposium. *Personnel Psychology*, 17(2):128–133, 1964.

453. GARBER, ROBERT. Outside consultants to industry: Strengths, problems, and pitfalls (symposium): III. When the president is the problem—a case study. *Personnel Psychology*, 17(2):114–119, 1964.

454. GARDNER, BURLEIGH B. The consultant to business—his role and his problems. In: Gouldner, Alvin, W., and Miller, S.M., eds. *Applied Sociology*. New York: The Free Press, 1965. pp. 79–85.

455. LEVINSON, HARRY. What can a psychiatrist do in industry? *Menninger Quarterly*, 9(2):21–30, 1955.

456. Women's Bureau. Guide to Conducting a Consultation on Women's Employment with Employers and Union Representatives. Washington, D.C.: Women's Bureau (DOL), 1971. (EDRS).

See also: 1, 22, 26, 31, 313, 631, 638, 645, 649, 681, 696, 724, 725, 730, 846, 949, 955, 992.

MILITARY

Articles and Periodicals

457. ANDERSON, JACK R. Psychiatric support of III and IV corps tactical zones. *USARV Medical Bulletin*, 40(7):37–39, 1968.

458. BACH, P.B. (Discussion) Change of command in combat: A locus of stress. *The American Journal of Psychiatry*, 129(6):702, December 1972.

459. BARRETT, C.F., and KERN, R.P. A field service program in military mental hygiene. *U.S. Armed Forces Medical Journal*, 6:1011–1020, 1955.

460. BEY, D.R., JR. Change of command in combat: A locus of stress. *The American Journal of Psychiatry,* 129(6):698–702, December 1972.

461. BEY, D.R., and SMITH, W.E. Organizational consultation in a combat unit. *The American Journal of Psychiatry.* 128(4):401–406, October 1971.

462. BOSTROM, JOHN A. Psychiatric consultation in the first cavalry. *USARV Medical Bulletin,* 40(7):24–26, 1968.

463. DATEL, WILLIAM E., and GIESEKING, C.F. A method for extending Army mental hygiene consultation. *Military Medicine,* 131(10):1299–1308, October 1966.

464. GORDON, EDWARD L. Division psychiatry: Documents of a tour. *USARV Medical Bulletin,* 40(8):62–69, 1968.

465. HAYNES, H.C. Psychiatric consultations and civil aviation medicine. *International Psychiatry Clinics,* 4(1):81–99, Winter 1967.

466. KRAKOWSKI, ADAM J. Psychiatric consultation to an Air Force hospital. *Diseases of the Nervous System,* 23(10):584–588, October 1962.

467. LITRIO, JOHN J. A suggested program for the establishment of a mental health consultant officer at Army level. In: *Collected Papers From a Short Course on Current Trends in Army Social Work.* Washington: Walter Reed Army Institute of Research, 1962.

468. SPENCER, CHARLES D. An approach to mental health consultation within the military. *Military Medicine,* 130(7):691–694, 1965.

469. VIELHABER, DAVID P. Mental health consultation in a combat division. In: *Collected Papers From a Short Course on Current Trends in Army Social Work.* Washington: Walter Reed Army Institute of Research, 1962.

See also: 350, 997, 1006, 1021, 1022, 1051, 1063.

SCHOOLS

Books

470. CLAIBORN, WILLIAM L., and COHEN, ROBERT. *School Intervention.* New York: Behavioral Publications, 1973.

471. JACOBSON, STANLEY. *Consultation Process in the Schools.* (School Project on Consultation Skills.) Washington: D.C. Public Schools and Washington School of Psychiatry, 1966.

472. JAMES, EDWARD W., and WEBER, ROBERT A. *School Consultants: Roles Assumed and Techniques Employed.* Austin, Texas: Southwestern Cooperative Programs in Education Administration, University of Texas, 1954.

473. NEWMAN, RUTH G. *Psychological Consultation in the Schools: A Catalyst for Learning.* New York: Basic Books, 1967.

474. NEWMAN, RUTH G.; REDL, F.; and KITCHENER, H.L. *Technical Assistance in a Public School System.* Washington: Washington School of Psychiatry, 1962.

Articles and Periodicals

475. ANSHIN, ROMAN N. The Role of a Psychiatric Consultant to a Public High

School in Racial Transition: Challenge and Response. Los Angeles: Cedars-Sinai Medical Center, 1970. (EDRS).

476. BARMAN, ALICEROSE S. Adding a new dimension to mental health services for a school community: A description of a consultant-coordinator position in a suburban school district. *American Journal of Orthopsychiatry*, 43(2): 221, March 1973.

477. BERKOVITZ, I.H. Varieties of mental health consultation for school personnel. *Journal of Secondary Education*, 45(3), 1970.

478. BERKOWITZ, HERSHEL. A collaborative approach to mental health consultation in school settings. In: Claiborn, William L., and Cohen, Robert, eds. *School Intervention*. New York: Behavioral Publications, 1973. pp. 54–63.

479. BERLIN, IRVING. Mental health consultation in schools as a means of communicating mental health principles. *Journal of the American Academy of Child Psychiatry*, 1(4):671–679, October 1962.

480. BERLIN, IRVING. Mental health consultation in the schools: Who can do it and why? *Community Mental Health Journal*, 1(1):19–22, Spring 1965.

481. BERLIN, IRVING. Preventive aspects of mental health consultation to schools. *Mental Hygiene*, 51(1):34–40, January 1967.

482. BERLIN, IRVING. Some learning experiences as psychiatric consultant in the schools. *Mental Hygiene*, 40(2):215–236, 1956.

483. BERLIN, IRVING. What help can the educator expect from the mental health specialist. *California Journal of Elementary Education*, 31(1):7–15, 1962.

484. BERNSTEIN, NORMAN R., and RICE, JACK O. Psychiatric consultation in a school for the retarded. *American Journal of Mental Deficiency*, 76(6): 718–725, 1972.

485. BLOCH, H. SPENCER. Experiences in establishing school consultation. *American Journal of Psychiatry*, 129(1):63–68, 1972.

486. BRAGG, R., and FREEMAN, W. Principles of mental health consultation to a school system. *American Journal of Orthopsychiatry*, 39(2):285–286, March 1969.

487. BRODY, MICHAEL, and SCHNEIDER, OWEN B. The psychiatrist as classroom teacher: School consultation in the inner city. *Hospital and Community Psychiatry*, 24(4):248–251, April 1973.

488. BROSKOWSKI, ANTHONY. Teacher-centered consultation in an inner-city junior high school. In: Claiborn, William L., and Cohen, Robert, eds. *School Intervention*. New York: Behavioral Publications, 1973. pp. 124–143.

489. CALLISTER, SHELDON L. A Behavior Modification Approach to Elementary School Consultation, 1970. (EDRS).

490. CAPLAN, G. Mental health consultation in schools. In: *The Elements of a Community Mental Health Program*. New York: Milbank Memorial Fund, 1956. pp. 77–85.

491. CHESS, STELLA, and FERNANDEZ, PAULINA. Through the looking glass: A school's view of psychiatric care. *American Journal of Orthopsychiatry*, 43(2):222–223, March 1973.

492. COHEN, RAQUEL E. Team consultation in a school system. *College Student Journal*, 6(1):100–105, February 1972.

493. COUCHMAN, ROBERT, and GOLOMBEK, HARVEY. Psychiatric consultation in a school counseling department. *School Counselor*, 19(1):38–42, September 1971.

494. CURTIS, JOHN R. Satellite psychiatry for the small college. *Journal of the American College Health Association*, 17(4):349–352, 1969.

495. DAVIDSON, JOAN. Psychiatric consultation in a school for problem girls. *Mental Hygiene*, 53(2):280–288, April 1969.

496. EMMET, GERALD M. The psychoanalyst, the community and the schools. *Contemporary Psychoanalysis*, 7(2):153–162, 1971.

497. FISCHER, HENRY L. School consultation in a special educational setting. *Psychology in the Schools*, VI(1):12–17, January 1969.

498. FORMAN, MARC A., and HETZNECKER, WILLIAM. Varieties and vagaries of school consultation. *Journal of the American Academy of Child Psychiatry*, 11(4):694–704, 1972.

499. GLASSCOCK, THOMAS T., and FLAX, MORTON L. Programs for consultations in schools. In: Beigel, Allan, and Levenson, Alan I. *The Community Mental Health Center*. New York: Basic Books, 1972. pp. 247–251.

500. GOLDBERG, S.; MOONEY, S.; DONOFRIO, I.; and PORTIN, R. A model for mental health services to schools. *American Journal of Orthopsychiatry*, 40(2): 305–306, March 1970.

501. HIRSCHOWITZ, R.G. Psychiatric consultation in the schools: Sociocultural perspectives. *Mental Hygiene*, 50:218–225, 1966.

502. HIRSCHOWITZ, RALPH G. Mental health consultation to schools. *Mental Hygiene*, 55(2):237–241, 1971.

503. HOLLISTER, WILLIAM G. The psychiatrist as a consultant to the school. In: Mendel, W.M., and Solomon, P., eds. *The Psychiatric Consultation*. New York: Grune & Stratton, 1968. pp. 86–97.

504. HORN, EUGENE A.; POLLACK, DONALD; ST. JOHN, BEREA; and HAWKINS, SUSIE C. School mental health services offered without invitation. *Mental Hygiene*, 53(4):620–624, 1969.

505. JAMES, Q. Mental health consultation in a black elementary school. In: Miller, L., ed., *Fourth International Congress of Social Psychiatry: Abstract of Papers*. Jerusalem: AHVA Cooperative, 1972. pp. 50–51.

506. KAUFFMAN, JAMES M. et al. Part-time consultants in the schools: Observations of a resource team for service to children with school problems. *Journal of School Health*, 42(8):446–449, October 1972.

507. KELLY, JAMES G., and BOONE, DOROTHY. Teacher consultations. In: *Mental Health Services for Nonachieving Children. Mental Health Study Center Reports*. Adelphi, Maryland: National Institute of Mental Health, 1964. pp. 12–15.

508. KLEIN, DONALD C., and LINDEMANN, E. Preventive intervention in individual and family crisis situations. In: Caplan, G., ed. *Prevention of Mental Disorders in Children*. New York: Basic Books, 1961. pp. 283–306.

509. LACEY, WILBERT. Consultation service to college students: A learning experience. *Journal of the National Medical Association*, 65(3):225, May 1973.

510. LAWRENCE, MARGARET M.; SPANIER, IRENE J.; and DUBOWY, MILDRED W. An analysis of the work of the school mental health unit of a community mental health board. *American Journal of Orthopsychiatry*, 32(1):99–108, January 1962.

511. LEVINE, MURRAY, and GRAZIANO, ANTHONY M. Intervention programs in elementary schools. In: Golann, Stuart E., and Eisdorfer, Carl, eds. *Handbook of Community Mental Health*. New York: Appleton-Century-Crofts, 1972. pp. 541–573.

512. MEYERS, JOEL. Mental Health Consultation and Reinforcement Principles in Teacher Consultation, 1971. (EDRS).

513. MUMFORD, EMILY. Promises and disaffections in mental health programs in schools. *Psychology in the Schools*, VII(1):20–27, 1970.

514. MUMFORD, EMILY. Teacher response to psychiatric consultants in the school. *Current Psychiatric Therapies*, 9:43–51, 1969.

515. NEWMAN, R.; BLOOMBERG, C.; EMERSON, R.; KEITH, M.; KITCHNER, H.; and REDL, F. Educational technical assistance. In: Long, Nicholas J.; Morse, William C.; and Newman, Ruth, eds. *Conflict in the Classroom*. Belmont, California: Wadsworth Publishing Company, 1965. pp. 228–243.

516. PERKINS, KEITH J. Consultation services to public schools by a mental health team. *Mental Hygiene*, 37:585–595, 1953.

517. PFEIFFER, ERIC. Multiplying the hands of the psychiatrist: The use of limited psychiatric manpower in a small college setting. *Journal of the American College Health Association*, 17(1):76–79, 1968.

518. ROSENBLUM, GERSHWIN. The role of the mental health consultant in the public schools. *Boston University Journal of Education*, 146(3):48–52, February 1964.

519. SCHARFF, DAVID E. Mental health consultation in an urban community school system. *American Journal of Orthopsychiatry*, 42(2):310–311, 1972.

520. SKUROW, NATALIE R., and DIZENHUZ, ISRAEL M. New dimensions of psychiatric consultation with teachers: A conceptual approach to the helping alliance. *American Journal of Orthopsychiatry*, 43(2):226–227, March 1973.

521. SUSSMAN, ROBERT B., and ZIMBERG, SHELDON. Psychiatric Consultation with Public Schools in an Underprivileged Neighborhood. Paper presented at a meeting of the American Orthopsychiatric Association. Washington, D.C., April 22, 1967. (EDRS).

522. TETREAULT, JEANNE M. Informal consultation: Social work activity with the elementary school teacher. *Smith College Studies in Social Work*, 39(1):85–86, November 1968.

523. TUCKER, R. Consumer oriented consultation and training. *American Journal of Orthopsychiatry*, 41(2):262–263, March 1971.

524. WHITTINGTON, H.G. Consultation with educational agencies. In: Whittington, H.G. *Psychiatry in the American Community*. New York: International Universities Press, 1966. pp. 153–177.

525. WILLIAMS, MARY ELLEN KNAPP. Help for the teacher of disturbed children in the public school: The use of consultation for problem solving and personal growth. *Exceptional Children*, 34(2):87–91, 1967.

526. WILLIS, JERRY W. Consultation in an urban ghetto school. *Mental Hygiene*, 56(1):31–38, Winter 1972.

See also: 85, 171, 176, 187, 203, 287, 305, 311, 317, 318, 322, 324, 325, 326, 328, 329, 330, 332, 333, 349, 363, 551, 588, 591, 597, 599, 612, 619, 623, 625, 628, 634, 641, 642, 644, 650, 653, 656, 661, 737, 746, 755, 763, 800, 829, 834, 835, 836, 850, 855, 857, 858, 864, 866, 907, 908, 909, 946, 959, 963, 996, 1016, 1020, 1033, 1043, 1048, 1050, 1051, 1055, 1078, 1079, 1095, 1110, 1111, 1113.

SOCIAL AGENCIES

Books

527. Family Service Association of America. *Psychiatric Consultation in the Family Service Agency*. New York: Family Service Association of America, 1956.

528. Group for the Advancement of Psychiatry. *The Consultant Psychiatrist in a Family Service Agency*. Report No. 34. New York: Group for the Advancement of Psychiatry, 1956.

529. ROSENTHAL, M.J., and SULLIVAN, M.E. *Psychiatric Consultation in a Public Child Welfare Agency*. U.S. Children's Bureau Publication No. 372. Washington: Superintendent of Documents, U.S. Government Printing Office, 1959.

530. University of Hawaii, School of Social Work. *Proceedings of the Institute for Social Workers' Use of Psychiatric Consultation and Treatment of Adolescents*. Princess Kainlani Hotel, Hawaii: May 1958.

Articles and Periodicals

531. AIKIN, DOROTHY. Psychiatric consultation in social agencies. *Canada's Mental Health*, 13(6):45–50, 1965.

532. BERNARD, VIOLA N. Psychiatric consultation in the social agency. *Child Welfare*, 33(9):3–8, November 1954.

533. BRODY, CELIA. Psychiatric consultation in a family counseling agency. *Jewish Social Service Quarterly*, 28:151–157, 1951.

534. COHEN, MARIETTE B.; ABMA, GAIL; and SELTERMAN, PHYLLIS. A position paper on psychiatric consultation in a public child welfare agency. *Public Welfare*, 30(3):11–15, 1972.

535. COLEMAN, JULES V. Mental health consultation to agencies protecting family life. In: *The Elements of a Community Mental Health Program*. New York: Milbank Memorial Fund, 1956. pp. 69–76.

536. COLEMAN, JULES V. Psychiatric consultation in casework agencies. *American Journal of Orthopsychiatry*, 17(3):533–539, 1947.

537. HAVENS, LESTON L., and GUBELLI, E. GERALD. The psychiatrist and the State vocational rehabilitation agency. *American Journal of Psychiatry*, 123(9):1094–1099, March 1967.

538. KAPHAN, MARVIN N., and LITMAN, R.E. Suicide consultation: A psychiatric

service to social agencies. *American Journal of Psychiatry*, 122:1357–1361, 1966.

539. LEVINSON, FRANCES T., and GOMBERG, M. ROBERT. The social agency and the psychiatrist. *Jewish Social Service Quarterly*, 28:143–150, 1951.

540. LIFSCHUTZ, JOSEPH E.; STEWART, T.B.; and HARRISON, A.M. Psychiatric consultation in the public assistance agency. *Social Casework*, 39:3–9, 1958.

541. MADDUX, JAMES F. Psychiatric consultation in a public welfare agency. *American Journal of Orthopsychiatry*, 20(4):754–764, 1950.

542. MILLER, ARTHUR A. The psychiatric consultant in family counseling. *Marriage and Family Living*, 18(3):254–258, 1956.

543. NEUMANN, FREDERIKA. The use of psychiatric consultation by a casework agency. *Family*, 26(6):216–221, October 1945.

544. PRICE, MORRIS H. The agency psychiatrist as a teaching adjunct. *Jewish Social Service Quarterly*, 30:137–142, 1953.

545. PRICE, MORRIS H. The place of psychiatric consultation in a child placement agency. *Jewish Social Service Quarterly*, 28(4):366–374, 1951.

546. TANNENBAUM, DAVID E. Establishing psychiatric consultation for agency program. *Social Casework*, 32(5):196–202, 1951.

547. THOMPSON, W.C. Psychiatric consultation in social agencies. *Child Welfare*, 36(9):1–3, 1957.

548. WHITTINGTON, H.G. Consultation with welfare and social agencies. In: Whittington, H.G. *Psychiatry in the American Community*. New York: Universities Press, 1966. pp. 144–152.

See also: 161, 166, 167, 176, 202, 205, 253, 258, 343, 345, 352, 551, 595, 599, 604, 605, 620, 622, 627, 650, 705, 726, 731, 928, 941, 1030, 1114.

SPECIALIZED SETTINGS

Books

549. DUMONT, MATTHEW. *The Absurd Healer*. New York: Science House, 1968.

550. The Southern Regional Education Board and NIMH. *Training and Consultation in Aftercare; Final Report of the Pilot Project—A Training Program for Aftercare Workers*. Atlanta, Georgia: The Southern Regional Education Board, 1967.

551. U.S. Department of Health, Education and Welfare. *Consultation and Education*. Public Health Service Publication No. 1478. National Institute of Mental Health, Washington: Superintendent of Documents, U.S. Government Printing Office, 1966.

Dissertations

552. KREBS, DORIS E. "The North American Nurse Consultant in Latin America: Living and Working Conditions as Factors of Adjustment." Unpublished doctoral dissertation. Columbia University, 1969.

Articles and Periodicals

553. BERG, B. ROBERT. The casework consultant in camp. *Journal of Jewish Communal Service*, 35(4):409–413, 1959.

554. BERNSTEIN, S., and MacLENNAN, B. Community Psychiatry with the Communications Media. *The American Journal of Psychiatry*, 128(6):722–727, December 1971.

555. BIGGERS, MOZELLE. The use of mental health consultation in rural areas. *Smith College Studies in Social Work*, 36(1):81–82, October 1965.

556. BUTLER, R.N., and PERLIN, S. Psychiatric consultations in a research setting. *Medical Annals of the District of Columbia*, 27(10):503–506, 1958.

557. CHIARANDINI, IRENE, and SHANNON, BARBARA. Experience of an interdisciplinary, interracial consultation team in a black ghetto. *American Journal of Orthopsychiatry*, 41(2):259–260, 1971.

558. DUHL, LEONARD J.; LEOPOLD, R.L.; and ENGLISH, J.T. A mental health program for the Peace Corps. *Human Organization*, 23(2):131–136, 1964.

559. ENGLISH, JOSEPH T. Mental health consultation with a government agency. In: Mendel, Werner M., and Solomon, Philip, eds. *The Psychiatric Consultation*. New York: Grune and Stratton, 1968. pp. 109–118.

560. GREENBERG, IRWIN M. Approaches to psychiatric consultation in a research hospital setting. *Archives of General Psychiatry*, 3(6):691–697, 1960.

561. HOLDEN, H.M. The psychiatrist as consultant to an experimental youthwork project. *Psychotherapy and Psychosomatics*, 15(1):30, 1967.

562. HUESSY, HANS R. Mental health consultation in varied settings. In: Huessy, Hans R., ed. *Mental Health With Limited Resources*. New York: Grune and Stratton, 1966. pp. 73–79.

563. KINZIE, J. DAVID; SHORE, JAMES H.; and PATTISON, E. MANSELL. Anatomy of psychiatric consultation to rural Indians. *Community Mental Health Journal*, 8(3):196–207, 1972.

564. KRAMER, MILTON, and FRANK, E.C. Mental health consultation in Peace Corps training. Considerations regarding the acceptance of the psychiatrist by the training staff. *Archives of General Psychiatry*, 10(1):1–6, 1964.

565. MEYER, G. Psychiatric consultation for blind students preparing to enter college. *American Journal of Orthopsychiatry*, 39(2):303–304, March 1969.

566. MICHAELSON, MIKE. Psychiatry comes to the grass roots. *Today's Health*, 46(11):52–55, 83–84, 87, 1968.

567. MORDOCK, JOHN B. Urban renewal agencies: Guidelines for mental health consultation. *Professional Psychology*, 2(2):155–158, Spring 1971.

568. MORRISON, ANDREW P. Consultation and group process with indigenous neighborhood workers. *Community Mental Health Journal*, 6(1):3–11, February 1970.

569. PORT, DAVID M. Mental health consultation with a paramilitary youth group. *Mental Hygiene*, 53(4):513–520, 1969.

570. ROBERTS, ROBERT W. Some impressions of mental health consultation in a poverty area. *Social Casework*, 49(6):339–345, June 1968.

571. ROBERTSON, G.G., and BAIZERMAN, MICHAEL. Psychiatric consultation on two

Indian reservations. *Hospital and Community Psychiatry*, 20(6):186, June 1969.

572. SCHEIDLINGER, SAUL, and SARCKA, ANNE. A mental health consultation-education program with group service agencies in a disadvantaged community. *American Journal of Orthopsychiatry*, 38(2):366–367, March 1968.

573. SCHEIDLINGER, SAUL; SARCKA, ANNE; and MENDES, HELEN. A mental health consultation service to neighborhood organizations in an inner city area. *Community Mental Health Journal*, 7(4):264–271, 1971.

574. SCHEIDLINGER, SAUL; STRUENING, ELMER L.; and RABKIN, JUDITH G. Evaluation of a mental health consultation service in a ghetto area. *American Journal of Psychotherapy*, 24(3):485–93, 1970.

575. SELZER, M.L.; MELVIN, L.; and BENEDEK, E. Lawyer's use of psychiatry. *American Journal of Psychiatry*, 122:212–213, August 1965.

576. SMYTH, WILMA. Preventive aspects of medical social work consultation in a rural state. *Social Work*, 5(3):91–96, 1960.

577. SOLOW, CHARLES; WEISS, ROBERT J.; and BERGEN, BERNARD, J. A 24-hour psychiatric consultation via TV. *American Journal of Psychiatry*, 127(12): 1684–1687, 1971.

578. STUTTLEFIELD, ROBERT L. Comments on the preceding article: Psychiatric consultation in a rural setting. *American Journal of Orthopsychiatry*, 23 (4):783–784, 1953.

579. VISHER, JOHN S., and HARRIS, M. ROBERT. A psychiatric contribution to alleviating hard-core unemployment. *American Journal of Psychiatry*, 124 (11):1505–1514, 1968.

580. WALLACE, HELEN M.; COHEN, ROBERT; and SEFFERT, ROBERT. Advisory committees and consultants in programs for crippled children. *Public Health Reports*, 83(8):652–659, August 1968.

581. WEINANDY, JANET E. Family consultant service in Syracuse public housing. In: *Neighborhood Centers Serve the Troubled Family*. Chicago: National Federation of Settlements and Neighborhood Centers, 1964. pp. 35–42.

582. WHITE, LYMAN C. United Nations consultation with non-government organizations. *International Associations*, p. 539, November 1972.

See also: 174, 657.

FORMS OF CONSULTATION

*Although a number of attempts have been made to differ-
entiate types or patterns of consultation toward developing a
useful typology for the field, the aim here was much more
modest. It was simply to devise a way of classifying the many
items which dealt with different forms of consultation in a
manner that would be meaningful to the user. Since most of
the items were not actually seen for evaluation the categories
had to be kept fairly broad. The final grouping of items into
the four categories, i.e., Individual Case Consultation, Consultation with Groups, Program and Administrative Consultation and Community Consultation, was based primarily on
topical emphasis from an evaluation of the focus and content
of the item titles. For those who are interested in some of
the problems involved in formally developing a typology as
well as in some of the classification schemes actually devised by students of consultation, the following references
are suggested: 185, 194, 309, and 931.*

INDIVIDUAL CASE CONSULTATION

Books

583. Pennsylvania Department of Public Welfare. *Allenberry Conference on
Case Consultation for Mental Health.* Harrisburg, Pennsylvania: Bureau of
Community Mental Health Services, Pennsylvania Department of Public
Welfare, April 1959.

584. Texas State Department of Health, Division of Mental Health. *Extending
Clinic Services Into the Community.* Proceedings of an Institute for Texas
Psychiatric Clinic Personnel. Austin, Texas: Texas State Department of
Health, Division of Mental Health, October 13–14, 1960.

Articles and Periodicals

585. BABCOCK, CHARLOTTE G. Some observations on consultative experience.
Social Service Review, 23:347–357, September 1949.

586. BINDMAN, ARTHUR J. Some distinctive features of case consultation. In:
Conference on Case Consultation for Mental Health. Harrisburg, Pennsylvania: Department of Public Welfare, 1959. pp. 5–9.

587. COLEMAN, JULES V. Psychiatric consultation in perspective. *American
Journal of Orthopsychiatry,* 38(2):364–365, 1968.

588. COOPER, JO ANN. Application of the consultant role to parent-teacher management of school avoidance behavior. *Psychology in the Schools*, 10(2): 259–262, April 1973.

589. GROTJAHN, MARTIN, and TREUSCH, JEROME V. A new technique of psychosomatic consultations: Some illustrations of teamwork between an internist and a psychiatrist. *Psychoanalytic Review*, 44(2):176–192, 1957.

590. HARLOW, ROBERT G., and SALZMAN, LEONARD F. Toward the effective use of psychological consultation. *American Journal of Psychiatry*, 115(3): 228–231, 1958.

591. KLEIN, DONALD C. The prevention of mental illness. *Mental Hygiene*, 45(1):101–109, 1961.

592. KLEIN, DONALD C. Techniques of case consultation. In: *Proceedings of an Institute for Texas Psychiatric Clinic Personnel*. Austin, Texas: Texas State Department of Mental Health, October 1960. pp. 11–15.

593. LEADER, ARTHUR L. Social work consultation to psychiatry. *Social Casework*, 38(1):22–38, 1957.

594. LOWE, D.J.; SABOT, THEODORE J.; SUCHINSKY, RICHARD T.; WITTNER, WILLIAM K.; and ZARCONE, VINCENT P. Problems in achieving indirect psychiatric consultation. *Hospital and Community Psychiatry*, 22(3):91–94, March 1971.

595. McDANIEL, LEONARD J., and AHR, A. EDWARD. The school psychologist as a resource person initiating and conducting in-service teacher education. *Psychology in the Schools*, 2(2):220–224, 1965.

596. McDONALD, ELIZABETH. Techniques of case consultation with groups. In: *Proceedings of an Institute for Texas Psychiatric Clinic Personnel*. Austin, Texas: Texas State Department of Mental Health, October 1960. pp. 19–24.

597. McGEHEARTY, LOYCE. Case analysis: Consultation and counseling. *Elementary School Guidance and Counseling*, 4(3):218–222, 1970.

598. REDING, GEORGES R., and GOLDSMITH, ETHEL F. The nonprofessional hospital volunteer as a member of the psychiatric consultation team. *Community Mental Health Journal*, 3(3):267–272, Fall 1967.

599. ROSENFELD, JONA M., and CAPLAN, GERALD. Techniques of staff consultation in an immigrant children's organization in Israel. *American Journal of Orthopsychiatry*, 24(1):42–62, 1954.

600. SHAPIRO, LEON N. Psychiatric care and the public offender. In: Duhl, Leonard S., and Leopold, Robert L., eds. *Mental Health and Urban Social Policy*. San Francisco: Jossey-Bass, 1968. pp. 287–305.

601. SIGNELL, KAREN A. The crisis of unwed motherhood: A consultation approach. *Community Mental Health Journal*, 5(4):304–313, 1969.

602. SPIELBERGER, CHARLES D. A mental health consultation program in a small community with limited professional mental health resources. In: Cowen, E.L.; Gardner, E.A.; and Zax, M., eds. *Emergent Approaches to Mental Health Problems*. New York: Appleton-Century-Crofts, 1967. pp. 214–236.

603. TARNOWER, WILLIAM, and HALL, B.H. The psychiatric consultation. What? When? And for what purpose? *Journal of Kansas Medical Society*, 64(11): 505–508, November 1963.

604. TAYLOR, JOSEPH L. Psychiatric consultation in family counseling. *Marriage and Family Living*, 18(3):259–262, 1956.

605. VALENSTEIN, ARTHUR F. Some principles of psychiatric consultation. *Social Casework*, 36(6):253–256, 1955.

606. WEINER, MYRON F. Asking the psychiatrist for help—helpful hints to the referring physician. *Texas State Journal of Medicine*, 61:488–492, June 1965.

607. ZIEGLER, FREDERICK J. Liaison psychiatry and myocardial infarctions. *Postgraduate Medicine*, 35(3):263–269, March 1964.

608. ZWICK, PAUL A. Special problems in the consultation function of child guidance clinics. *American Journal of Orthopsychiatry*, 28(1):123–125, 1958.

See also: 170, 171, 172, 173, 175, 423, 430, 432, 436, 462, 515, 529, 538, 540, 551, 572, 749, 755, 762, 765, 777, 794, 804, 808, 849, 857, 901, 1004, 1025.

WITH GROUPS

Articles and Periodicals

609. ALTROCCHI, J.; SPIELBERGER, C.; and EISDORFER, C. Mental health consultation with groups. *Community Mental Health Journal*, 1(2):127–134, Summer 1965.

610. BECKHARD, RICHARD. Helping a group with planned change: A case study. *Journal of Social Issues*, 15(2):13–19, 1959.

611. BENNE, KENNETH D. Some ethical problems in group and organizational consultation. *Journal of Social Issues*, 15:60–67, 1959.

612. BERKOVITZ, IRVING H. Mental health consultation to school personnel: Attitudes of school administrators and consultant priorities. *Journal of School Health*, 40(7):348–354, 1970.

613. BLAHA, M. JAY. When and how the consultant can be used most effectively. *Educational Leadership*, 10:96–101, November 1952.

614. BRADFORD, LELAND P. The use of psychodrama for group consultants. *Sociatry*, 1(2):192–197, 1947.

615. CHAR, W.F., and McDERMOTT, J.F., JR. Abortions and acute identity crisis in nurses. *The American Journal of Psychiatry*, 128(8):952–957, February 1972.

616. GIBB, JACK R., and LIPPITT, RONALD, eds. Consulting with groups and organizations. *Journal of Social Issues*, 15(2): (whole issue), 1959.

617. ISSACHAROFF, AMMON; REDINGER, ROBERT; and SCHNEIDER, DIANE. The psychiatric consultation as an experience in group process. *Contemporary Psychoanalysis*, 8(2):260–272, 1972.

618. KEVIN, DAVID. Use of group method in consultation. In: Rapoport, Lydia, ed. *Consultation in Social Work Practice.* New York: National Association of Social Workers, 1963. pp. 69–84.

619. MACKEY, RICHARD A., and HASSLER, FERDINAND R. Group consultation with school personnel. *Mental Hygiene*, 50:351–353, 1966.

620. MAY, CARMILLA R. Community mental health consultation in a public agency. *Public Welfare*, 28(2):150–157, 1970.

621. MUSANTE, GERARD, and GALLEMORE, JOHNNIE, L., JR. Utilization of a staff development group in prison consultation. *Community Mental Health Journal*, 9(3):224–232, Fall 1973.

622. ORMSBY, RALPH. Group psychiatric consultation in a family casework agency. *Social Casework*, 31(9):361–365, November 1950.

623. ROWITCH, JEROME. Group consultations with school personnel. *Hospital and Community Psychiatry*, 19(8):261–266, 1968.

624. SCHULZ, ESTHER, and BROWN, DOROTHY. Preparing public health nurses for mental health problems. *Mental Hygiene*, 46(3):344–350, July 1962.

625. SOLNIT, ALBERT J., and STARK, MARY H. Learning with teachers. *Children*, 14(1):19–24, 1967.

626. SWITZER, ELAINE. The social group worker as a consultant. In: *New Perspectives on Services to Groups: Social Work With Groups, 1961.* New York: National Association of Social Workers, 1961. pp. 143–160.

627. ZINBERG, NORMAN, and EDINBURG, GOLDA. Psychiatric consultation in an interdisciplinary setting. *Smith College Studies in Social Work*, 34(2):126–139, 1964.

See also: 170, 171, 172, 377, 392, 424, 442, 471, 510, 515, 529, 568, 569, 572, 584, 595, 596, 599, 602, 662, 698, 726, 750, 752, 759, 768, 770, 866, 898, 909, 935, 972, 1004, 1013, 1021.

PROGRAM AND ADMINISTRATIVE

Books

628. LAWRENCE, MARGARET MORGAN. *The Mental Health Team in the Schools.* New York: Behavioral Publications, 1971.

629. U.S. Department of Labor. *The Consultative Approach to Safety.* Safety in Industry Bulletin 223. Washington: Bureau of Labor Standards, Superintendent of Documents, U.S. Government Printing Office, 1962.

Articles and Periodicals

630. ADAMSON, FRANCES K. A mental health consultant at work. *American Journal of Nursing*, 70(10):2164–2166, 1970.

631. AHERN, MARGUERITE S. The occupational health nurse's role in absentee control. *American Association of Industrial Nurses Journal*, 16(5):7–10, 1968.

632. BEAUMONT, JOHN A.; KOZELKA, R.; and MULLANEY, W. Consultant service report as a function of administration. *National Business Education Quarterly*, 21(4):15–21, 1953.

633. BLAKE, ROBERT R.; MOUTON, JANE S.; BARNES, LOUIS B.; and GREINER, LARRY E. Breakthrough in organization development. *Harvard Business Review*, 42(6):133–155, 1964.

634. BRADSHAW, WALTER H., JR.; BORUS, JONATHAN F.; O'NEILL, PATRICIA H.;

and MacLennan, Beryce W. Mental health consultants in an educational charrette. *Psychiatry*, 35(4):317–335, 1972.

635. Byram, H.M. Choosing and using consultants in program planning. *The Agricultural Education Magazine*, 38:138–139, December 1965.

636. Byrd, Richard E. Planning with volunteers; a consulting design. *Adult Leadership*, 14(1):5–7, 1965.

637. Clendenen, Richard J. The use of national consultants. In: *Selected Papers From a Workshop on Consultation*. Washington: Children's Bureau, U.S. Department of Health, Education, and Welfare, 1965. pp. 1–8.

638. Collins, Ralph T. Neuropsychiatry in a company. In: Collins, Ralph T., ed. *Occupational Psychiatry*. Boston: Little, Brown and Company, 1969. pp. 93–109.

639. Davis, Alice Taylor. Consultation: A function in public welfare administration. *Social Casework*, 37:113–119, 1956.

640. Frankel, Fred H., and Clark, Eleanor. Mental health consultation and education in nursing homes. *Journal of the American Geriatrics Society*, 17(4):360–365, 1969.

641. Gallessich, June. A system model of mental health consultation. *Psychology in the Schools*, 9(1):13–15, 1972.

642. Harris, Jan Owen. Mental health services to a racially troubled school. *Health and Community Psychiatry*, 22(5):140–143, 1971.

643. Insley, V. Program consultation. In: Caplan, Gerald, ed. *Concepts of Mental Health and Consultation*. Washington: Children's Bureau, U.S. Health, Education, and Welfare Department, 1959. pp. 235–246.

644. Kluger, J.M. The classroom as an outpatient kibbutz. *The American Journal of Psychiatry*, 128(11):1395–1399, May 1972.

645. Lazer, William, and Warner, Arthur E. The knowledge industry: What does management think of the outside consultants it employs? *Business Topics*, 13(2):73–80, Spring 1965.

646. Lyons, J. Daniel. Factors Influencing Utilization of Research Findings in Institutional Change. HumRRO Professional Paper 2–66, April 1966. (Human Resources Research Organization, Alexandria, Va.)

647. McGarry, A. Louis; Curran, W.J.; and Kenefick, D.P. Problems of public consultation in medicolegal matters: A symposium. *American Journal of Psychiatry*, 125(1):42–59, July 1968.

648. Meehan, M. Administrative staff consultant as a resource to the school administrator for the improvement of interpersonal relations. *American Journal of Orthopsychiatry*, 39(2):286–288, March 1969.

649. Munter, Preston K. Management training and psychiatry in a company. In: Collins, Ralph T., ed. *Occupational Psychiatry*. Boston: Little, Brown and Company, 1969. pp. 113–122.

650. Nir, Yehuda. Consultation to schools in poverty areas. *Child Welfare*, 52(7):425–430, July 1973.

651. O'Toole, James K. Psychiatric consultation to a State welfare department. *American Journal of Orthopsychiatry*, 38(2):365–366, 1968.

652. Quittmeyer, Charles L. Management looks at consultants: A survey of company opinion and experience. *Management Review*, 50(3):4–10, 1961.

653. Reavis, W.C. The place of the consultant: The school administrator needs the expert for special problems. *Nation's Schools*, 41:24–25, 1948.

654. Rehage, K.J., and Heywood, S.J. Consultant services to administrators. *Elementary School Journal*, 53:131–133, November 1952.

655. Roos, H. Warner. How to make the best use of consultants. *Management Review*, 41(7):421–422, 1952.

656. Shearer, Marshall. The principal is often overlooked. *Community Mental Health Journal*, 4(1):47–52, 1968.

657. Sloman, Leon. Consultation to a special school. *Hospital and Community Psychiatry*, 22(12):375–378, 1971.

658. Spencer, Esther C., and Croley, H.T. Administrative consultation. In: Rapoport, Lydia, ed. *Consultation in Social Work Practice*. New York: National Association of Social Workers, 1963. pp. 51–68.

659. Wallis, Robert S., and Katf, Nicola Y. The 50-mile bridge: Consultation between State hospital and community mental health center staffs. *Hospital and Community Psychiatry*, 23(3):73–76, March 1972.

660. Williams, Martha. The problem profile technique in consultation. *Social Work*, 16(3):52–59, July 1971.

661. Zegans, F.S.; Schwartz, M.S.; and Dumas, R. A mental health center's response to racial crisis in an urban high school. *Psychiatry*, 32(3):252–264, August 1969.

See also: 170, 171, 172, 173, 233, 407, 414, 415, 451, 452, 460, 471, 473, 475, 510, 554, 563, 570, 587, 601, 616, 680, 698, 709, 731, 765, 782, 789, 810, 819, 824, 846, 874, 944, 945, 962, 965, 974, 985, 1004.

COMMUNITY

Books

662. Massachusetts Department of Public Health. *Social Work Activities in Public Health*. Report of workshop sponsored by Medical Social Training Project, Social Work Section. Boston: Massachusetts Department of Public Health, 1961. pp. 49–55.

663. U.S. Department of Health, Education, and Welfare. *Proceedings of the Ninth Annual Conference of Chief Social Workers from State Mental Health Programs, Philadelphia*. Bethesda, Maryland: National Institute of Mental Health, May 16–18, 1957.

Articles and Periodicals

664. Armstrong, R.M. Mental health consultation in the community: The home scene. *Australian Psychologist*, 4(1):13–19, 1969.

665. Chamberlain, H.E., and De Schweinitz, Elizabeth. A program of statewide consultation. In: Kotinsky, Ruth, and Witmer, Helen L., eds. *Community Programs for Mental Health*. Cambridge: Harvard University Press, 1955. pp. 119–128.

666. COHNSTAEDT, MARTIN L., and PHILLIPSON, THOMAS K. The urban extension agent. *Adult Leadership*, 10(8):225–226, 1962.

667. DUBOIS, EUGENE E. Community research and consultation for the community—junior college. *Adult Leadership*, June 1969. pp. 49–50.

668. FORBES, JOHN L. The Dorchester inservice training and consultation project. In: *The Mental Health Role of Settlement and Community Centers*. Proceedings of a conference held at Swampscott, Mass., October 23–25, 1963. Boston: Massachusetts Department of Mental Health, 1964. pp. 52–58.

669. HALLOCK, ARTHUR C.K., and VAUGHAN, WARREN. Community organization —a dynamic component of community mental health practice. *American Journal of Orthopsychiatry*, 26(4):691–706, 1956.

670. HOIBERG, OTTO G. Problems of the consultant in small communities. *Journal of Educational Sociology*, 29(4):164–172, December 1955.

671. KLAPMAN, HOWARD J., and BADOWSKI, PAUL. The Adlerian as consultant in the general community. *Journal of Individual Psychology*, 29(1):72, May 1973.

672. MOE, EDWARD O. Consulting with a community system: A case study. *Journal of Social Issues*, 15(2):28–35, 1959.

673. NELEIGH, JANICE R. Nonprofessional community project leaders: Consultation. *Community Mental Health Journal Monograph Series*, 6:19–28, 1971.

674. ROCKMORE, MYRON J. Consultation: Illustrating a problem of State hospital and community relations in after-care planning. In: *Proceedings of the Ninth Annual Conference of Chief Social Workers from State Mental Health Programs, Philadelphia, Pennsylvania*. Bethesda, Maryland: National Institute of Mental Health, U.S. Department of Health, Education, and Welfare, May 1957.

675. SCHIFF, SHELDON, and KELLAM, SHEPPARD. A community mental health program of prevention and early treatment in first grade. In: Greenblatt, Milton, ed. *Poverty and Mental Health*. Psychiatric Research Report No. 21. Washington: American Psychiatric Association, 1967. pp. 92–102.

676. SEARS, WILLIAM F., and LIBO, LESTER M. Consultation in areas without psychiatric facilities. In: Duhl, Leonard S., and Leopold, Robert L., eds. *Mental Health and Urban Social Policy*. San Francisco: Jossey-Bass, 1968. pp. 75–88.

677. SENOR, JAMES M. Applicability of selected consultation concepts to community development. *Indian Journal of Social Work*, 25(3):261–267, 1964.

678. WILLIAMS, BETH T. Problems in consultation posed by one community. In: *Proceedings of the Ninth Annual Conference of Chief Social Workers from State Mental Health Programs, Philadelphia, Pa.* Bethesda, Maryland: National Institute of Mental Health, U.S. Department of Health, Education, and Welfare, May 1957.

679. YANKAUER, ALFRED. An American pediatrician in India reflects on problems of intercultural communication in technical consultation. *Community Development Review*, 5(2):9–17, 1960.

See also: 172, 173, 361, 572, 573, 602, 687, 691, 707, 722, 744, 746, 765, 766, 776, 814, 830, 831, 837, 839, 841, 842, 845, 847, 856, 873, 930, 962, 1008, 1108.

PROFESSIONAL ROLES IN CONSULTATION

The practice of consultation is implemented by a number of expectations which manifest themselves in the form of roles, i.e., certain rights, duties, and responsibilities assigned to both the consultant and consultee. It is the reciprocal nature of these roles and expectations that is pertinent to the actual work of consultation. Operationally, effective consultation is dependent upon, (1) the degree of complementarity between the perception each has of his role and that of the other and (2) the degree of complementarity which exists between the expectations each has of the other. If there are marked discrepancies between these perceptions or expectations, it is almost certain to create serious difficulties in carrying on the consultation. Although there is, as yet, no clear picture of the behaviors or actions required in the consultation situation for either the consultant or the consultee, quite a number of writers have focused their attention on this aspect of consultation. The 65 items in this section represent that part of the consultation literature which focuses upon professional roles in consultation practice.

PROFESSIONAL ROLES

Books

680. WARREN, ROLAND L. *Social Research Consultation.* New York: Russell Sage Foundation, 1963.

Dissertations

681. BOCKE, JOE B. "Perceptions of Duties of State Consultants and Local Supervisors of Educable Mentally Retarded." Unpublished doctoral dissertation. University of Northern Colorado, 1970.

682. PETTY, GARY F. "The Role of the Educational Consultant in Community College Facilities Planning." Unpublished doctoral dissertation. University of Michigan, 1969.

Articles and Periodicals

683. ANDERSON, FLORENCE, and SHANGOLD, B. The role of the consultant in adult education. *Adult Education,* 14:114–120, April 1950.

684. BETZ, ROBERT. The Project Consultant: His Unique Role. Paper presented at the American Personnel and Guidance Association Convention, Las Vegas, Nevada, March 30-April 3, 1969. Washington, D.C.: American Personnel and Guidance Association. (EDRS).

685. BLUMBERG, A. The role of the consultant. In: *Some Papers on Consultation.* New York: National League for Nursing, 1959. pp. 2–5.

686. BOGUSLAW, ROBERT, and BACH, GEORGE R. "Work culture management" in industry: A role for the social science consultant. *Group Psychotherapy,* 12(2):134–142, 1959.

687. BOWMAN, PAUL H. The role of the consultant as a motivator of action. *Mental Hygiene,* 43(1):105–110, 1959.

688. BOWMAN, PAUL H.; DeHANN, ROBERT F.; KOUGH, JOHN K.; and LIDDLE, GORDON P. Mobilizing community resources for youth. Part III. The consultant role. *Supplementary Educational Monographs No. 85.* Chicago: The University of Chicago Press, October 1956. pp. 99–117.

689. CALDWELL, LYNTON K. The role of the technical expert. *Annals of the American Academy of Political and Social Science,* 323:91–99, 1959.

690. CAPLAN, GERALD. The role of the social worker in preventive psychiatry, *Medical Social Work,* 4:144–159, 1955.

691. CHIN, R. Community team. *Adult Leadership,* 2(1):17–20, 1954.

692. COCKING, WALTER D. Role of the educational consultant. *School Executive,* 75(10):7, 1956.

693. Committee on Child Psychiatry of Childhood and Adolescence, R.I. District Branch, American Psychiatric Association. Consultation in child psychiatry. *Rhode Island Medical Journal,* 56(2):61–65, 1973.

694. CUSHING, J.G.N. Role of the psychiatrist as a consultant. *American Journal of Psychiatry,* 106(11):861–864, 1950.

695. DAVIS, JOHN. Role of the field representative. *Adult Leadership,* 14(5):165–166, 1965.

696. DAYAL, ISHWAR, and THOMAS, JOHN M. Operation KPE: Developing a new organization. *The Journal of Applied Behavioral Science,* 4(4):473–506, October-December 1968.

697. DELOUGHERY, GRACE W.; GEBBIE, KRISTINE M.; and NEUMAN, BETTY M. Application to Practice. In: Deloughery, G., ed. *Community Mental Health Nursing.* Baltimore: Williams and Wilkins, 1971. pp. 92–116.

698. FERGUSON, CHARLES K. Concerning the nature of human systems and the consultant's role. *Journal of Applied Behavioral Science,* 4(2):179–193, 1968.

699. FORTI, THERESA. Mental health consultation: One key to planned change. *Nursing Outlook,* 18(7):42–45, 1970.

700. FREEMAN, VICTOR J. Dual role of the psychiatric consultant in the community. *Archives of General Psychiatry,* 1:561–564, 1959.

701. GATES, S.G. Role of the North Central Association examiner and consultant. *North Central Association Quarterly,* 39:252–258, Winter 1965.

702. GEBBIE, KRISTINE M.; DELOUGHERY, GRACE; and NEUMAN, BETTY M. Levels

of utilization: Nursing specialists in community mental health. *Journal of Psychiatric Nursing and Mental Health Services*, 8(1):37–39, 1970.

703. GIBB, JACK R. The role of the consultant. *Journal of Social Issues*, 15(2): 1–4, 1959.

704. GILBERT, RUTH. Functions of the consultant. *Teachers College Record*, 61(4):177–187, January 1960.

705. GOLDBERG, RICHARD T., and STEIN, JANE. The role of the psychiatric consultant in the State rehabilitation agency. *Mental Hygiene*, 54(4):553–558, 1970.

706. GORDON, DOROTHY E. The functions of a consultant. *Nursing Outlook*, 1(10): 575–577, 1953.

707. GOTTLIEB, BENJAMIN H., and RIGER, STEPHANIE. Social interventions in the community: Three professional roles. *Professional Psychology*, 3(3): 231–240, 1972.

708. GREENBERG, P. Role of the art consultant. *School Arts*, 63:21–38, April 1964.

709. HANLON JULIAN. The consultant's role in program evaluation. In: *Proceedings of the Ninth Annual Conference of Chief Social Workers from State Mental Health Programs, Philadelphia, Pa.* Bethesda, Maryland: National Institute of Mental Health, U.S. Department of Health, Education, and Welfare, May 1957.

710. HEREFORD, KARL T., and LEU, DONALD J. The role of the educational consultant. *The School Executive*, 75:99–100, January 1956.

711. HOLCOMB, EMERSON. An analysis of the supervisory job. *Social Casework*, 37(3):126–131, 1956.

712. HORNUNG, JACK. Consultants' renewal role and problems reviewed, evaluated. *Journal of Housing*, 20:516–518, 1963.

713. Hospital Progress. What is the role of the consultant? *Hospital Progress*, 34(2):56–60, 1953.

714. Human Organization. The role of the consultant. *Human Organization*, 13 (1):3–4, Spring 1954. (Editorial)

715. HUME, KATHERINE. Counseling and consulting: Complementary functions. *Elementary School Guidance Counseling*, 5(1):3–11, October 1970.

716. JONES, A.L. Role of the college consultant in curriculum planning. *The High School Journal*, 47:274–279, April 1964.

717. KAUFMAN, IRVING. The role of the psychiatric consultant. *American Journal of Orthopsychiatry*, 26(2):223, 1956.

718. KAUFMAN, M. RALPH. The role of the psychiatrist in a general hospital. *Psychiatric Quarterly*, 27(3):367–381, 1953.

719. KIDNEIGH, JOHN C. The philosophy of administrative process and the role of the consultant. *Public Health Nursing*, 43(8):474–478, 1951.

720. KOCH, WILLIAM H., JR. Stance toward helping: Reflections on the role of a consultant. *Adult Leadership*, 16(6):202–204, 1967.

721. LAWLER, MARCELLA R. Role of the consultant in curriculum improvement. *Educational Leadership*, 8:219–225, January 1951.

722. LIBO, LESTER M. Multiple functions for psychologists in community consultation. *American Psychologist*, 21(6):530–534, June 1966.

723. LIPPITT, RONALD. Dimensions of the consultant's job. *Journal of Social Issues*, 15(2):5–12, 1959.

724. LYNTON, ROLF P. Comments on the preceding article: Operation KPE: Developing a new organization. *The Journal of Applied Behavioral Science*, 4(4):507–509, October-December 1968.

725. McGREGOR, DOUGLAS; KNICKERBOCKER, I.; HAIRE, M.; and BAVELAS, A. The consultant role and organizational leadership: Improving human relations in industry. *Journal of Social Issues*, 4(3):3–53, 1948.

726. NITZBERG, HAROLD, and KAHN, MARVIN W. Consultation with welfare workers in a mental health clinic. *Social Work*, 7(3):84–93, 1962.

727. NORMAN, EDWARD C. Role of the mental health consultee. *Mental Hygiene*, 52(2):304–308, April 1968.

728. NORTHROP, JAMES C. Guidance Consultant: Questions and Directions. Paper presented at the American Personnel and Guidance Association Convention in New Orleans, Louisiana, March 22–26, 1970. Washington, D.C.: American Personnel and Guidance Association. (EDRS).

729. PENNINGROTH, PAUL W. The role of the consultant in community mental health programs. In: Riess, Bernard F., ed. *New Directions in Mental Health, Vol. 1*. New York: Grune and Stratton, 1968. pp. 268–279.

730. PETER, HOLLIS W. Comments on the preceding article: Operation KPE: Developing a new organization. *The Journal of Applied Behavioral Science*, 4(4):510–512, October-December 1968.

731. PLEYDELL, ALBERT. The role of the management consultant in the social work field. In: *Administration, Supervision and Consultation*. New York: Family Service Association of America, 1955. pp. 92–97.

732. ROBERTS, C.A. Psychiatric and mental health consultation. *Canadian Journal of Public Health*, 61(1):17–24, 1970.

733. SCHIFFMAN, G.B. Role of a State reading consultant. *Reading Teacher*, 20:487–493, March 1967.

734. SCHWARTZ, EMANUEL K., and LEDER, RUTH. The role of the mental health consultant in community psychology. In: Riess, Bernard F., ed. *New Directions in Mental Health, Vol. II*. New York: Grune and Stratton, pp. 41–45.

735. SEASHORE, CHARLES, and VAN EGMOND, ELMER. The consultant-trainer role in working directly with a total staff. *Journal of Social Issues*, 15(2):36–42, 1959.

736. SHLENSKY, RONALD. Role of the psychiatric consultant at a rehabilitative agency. *Illinois Medical Journal*, 143(1):25–26, 1973.

737. STACHOWIAK, JAMES G. Toward the Management of Classroom Behavior Problems: An Approach to Intervention in a School System. Paper presented at the American Psychological Association meetings, San Francisco, California, August 30–September 3, 1968. Washington, D.C.: American Psychological Association. (EDRS).

738. STEINLE, R.L. Consultants corner: Use and function of hospital consultants. *Hospital Topics*, 36:36–54, 1958.

739. STEPHENSON, RACHEL B. Role of the regional psychiatric social work consultant. In: *Conference of Chief Social Workers from State Mental Health Programs, Cleveland, Ohio, June, 1949.* Bethesda, Maryland: National Institute of Mental Health, U.S. Department of Health, Education, and Welfare, 1950.

740. TANAY, EMANUEL. Psychiatric aspects of the role of industrial physicians. *Journal of Occupational Medicine,* 14(3):207–211, 1972.

741. TILLES, SEYMOUR. Understanding the consultant's role. *Harvard Business Review,* 39(6):87–99, 1961.

742. VAN VLEET, PHYLLIS, and BROWNBRIDGE, ROBERT. Investments in Prevention. The Prevention of Learning and Behavior Problems in Young Children. Intervention Report II. Washington, D.C.: U.S. Department of Health, Education, and Welfare, Office of Education, June 1969. (EDRS).

743. WILMER, HARRY A. The role of the psychiatrist in consultation and some observations on video tape learning. *Psychosomatics,* 8(4):193–195, July-August 1967.

744. WOLFF, MAX. The role of the sociologist as a community consultant. *Journal of Educational Sociology,* 29(4):146–150, December 1955.

See also: 5, 170, 171, 172, 176, 193, 194, 201, 229, 233, 345, 361, 402, 409, 410, 411, 412, 420, 426, 454, 472, 475, 491, 515, 518, 529, 534, 540, 551, 609, 614, 745, 749, 752, 758, 759, 765, 784, 801, 805, 811, 813, 827, 834, 852, 865, 886, 904, 919, 937, 938, 945, 947, 958, 959, 961, 962, 968, 970, 974, 976, 983, 984, 986, 990, 1002, 1004, 1033, 1039, 1085, 1086, 1094.

THE PROCESS OF CONSULTATION:
PROBLEMS AND CHARACTERISTICS

In the 84 items in this section the concern is with the consultation process or the developmental sequences which characterize those activities which take place in the name of consultation. Various students have divided the consultation process into a number of phases, which usually range from a preparatory phase, prior to actually beginning the consultation relationship, to an evaluation phase after the consultation relationship has terminated. In each of these phases a number of issues and problems have been considered and discussed in the literature. These include issues around distance and proximity, handling resistance, the need for sanction, the contract, defining boundaries, nature of authority in the relationship, issues around initiation, transference and countertransference elements, the entry problem, the dynamics of consultation, etc. The items in this section are intended to portray some of the characteristics and problems of the consultation process, which have been identified and discussed in the literature.

CONSULTATION PROCESS

Books

745. Group for the Advancement of Psychiatry. The psychiatric consultant on public issues. In: *The Psychiatrist and Public Issues.* New York: Group for the Advancement of Psychiatry, October 1969. pp. 179–182.

746. SARASON, SEYMOUR B.; LEVINE, MURRAY; GOLDENBERG, IRA; CHERLIN, DENNIS L.; and BENNETT, EDWARD M. *Psychology in Community Settings.* New York: John Wiley & Sons, 1966.

747. SCHEIN, EDGAR H. *Process Consultation: Its Role in Organization Development.* Reading, Massachusetts: Addison-Wesley Publishing Co., 1969.

748. TOWLE, CHARLOTTE. *The Consultation Process.* Chicago: University of Chicago, 1951.

749. Washington Department of Health. *A Pattern for Effective Consultation.* Seattle: Washington Department of Health, 1961.

Articles and Periodicals

750. ABRAM, HARRY S. Interpersonal aspects of psychiatric consultations in a general hospital. *Psychiatry in Medicine,* 2(4):321–326, 1971.

751. ABRAMOVITZ, A.B. Methods and techniques of consultation. *American Journal of Orthopsychiatry,* 28(1):126–133, January 1958.

752. ARGYRIS, CHRIS, Explorations in consulting-client relationships. *Human Organization,* 21:121–133, Fall 1961.

753. BARTEMEIER, LEO H. Psychiatric consultations. *American Journal of Psychiatry,* 111:364–365, 1954.

754. BERGAN, JOHN R. A systems approach to psychological services. *Psychology in the Schools,* VII(4):315–319, 1970.

755. BERLIN, IRVING N. Mental health consultation for school social workers: A conceptual model. *Community Mental Health Journal,* 5(4):280–288, 1969.

756. BERLIN, IRVING N. The theme in mental health consultation sessions. *American Journal of Orthopsychiatry,* 30(4):827–828, October 1960.

757. BOEHM, WERNER W. The professional relationship between consultant and consultee. *American Journal of Orthopsychiatry,* 26(2):241–248, April 1956.

758. BOLIAN, GEORGE C. Wanted: Identity for a community psychiatrist. *Mental Hygiene,* 52(3):431–438, 1968.

759. BROCKBANK, REED. Aspects of mental health consultation. *Archives of General Psychiatry,* 18(3):267–275, March 1968.

760. BROSIN, HENRY W. Communication systems of the consultation process. In: Mendel, Werner M., and Solomon, Philip, eds. *The Psychiatric Consultation.* New York: Grune & Stratton, 1968. pp. 1–12.

761. BURKE, MIRIAM G. On Becoming A Consultant. Paper presented at American Personnel and Guidance Association's 20th Annual Convention, Atlantic City, N.J., April 4–8, 1971. Michigan: Michigan State University. (EDRS).

762. CAPLAN, GERALD. A method of mental health consultation. In: Caplan, G., ed. *Principles of Preventive Psychiatry.* New York: Basic Books, 1964. pp. 232–265.

763. CARVER, JOHN. Behavior modification in the consultation-education element of service. In: Beigel, Allan, and Levenson, Alan I., eds. *The Community Mental Health Center.* New York: Basic Books, 1972. pp. 263–271.

764. CHARTERS, W.W., JR. Stresses in consultation. *Adult Leadership,* 3(10):21–22, 1955.

765. COHEN, LOUIS D. Consultation as a method of mental health intervention. In: Abt, L.E., and Riess, B.F., eds. *Progress in Clinical Psychology.* New York: Grune and Stratton, 1966. pp. 107–128.

766. COLLINS, JEROME A. Mental health consultation to Boston's Model Cities Program. *Hospital and Community Psychiatry,* 21(7):213–216, July 1970.

767. COOK, MAXWELL A. Ten commandments of consultation. *Journal of American Public Welfare Association,* 8(3):303–305, 1970.

768. COVNER, BERNARD J. Principles for psychological consulting with client organizations. *Journal of Consulting Psychology,* 11(5):227–244, September–October 1947.

769. CROLEY, H.T. The consultative process. In: *The Voluntary Health Agency—Meeting Needs. Continuing Education Monograph No. 1.* San Francisco: Western Regional Office, American Public Health Association, 1961. pp. 39–45.

770. DELOUGHERY, GRACE W.; GEBBIE, KRISTINE M.; and NEUMAN, BETTY M. Consultation process in groups. In: Deloughery, G., ed. *Community Mental Health Nursing.* Baltimore: Williams and Wilkins, 1971. pp. 75–91.

771. DELOUGHERY, GRACE W.; GEBBIE, KRISTINE M.; and NEUMAN, BETTY M. Framework of mental health consultation: Theoretical framework. In Deloughery, G., ed. *Community Mental Health Nursing.* Baltimore: Williams and Wilkins, 1971. pp. 53–74.

772. DYER, WILLIAM G.; MADDOCKS, ROBERT F.; MOFFITT, J. WELDON; and UNDERWOOD, WILLIAM T. A laboratory-consultation model for organization change. *Journal of Applied Behavioral Science,* 6(2):211–227, April, May, June 1970.

773. EISDORFER, CARL; ALTROCCHI, JOHN; and YOUNG, ROBERT F. Principles of community mental health in a rural setting: The Halifax County Program. *Community Mental Health Journal.* 4(3):211–220, 1968.

774. EISDORFER, CARL, and BATTON, LOIS. The mental health consultant as seen by his consultees. *Community Mental Health Journal,* 8(3):171–177, August 1972.

775. EKSTEIN, R.; MOTTO, R.; ROSENFIELD, H.; HEINECKE, C.; and GILMAN, L. Issues in consultation: The mental health worker and educator. *American Journal of Orthopsychiatry,* 41(2):312–314, March 1971.

776. EVANS, DOROTHY A. Problems and challenges for the mental health professional consulting to a community action organization. *Community Mental Health Journal,* 9(1):46–52, Spring 1973.

777. FERNEAU, ERNEST W., JR., and KLEIN, DONALD C. Mental health consultation and sector psychotherapy. *Psychoanalytic Review,* 56(2):327–339, 1969.

778. GAUPP, PETER G. Authority, influence and control in consultation. *Community Mental Health Journal,* 2(3):205–210, Fall 1966.

779. GEBBIE, KRISTINE M. Consultation contracts. Their development and evaluation. *American Journal of Public Health,* 60(10):1916–1920, October 1970.

780. GLASSCOTE, RAYMOND, M.; FISHMAN, MICHAEL E.; and SONIS, MEYER. Consultation. In: *Children and Mental Health Centers.* Washington, D.C.: The Joint Information Service of the American Psychiatric Association and the National Association for Mental Health, 1972. pp. 36–39.

781. GLIDEWELL, JOHN C. The entry problem in consultation. *Journal of Social Issues,* 15:51–59, 1959.

782. GOODSTEIN, LEONARD D., and BOYER, RONALD K. Crisis intervention in a municipal agency: A conceptual case history. *Journal of Applied Behavioral Science,* 8(3):318–340, May-June 1972.

783. GORMAN, JOANNA F. Some characteristics of consultation. In: Rapoport, Lydia ed. *Consultation in Social Work Practice.* New York: National Association of Social Workers, 1963. pp. 21–31.

784. GREEN, ROSE. The consultant and the consultation process. *Child Welfare*, 44(8):425–430, October 1965.

785. GROSSMAN, FRANCES K., and QUINLAN, DONALD. Mental health consultation to community settings: A case study of a failure to achieve goals. In: Golann, Stuart E., and Eisdorfer, Carl, eds. *Handbook of Community Psychiatry*. New York: Appleton-Century-Crofts, 1972. pp. 617–640.

786. HANEGBI, RIVKAH. Professional assistance to the more disturbed child: Toward a theory of counselling techniques. In: Wolins, M., and Gottesmann, M., eds. *Group Care: An Israeli Approach*. New York: Gordon and Breach, 1971, pp. 290–297.

787. HAYLETT, CLARICE H. Evolution of indirect services. In: Lamb, H. Richard; Heath, Don; and Downing, Joseph J., eds. *Handbook of Community Mental Health Practice*. San Francisco: Jossey-Bass, 1969. pp. 289–304.

788. HAYLETT, CLARICE H. Issues of indirect services. In: Lamb, H. Richard; Heath, Don; and Downing, Joseph J. *Handbook of Community Mental Health Practice*. San Francisco: Jossey-Bass, 1969. pp. 305–321.

789. HIRSCHOWITZ, RALPH G., and RALPH, DONALD E. Communication about communication problems in psychiatric organizations: An intervention model. *Adult Leadership*, 21(9):285–288, March 1973.

790. HITCHCOCK, JOHN, and MOONEY, WILLIAM E. Mental health consultation: A psychoanalytic formulation. *Archives of General Psychiatry*, 21(3):353–358, 1969.

791. HODGES, ALLEN. How not to be a consultant. *Mental Hygiene*, 54(1):147–148 Winter 1970.

792. HOLLANDER, MARC H., and HERSH, S.P. Impossible consultation made possible. *Archives of General Psychiatry*, 23:343–345, October 1970.

793. JARVIS, PAUL E., and NELSON, SHERMAN E. Familiarization: A vital step in mental health consultation. *Community Mental Health Journal*, 3(4):343–348, Fall 1967.

794. KARP, NEIL H., and KARLS, JAMES M. Combining crisis therapy and mental health consultation. *Archives of General Psychiatry*, 14:536–542, May 1966.

795. KHAJAVI, FARROKH; BROSKOWSKI, ANTHONY; and MERMIS, WILLIAM. Team consultation to complex organizations: Some emerging issues for mental health workers. *Hospital and Community Psychiatry*, 23(8):235–239, 1972.

796. KING, MURIEL. Coordinated patient care: A consultant's view. *Mental Hygiene*, 55(4):461–466, 1971.

797. LIPPITT, GORDON L. Operational climate and individual growth: The consultative process at work. *Personnel Administration*, 23(5):12–19, 1960.

798. LONG, MARIE ANN. Action versus advice: Conflict in consulting. *ALA Bulletin*, 60(4):357–361, April 1966.

799. MENDELSON, MYER, and MEYER, EUGENE. Countertransference problems of the liaison psychiatrist. *Psychosomatic Medicine*, 23(2):115–121, 1961.

800. MILLER, F.T.; PINKERTON, ROLFF S.; and HOLLISTER, W.G. An "action-facilitation" entry pattern of mental health consultation. *Professional Psychology*, 1(4):359–362, 1970.

801. MOED, GEORGE, and MUHICH, DONALD E. Some problems and parameters of

mental health consultation. *Community Mental Health Journal*, 8(3):232–239, 1972.

802. NAGLER, SYLVAIN, and COOPER, SAUL. Influencing social change in community mental health. *Canada's Mental Health*, 18(5):6–12, 1969.

803. OGURA, KIYOSH, and BRADLEY, V. A look at the consultative process: The psychiatric team and community agencies. *The Psychiatric Quarterly Supplement*, 41(1):17–35, 1967.

804. PAPANEK, GEORGE O. Dynamics of community consultation. *Archives of General Psychiatry*, 19(2):189–196, August 1968.

805. PERLMUTTER, FELICE, and SILVERMAN, HERBERT A. Conflict in consultation-education. *Community Mental Health Journal*, 9(2):116–122, Summer 1973.

806. PLAUT, T. Techniques and problems of mental health consultation. In: *Consultation in Community Mental Health*. Chapel Hill: North Carolina Board of Health, 1961.

807. PLAUT, T. Theory and purposes of mental health consultation. In: *Consultation in Community Mental Health*. Chapel Hill: North Carolina Board of Health, 1961.

808. PORTNOI, TIKVAH S.; LAM, DIANNE J.; ROSENHEIM, ELIYAHU; LIVINGSTONE, JOHN B.; SHERRY, S. NORMAN; NORTH, BETTY; and ONESTI, SILVIO J. Consultation by participation in child psychiatry. *Social Casework*, 54(7):412–417, July 1973.

809. RABINER, CHARLES J.; SILVERBERG, SEYMOUR; GALVIN, JOHN W.; and HANKOFF, LEON D. Consultation or direct service. *American Journal of Psychiatry*, 126(9):1321–1325, 1970.

810. ROBINS, ARTHUR J. Principles of consultation applied to international aid programme. *The Indian Journal of Social Work*, XXIV(3):152–160, October 1963.

811. ROSENBLUM, GERSHEN. Social intervention: Consultation to organizations. *Mental Hygiene*, 54(3):393–396, 1970.

812. RUBENSTEIN, GERALD. Towards authenticity in the consulting process. In: Claiborn, William L., and Cohen, Robert, eds. *School Intervention*. New York: Behavioral Publications, 1973. pp. 31–49.

813. RUDD, J.L., and MARGOLIN, R.J. Nonmedical consultant in a medical specialty. *Adult Leadership*, 12(7):197–198, 1964.

814. SCHILD, SYLVIA; ROCK, HERBERT; and KOCH, RICHARD. Dynamics of the traveling consultation clinic. *Mental Retardation*, 4(5):23–25, 1966.

815. SCHWAB, JOHN J., and BROWN, JUDITH. Uses and abuses of psychiatric consultation. *Journal of the American Medical Association*, 205(2):65–68, 1968.

816. SHELDON, ALAN. On consulting to new, changing, or innovative organizations. *Community Mental Health Journal*, 7(1):62–71, March 1971.

817. SIEGEL, DORIS. Consultation: Some guiding principles. In: *Administration, Supervision and Consultation*. New York: Family Service Association of America 1955. pp. 98–114.

818. SIGNELL, KAREN A., and SCOTT, PATRICIA A. Mental health consultation: An interaction model. *Community Mental Health Journal*, 7(4):288–302, 1971.

819. SIMONS, RICHARD C. Mental health consultation and the phenomenon of counteridentification. *Comprehensive Psychiatry*, 6(6):410–419, December 1965.

820. SMITH, CLAGETT G. Consultation and decision processes in a research and development laboratory. *Administrative Science Quarterly*, 15(2):203–215, June 1970.

821. STEELE, FRED I. Consultants and detectives. *Journal of Applied Behavioral Science*, 5(2):187–202, 1969.

822. STEELE, FRITZ. Potter unearthed for the consultant. *Journal of Applied Behavioral Science*, 8(5):513–526, September-October 1972.

823. STRINGER, LORENE A. Consultation: Some expectations, principles, and skills. *Social Work*, 6(3):85–90, 1961.

824. TATAR, HAROLD R. Use and abuse of psychiatric consultation in the college administrative process: A panel discussion. *Journal of American College Health Association*, 15:54–61, October 1966.

825. TIEMAN, GERALD R. Toward collaborative mental health consultation. *Journal of Religion and Health*, 9(4):371–376, 1970.

826. TIPTON, JAMES H. Consulting under fire. *Adult Leadership*, 3(9):17–20, April 1955.

827. WOLFE, H.E. Consultation: Role, function, and process. *Mental Hygiene*, 50:132, 1966.

828. YAMAMOTO, KAZUO. Mental health consultation method and the issues in Japanese culture. *Journal of Mental Health*, 15:59–68, 1967.

See also: 170, 171, 172, 173, 175, 193, 194, 199, 309, 331, 340, 361, 376, 392, 397, 439, 471, 473, 474, 485, 492, 498, 503, 510, 515, 529, 541, 570, 832, 835, 837, 838, 843, 848, 849, 850, 862, 864, 873, 874, 878, 890, 920, 922, 937, 938, 948, 950, 967, 973, 1004, 1055, 1062, 1067, 1069, 1079, 1080, 1087, 1089.

PLANNING
CONSULTATION PROGRAMS

Planning consultation programs cannot be done in a vacuum. Consultation must be an integral part of an agency's program, designed to facilitate the attainment of agency objectives. Hence, a clear description of agency goals, both immediate and long-range, are needed prior to considering what forms of intervention are needed to achieve these goals. If it is decided to include consultation as a part of an agency's service program, considerable knowledge about the community is required in order to establish priorities in terms of agency objectives. Despite the necessity of careful planning in setting up consultation programs, this is not an area in which authors have given a great deal of attention in recording their experiences in the literature. Because of its importance, however, we have attempted to select in the 30 items in this section references that do deal with some of the problems and issues involved in planning and implementing consultation programs.

PLANNING CONSULTATION

Books

829. California State Departments of Public Health and Education. *Programming Consultation to Schools by Mental Health Specialists.* Technical Assistance Project. Sacramento: California State Departments of Public Health and Education, 1961.

830. RIEMAN, DWIGHT W. *Organization, Operation and Extension of Consultation Services.* Austin: Division of Mental Health, Texas State Department of Health, 1965.

831. TOLAND, ROBERT A. *Daniel Fights His Phantoms: How a Psychiatric Consultation Service Came to a Middle-sized Community.* Austin: Hogg Foundation for Mental Health, 1966. 42 pp.

Articles and Periodicals

832. American Association of Junior Colleges. On Using and Being a Consultant. Washington, D.C.: American Association of Junior Colleges, 1967. (EDRS).

833. BINDMAN, ARTHUR J., and KLEBANOFF, L.B. Administrative Problems in Establishing a Community Mental Health Program. *American Journal of Orthopsychiatry,* 30:696–711, 1960.

834. BRICKMAN, HARRY, and MEEKER, MARCHIA. Mental health consultation in schools: Preliminary appraisal of an urban program. *Journal of School Health*, 37(2):79–85, February 1967.

835. BRIGANTE, THOMAS R. Issues In Implementing Campus Community Mental Health Programs. (EDRS).

836. BRIGANTE, THOMAS R. Toward campus community mental health programs. In: Golann, Stuart E., and Eisdorfer, Carl, eds. *Handbook of Community Mental Health*. New York: Appleton-Century-Crofts, 1972. pp. 575–594.

837. BROWN, JONATHAN W. Pragmatic notes on community consultation with agencies. *Community Mental Health Journal*, 3(4):399–405, Winter 1967.

838. BURNHEIM, RONALD L. Symposium: Mental health consultation in the community. *Australian Psychologist*, 4(1):5–12, 1969.

839. DÖRKEN, HERBERT. A dimensional strategy for community focused mental health services. In: Task Force on Community Mental Health, Div. 27 of the American Psychological Association. *Issues in Community Psychology and Preventive Mental Health*. New York: Behavioral Publications, 1971. pp. 85–86.

840. GUREVITZ, H. Programming for consultation services. *Hospitals*, 38:93–100, February 1964.

841. HALPERN, HOWARD, and LOVE, RONALD W. Initiating community consultation in rural areas. *Hospital and Community Psychiatry*, 22(9):274–277, September 1971.

842. KELLY, JAMES G. Ecological constraints on mental health services. *American Psychologist*, 21:535–539, 1966.

843. KHANTZIAN, EDWARD J., and MACK, JOHN E. The initiation and practice of psychiatric consultation in the general hospital. In: Grunebaum, Henry, ed. *The Practice of Community Mental Health*. Boston: Little, Brown and Company, 1970. pp. 735–747.

844. LAMB, H. RICHARD, and McGENNIS, THURMAN. Consultation to the police. In: Beigel, Allan, and Levenson, Alan I., eds. *The Community Mental Health Center*. New York-London: Basic Books, 1972. pp. 251–263.

845. LEMKAU, PAUL. The planning project for Columbia, In: Shore, Milton F., and Mannino, Fortune V., eds. *Mental Health and the Community: Problems, Programs, and Strategies*. New York: Behavioral Publications, 1969. pp. 193–204.

846. LEVINSON, HARRY. Psychiatric consultation in industry. In: Mendel, Werner M., and Solomon, Philip, eds. *The Psychiatric Consultation*. New York: Grune and Stratton, 1968. pp. 159–180.

847. LIBO, LESTER M., and GRIFFITH, CHARLES R. Developing mental health programs in areas lacking professional facilities: The community consultant approach in New Mexico. *Community Mental Health Journal*. 2(2):163–169, Summer 1966.

848. MANN, PHILIP A. Establishing a mental health consultation program with a police department. *Community Mental Health Journal*, 7(2):118–126, 1971.

849. MANNINO, FORTUNE V. Developing consultation relationships with community agents. *Mental Hygiene*, 48(3):356–362, 1964.

850. RAE-GRANT, QUENTIN, and STRINGER, L.A. Mental health programs in schools. In: Shore, Milton F., and Mannino, Fortune V., eds. *Mental Health and the Community: Problems, Programs and Strategies.* New York: Behavioral Publications, 1969.

851. ROONEY, H.L., and MILLER, A.D. A mental health clinic intake policy project. *Mental Hygiene*, 39:391–405, July 1955.

852. SCHUMACHER, HENRY C. Nature of mental health programs in health and educational agencies under the mental health act—role of the consultant. *American Journal of Public Health*, 40:131–135, 1950.

853. SUSSELMAN, SAMUEL, and BLUM, HENRIK. Origins and progress of a mental health program. In: Duhl, L., and Leopold, R., eds. *Mental Health and Urban Social Policy.* San Francisco: Jossey-Bass, 1968. pp. 35–55.

854. WEISMAN, A.D., and HACKETT, T.P. The organization and function of a psychiatric consultation service. *International Record of Medicine*, 173: 306–311, May 1960.

855. WHITTINGTON, HORACE G. Consultation practice in colleges and universities. In: Mendel, Werner M., and Solomon, Philip, eds. *The Psychiatric Consultation.* New York: Grune and Stratton, 1968. pp. 98–108.

856. WOODWARD, L.E., and ARRINGTON, W.W. Consultation in the planning and expansion of clinics. *American Journal of Orthopsychiatry*, 24(1):153–163, 1954.

857. WYLE, HOWARD LEE, and SILLS, MALCOLM. Psychodynamically oriented procedures in school consultation. In: Gottsegen, Monroe G., and Gottsegen, Gloria B., eds. *Professional School Psychology.* New York: Grune & Stratton, 1960. Volume I, pp. 148–161.

858. ZRULL, JOEL P. An experience in developing a program of consultation with a county board of education. *Journal of the American Academy of Child Psychiatry*, 5(3):490–495, July 1966.

See also: 170, 171, 172, 173, 175, 193, 194, 201, 429, 431, 567, 766, 909, 930.

CONSULTATION TRAINING AND EDUCATION

The items in this section deal primarily with two facets of training and education in relationship to consultation. First, there are those items which focus on the various aspects of the training of professionals in the art of doing consultation, i.e., to become practitioners of consultation. This has become increasingly important, particularly in the area of mental health, in light of the inclusion of consultation as one of the essential services required for Federal assistance under the Community Mental Health Centers Act. However, it is also true in a number of other fields due to the increasing demands being made upon available professional manpower.

Second, there are those items which deal with the use of consultation to supplement training in other areas. When used in this fashion consultation becomes part of a formal educational training program. Examples of the use of consultation to achieve educational objectives, such as in teaching psychiatric and psychological concepts to residents and medical students, are constantly increasing. A large number of the 67 items in this section deal with this aspect of training and education in relation to consultation.

TRAINING AND EDUCATION

Books

859. American Psychological Association. *Training Opportunities in Community Psychology and Mental Health.* Washington, D.C.: Committee on Manpower and Training, Div. 27, 1969–1970.

860. PARKER, BEULAH. *Mental Health Inservice Training.* New York: International Universities Press, 1968.

861. ROBBINS, PAUL R.; SPENCER, ESTHER C.; and FRANK, DANIEL A. *A Casebook of Consultations.* Berkeley, Calif.: California State Department of Public Health, 1969.

862. SINGH, R.K. JANMEJA. *Community Mental Health Consultation and Crisis Intervention.* Berkeley, Calif.: Book People, 1971.

863. SPECTER, GERALD J.; TAYLOR, IRVING A.; and ANDREWS, JUDITH E. *Utiliza-

tion Review Casebook. Pittsburgh, Pa.: Hospital Utilization Project, November 1972.

864. ZUSMAN, JACK, and DAVIDSON, DAVID L. *Practical Aspects of Mental Health Consultation.* Springfield, Ill.: Charles C Thomas, 1972.

Dissertations

865. WILSON, JAMES BRIAN. "Rationale and Design for the Practicum Experiences in an Internship for Instructional Consultants." Unpublished doctoral dissertation. Pittsburgh: University of Pittsburgh, 1968.

Articles and Periodicals

866. ADAMS, ROBERT S., and WEINICK, HOWARD M. Consultation: An inservice training program for the school. *Journal of the American Academy of Child Psychiatry,* 5(3):479–489, July 1966.

867. ALDRICH, C. KNIGHT. A specialized teaching program for residents in psychiatry. In: Mendel, Werner M., and Solomon, Philip. *The Psychiatric Consultation.* New York: Grune and Stratton, 1968. pp. 26–32.

868. BAER, DONALD M. The consultation process model as an irrational state of affairs. *Psychology in the Schools,* 7(4):341–344, 1970.

869. BARNES, ROBERT H.; BUSSE, E.W.; and BRESSLER, B. The training of psychiatric residents in consultative skills. *Journal of Medical Education,* 32: 124–130, 1957.

870. BATMAN, ROBERT H. Consultation as an educational technique in psychiatric nursing. *Mental Hygiene,* 52(4):617–621, October 1968.

871. BENSCHOTER, REBA ANN; WITTSON, C.L.; and INGHAM, C.G. Teaching and consultation by television: I. Closed-circuit collaboration. *Mental Hospitals,* 16(3):99–100, March 1965.

872. BERBLINGER, KLAUS W. The teaching of psychiatric consultation techniques. In: Mendel, Werner M., and Solomon, Philip, eds. *The Psychiatric Consultation.* New York: Grune and Stratton, 1968. pp. 13–17.

873. BERKEN, GILBERT, and EISDORFER, CARL. Closed ranks in microcosm: Pitfalls of a training experience in community consultation. *Community Mental Health Journal,* 16(2), 1970.

874. BERLIN, IRVING NORMAN. Learning mental health consultation history and problems. *Mental Hygiene,* 48:257–266, April 1964.

875. CAPLAN, GERALD. An approach to the education of community mental health specialists. *Mental Hygiene,* 43:268–280, 1959.

876. CAPLAN, GERALD. Problems of training in mental health consultation. In: Goldston, Stephen E., ed. *Concepts of Community Psychiatry.* Public Health Service Publication No. 1319. Bethesda, Maryland: National Institute of Mental Health, U.S. Department of Health, Education, and Welfare, 1965. pp. 91–108.

877. CARTER, JERRY W., JR. The training needs of psychologists in community mental health programs at State and local levels. In: Strother, Charles R., ed. *Psychology and Mental Health.* Washington: American Psychiatric Association, 1956. pp. 21–40.

878. CATHELL, J.L., and STRATAS, N.E. Mobile psychiatric consultation-education for primary physicians. *Community Mental Health Journal*, 3(3):226–230, Fall 1967.

879. CHESLER, MARK, et al. Resources for School Change I: A Manual on Issues and Programs in Training Education Change. Sponsored by the National Center for Educational Research and Development, Department of Health, Education, and Welfare. Ann Arbor, Michigan: University of Michigan School of Education, 1972. (EDRS).

880. CLEMMONS, ROY S. Consultation as a two-way process: Psychiatric education through consultation. *Southern Medical Journal*, 59(8):975–978, August 1966.

881. DIAMOND, H. Urban problems and the community mental health center: Multiple mandates; difficult choices: Consultation and education. *American Journal of Orthopsychiatry*, 40(2):270–271, March 1970.

882. ENELOW, ALLEN J. Teaching consultation psychiatry in a county general hospital. In: Mendel, Werner M., and Solomon, Philip, eds. *The Psychiatric Consultation*. New York: Grune and Stratton, 1968. pp. 59–64.

883. ENELOW, A.; FINKELSTEIN, I.; HUGHES, C.; and WORBY, C. Teaching social psychiatry to psychiatric residents in a community-based medical school. In: Miller, L., *Fourth International Congress of Social Psychiatry: Abstract of Papers*. Jerusalem: AHVA Cooperative, 1972. pp. 109–110.

884. FISHER, LAWRENCE. Training in school consultation. In: Claiborn, William L., and Cohen, Robert, eds. *School Intervention*. New York: Behavioral Publications, 1973. pp. 76–93.

885. GARRIS, A.G., and KOONCE, K.D. Technical Consultant Services to Innovate More Adequate Rehabilitation Services to Clients with Catastrophic Disabilities. Rehabilitation Research Report. Final Survey, August 11, 1966 to June 30, 1969. Sacramento: California State Department of Rehabilitation. (EDRS).

886. GOLDIN, PAUL. Preparing mental health professionals as race relations consultants. *Professional Psychology*, 1(4):343–350, Summer 1970.

887. GREEN, ROSE, and HAMOVITCH, MAURICE B. Education of social workers for mental health consultation. *American Journal of Orthopsychiatry*, 32(2):225–226, 1962.

888. GROTJAHN, MARTIN. Psychiatric consultations for psychiatrists. *American Journal of Psychiatry*, 126(7):932–7, 1970.

889. HANSEN, A. VICTOR, JR. The psychotherapist as a consultant. *International Psychiatry Clinics*, 1(2):475–482, April 1964.

890. HOLLISTER, WILLIAM G. Some administrative aspects of consultation. *American Journal of Orthopsychiatry*, 32(2):224–225, 1962.

891. ITKIN, WILLIAM, and ROSENTHAL, VIN. A model for the training of child development consultants. *Psychology in the Schools*, 6(3):273–279, July 1969.

892. JUNG, CHARLES C. Preparing Educational Training Consultants. Paper presented at American Educational Research Association Convention, Minneapolis, Minnesota, March 2–6, 1970. Washington, D.C.: American Educational Research Association. (EDRS).

893. KAHANA, RALPH J. Teaching medical psychology through psychiatric consultation. *Journal of Medical Education,* 34:1003–1009, 1959.

894. KENNETH, HESTER YOUNG. Students learn to use consultants. *Nursing Outlook,* 15(12):39–41, December 1967.

895. KERN, HOWARD M., JR. The new emphasis on mental health consultation. In: Bellak, Leopold, and Barten, Harvey H., eds. *Progress in Community Mental Health,* Vol. 1. New York-London: Grune and Stratton, 1969. pp. 232–251.

896. LEADER, ARTHUR L. Supervision and consultation through observed interviewing. *Social Casework,* 49(5):288–293, May 1968.

897. LENZNER, ABRAHAM S. The liaison psychiatric service. *Psychosomatics,* 9(6):326–330, 1968.

898. LEON, ROBERT L. A participant-directed experience as a method of psychiatric teaching and consultation. *Mental Hygiene,* 44:375–381, 1960.

899. LIPOWSKI, Z.J. Psychiatric liaison with neurology and neurosurgery. *American Journal of Psychiatry,* 129(2):136–140, August 1972.

900. McKEGNEY, F. PATRICK. Consultation-liaison teaching of psychosomatic medicine: *Journal of Nervous and Mental Disease,* 154(3):198–205, 1972.

901. MALLOTT, I. FLOYD, and EARLEY, WILLIAM L. The consultation situation and program content. In: Mendel, Werner M., and Solomon, Philip, eds. *The Psychiatric Consultation.* New York: Grune and Stratton, 1968. pp. 18–25.

902. MARSHALL, P.; COLEMAN, L.; DAEDLER, R.; and LaBaw, W. Rural community consultation in child psychiatric training. *American Journal of Orthopsychiatry,* 40(2):294–295, March 1970.

903. MEYER, EUGENE, and MENDELSON, MYER. The psychiatric consultation in postgraduate medical teaching. *Journal of Nervous and Mental Disease,* 130:78–81, 1960.

904. NOLAN, LYDIA G. The faculty consultant in relation to the social work student. *Social Casework,* 34(4):156–161, 1953.

905. NOLAN, LYDIA G. The faculty consultant in relation to supervisor and agency. *Social Casework,* 35(2):62–68, February 1954.

906. PANTHER, EDWARD E. Simulated consulting experiences in counselor preparation. *Counselor Education and Supervision,* 11(1):17–23, September 1971.

907. PARKER, BEULAH. The value of supervision in training psychiatrists for mental health consultation. *Mental Hygiene,* 45:94–100, 1961.

908. POWELL, GARRY, and MESMER, ROGER. School consultation experience in a residency program. *Hospital and Community Psychiatry,* 24(3):170–171, March 1973.

909. ROGAWSKI, ALEXANDER S. Teaching consultation techniques in a community agency. In: Mendel, Werner M., and Solomon, Philip, eds. *The Psychiatric Consultation.* New York: Grune and Stratton, 1968. pp. 65–85.

910. RYAN, JAMES. Teaching and consultation by television. II. Teaching by video-tape. *Mental Hospitals,* 16(3):101–104, 1965.

911. SCHULZ, ESTHER, D., and BROWN, DOROTHY. Preparing public health nurses for mental health problems. *Mental Hygiene*, 46(3):344–350, July 1962.

912. SCHWAB, JOHN J. Consultation-liaison training program. In: Mendel, Werner M., and Solomon, Philip, eds. *The Psychiatric Consultation*. New York: Grune and Stratton, 1968. pp. 33–40.

913. SCHWAB, JOHN J.; CLEMMONS, R. S.; and MARDER, L. Training psychiatric residents in consultation work. *Journal of Medical Education*, 41(11):1077–1082, November 1966.

914. SEITZ, PHILIP F.; JACOB, E.; KOENIG, H.; KOENIG, R.; McPHERSON, W.; MILLER, A.; STEWART, R.; and STOCK, D. A coordinated consultant team for remote State hospitals. *Archives of General Psychiatry*, 8(3):283–288, 1963.

915. SIGNELL, KAREN A., and SCOTT, PATRICIA A. Training in consultation: A crisis of role transition. *Community Mental Health Journal*, 8(2):149–160, 1972.

916. SMALL, IVER F.; FOSTER, LOWELLIG; and SMALL, JOYCE G. Teaching the art and skill of psychiatric consultation: An experimental curriculum for a general hospital. *Diseases of the Nervous System*, 29(12):817–823, 1968.

917. STEARNS, NORMAN S.; GETCHELL, M.E.; and GOLD, R.A. Continuing Medical Education in Community Hospitals: A Manual for Program Development. Postgraduate Medical Institute, 30 The Fenway, Boston, Massachusetts 02215, 1971.

918. STEWART, R.L.; JACOB, E.; KOENIG, H.; KOENIG, R.; McPHERSON, W.; MILLER, A.A.; SEITZ, P.; and STOCK, D. The State hospital consultant team as an education instrument. *Current Psychiatric Therapies*, 3:264–271, 1963.

919. SUTHERLAND, J.D. The consultant psychotherapist in the National Health Service: His role and training. *British Journal of Psychiatry*, 114:509–515, April 1968.

920. THEIMER, WILLIAM C., JR. Utilization of Consultants in Inservice Training. Paper presented at the American Educational Research Association, Chicago, Ill., April 1972. (EDRS).

921. TUTTLE, LESTER E., and HOOKER, DENNIS A., eds. Consultants' Handbook. Boca Raton, Florida: Florida State Department of Education, Tallahassee Division of Curriculum and Instruction, 1969. (EDRS).

922. WARME, G.E. Consulting with aide-therapists: A revised role for the mental hospital psychiatrist. *Archives of General Psychiatry*, 13(5):432–438, November 1965.

923. WILLIAMS, ROBERT L. The educational potential of the psychiatric consultation. *Psychosomatics*, 9:63–66, March-April 1968.

924. WITTSON, C.L., and BENSCHOTER, R. Two-way television, helping the medical center reach out. *The American Journal of Psychiatry*, 129(5):624–627, November 1972.

925. WOLBERG, A., and LAWSON, E.P. The training of mental health consultants at the postgraduate center for psychotherapy. *International Mental Health Research Newsletter*, 4(3):1962.

See also: 173, 193, 201, 309, 370, 372, 433, 515, 577, 579, 953, 961, 1004, 1018, 1019, 1029, 1037, 1075, 1076, 1080, 1092, 1102.

RESEARCH, EVALUATIONS, SURVEYS, AND REVIEWS

The number of entries in this section is 193. As the title of the section indicates, not all of these are reports of research. Included as well are literature reviews, bibliographies, and a few surveys of consultation practice. Nevertheless, it is clear from the number of entries here that considerable effort has gone into the general area of evaluating consultation practice.

RESEARCH

Books

926. COHEN, L.D. *Consultation: A Community Mental Health Method, Report of a Survey of Practice in 16 Southern States.* Bethesda, Maryland: Southern Regional Education Board and National Institute of Mental Health, 1964.

927. CUTLER, RICHARD L., and MCNEIL, ELTON B. *Mental Health Consultation in Schools: A Research Analysis.* Ann Arbor: Department of Psychology, University of Michigan, 1966.

928. Family Service Association of America. *Practice in the Use of Purchased Psychiatric Consultation in 17 Private Family Service Association of America Member Agencies.* New York: Family Service Association of America, 1953.

929. GOLANN, STUART E. *Mental Health Consultation, A Bibliography.* College Park, Maryland: Department of Psychology, University of Maryland, 1965.

930. GRIFFITH, CHARLES R., and LIBO, LESTER M. *Mental Health Consultants: Agents of Community Change.* San Francisco: Jossey-Bass, 1968.

931. MCCLUNG, FRANKLIN B., and STUNDEN, ALASTAIR, A. *Mental Health Consultation to Programs for Children.* Washington, D. C.: National Clearinghouse for Mental Health Information, National Institute of Mental Health, 1970.

932. MACKEY, RICHARD A. *The Meaning of Mental Illness to Caregiving and Mental Health Agents: A Study of Four Different Occupational Groups.* Final report of Project M–MHSC–53(c). Adelphi, Maryland: Mental Health Study Center, 1966.

933. MANNINO, FORTUNE V., and SHORE, M.F. *Consultation Research in Mental Health and Related Fields.* Public Health Monograph No. 79. National Institute of Mental Health. Public Health Service Publication 2122. Washington, D.C.: U.S. Government Printing Office, 1971.

934. MONTAGUE, ERNEST K., and TAYLOR, ELAINE N. *Preliminary Handbook on Procedures for Evaluating Mental Health Indirect Service Programs in Schools.* PB–210091. Springfield, Virginia: NTIS, 1971.

935. PARKER, BEULAH. *Psychiatric Consultation for Nonpsychiatric Professional Workers.* Public Health Monograph No. 53. U.S. Department of Health, Education, and Welfare. Public Health Service Publication No. 588. Washington, D.C.: Superintendent of Documents, U.S. Government Printing Office, 1958.

936. PIERCE-JONES, J.; ISCOE, I.; and CUNNINGHAM, G. *Child Behavior Consultation in Elementary Schools, a Demonstration and Research Program.* Austin, Texas: University of Texas, 1968.

937. SAVAGE, WILLIAM W. *Consultative Services to Local School Systems.* Chicago: Mid-West Administration Center, University of Chicago, 1959.

938. SAVAGE, WILLIAM W. *Educational Consultants and Their Work in Mid-Western State Departments of Education.* Chicago: Mid-West Administration Center (Cooperative Program in Educational Administration), University of Chicago, 1952.

939. SENEY, WILSON. *Effective Use of Business Consultants, a Research Study and Report Prepared for Financial Executives Research Foundation.* New York: Financial Executives Research Foundation, 1963.

940. TATHAM, LAURA ESTHER. *The Efficiency Experts: An Impartial Survey of Management Consultancy.* London: Business Publications Ltd., 1964.

Dissertations

941. AIKIN, DOROTHY. "Psychiatric Consultation in the Family Agency." Unpublished doctoral dissertation. Chicago: University of Chicago, 1957.

942. ALBRIGHT, DAROLD E. "The Role of Private Educational Consultants in Public Education." Unpublished doctoral dissertation. Ames: The University of Iowa, 1970.

943. ALFORD, ROBERT LEE. "Organizational Patterns and Analysis of Consultant Supervisory Services for Educable Mentally Retarded (E.M.R.) Programs in the State of Ohio with Implications for National Standards." Unpublished doctoral dissertation. Miami University, 1972.

944. ANTON, TOD AUSTIN. "Outside Specialists and School Districts." Unpublished doctoral dissertation. Los Angeles: University of Southern California, 1964.

945. BANISTER, RICHARD EUGENE. "The Role of the Elementary Consultant in Iowa." Unpublished doctoral dissertation. Lincoln: University of Nebraska, Teachers College, 1962.

946. BERK, MARY R. "Effects of Mental Health Consultation on Teacher-Child Interactions." Unpublished doctoral dissertation. Austin: The University of Texas, 1971.

947. BJORK, WALTER E. "A Study of the Influence of the Role of the Curriculum Consultant on Curriculum." Unpublished doctoral dissertation. Evanston, Illinois: Northwestern University, 1970.

948. BLUMBERG, ARTHUR. "Some Human Relations Problems of the Educational

Consultant." Unpublished doctoral dissertation. New York: Teachers College, Columbia University, 1954.

949. BRODSHATZER, ARTHUR. "The Certified Public Accountant as a Management Consultant to Small Business." Unpublished doctoral dissertation. Los Angeles: University of Southern California, 1964.

950. BURKE, MIRIAM A. G. "The Institution of the Consultation Process Within a University Context." Unpublished doctoral dissertation. Austin: The University of Texas, 1970.

951. CARL, ROBERT L., JR. "A Study of Selected Classroom Teachers' Perceptions of Educational Consultants and Implications for Further Study." Unpublished doctoral dissertation. Ann Arbor: The University of Michigan, 1971.

952. CEBULA, JOSEPH P. "The Use of Consultants in Massachusetts Public Schools (1967–1970)." Unpublished doctoral dissertation. Amherst: University of Massachusetts, 1971.

953. CHAMPAGNE, DAVID W. "Rationale and Design of the University Phase of an Internship for Instructional Consultants." Unpublished doctoral dissertation. Pittsburgh: University of Pittsburgh, 1968.

954. DAVIS, KENNETH M. "An Experimental Study of Group Guidance Procedures Using the Elementary Guidance Worker, Consulted Teacher and Nonconsulted Teacher to Present Selected Mental Health Materials to Rural Fourth Grade Students." Unpublished doctoral dissertation. De Kalb: Northern Illinois University, 1972.

955. DOBSON, JACK THOMAS. "The Possibilities and Limitations of Management Consulting as an Aid to Small Business." Unpublished doctoral dissertation. Gainesville: University of Florida, 1962.

956. EASTON, HARRY K. "Forensic Issues as Related to the Vocational Consultants' Participation in Social Security Disability Hearings." Unpublished doctoral dissertation. Evanston: Northwestern University, 1969.

957. ERICKSON, MILDRED HILDEGARD. "Consultation Practice in Community Mental Health Services." Unpublished doctoral dissertation. Los Angeles: University of Southern California, June 1966.

958. FERNEAU, ELMER F. "Role Expectations in Consultations." Unpublished doctoral dissertation. Chicago: University of Chicago, 1954.

959. FISHER, JAMES CHARLES ROSS. "Expectations of Professional Education Personnel for the Role and Function of Mental Health Consultants to Schools." Unpublished doctoral dissertation. Lafayette, Indiana: Purdue University.

960. FISHER, RONALD J. "Third Party Consultation Between High School Students and Teachers, Volumes I and II." Unpublished doctoral dissertation. Ann Arbor: University of Michigan, 1972.

961. FITCH, THOMAS C. "Role Expectations for Intern Consultants: Views of Intern Teachers and Intern Consultants in the Michigan State University Elementary Intern Program." Unpublished doctoral dissertation. East Lansing: Michigan State University, 1969.

962. FRIST, ROBERT JEDIAH. "A Study of State Extension Specialists' Functions and Tasks in Program Development in Indiana." Unpublished doctoral dissertation. Madison: University of Wisconsin, 1965.

963. GOTTI, RICHARD E. "An Analysis of Community Mental Health and Retardation Consultation to Public Schools." Unpublished doctoral dissertation. The Florence Heller Graduate School for Advanced Studies in Social Welfare, Brandeis University, 1972.

964. HARTY, HAROLD. "The Consultant and the Implementation of a Process-Oriented Curriculum." Unpublished doctoral dissertation. Syracuse: Syracuse University, 1972.

965. HILTON, LYNN M. "Consultant Services Offered the Three State Departments of Education to School Administrators." Unpublished doctoral dissertation. Chicago: University of Chicago, 1952.

966. INMAN, GERALD D. "A Study of Expectations Held by Intern Teachers with Selected Personal Characteristics for Intern Consultant Role." Unpublished doctoral dissertation. East Lansing: Michigan State University, 1970.

967. KAZANJIAN, VARD. "A Study of the Elements of Process as They Are Revealed in Mental Health Consultation." Unpublished doctoral dissertation. San Francisco: California School of Professional Psychology, 1972.

968. KINDELSPERGER, WALTER L. "Differentiating the Role of Child Welfare Consultant From the Role of Public Assistance Casework Supervisor." Unpublished doctoral dissertation. Chicago: University of Chicago, June 1958.

969. KOSIER, KENNETH P. "Effects on Task-Oriented Behavior of Teacher In-service Charted and Video-Taped Feedback, and Individual Consultation." Unpublished doctoral dissertation. Madison: The University of Wisconsin, 1970.

970. LAWLER, M. R. "Work of the Consultant." Unpublished doctoral dissertation. New York: Columbia University Teachers College, 1949.

971. LEWIS, MICHAEL D. "A Study of the Relative Effects of Counseling and Consultation Upon Personal and Social Adjustment, Sociometric Status, and Achievement-Oriented Behavior of Third Grade Children." Unpublished doctoral dissertation. Ann Arbor: The University of Michigan, 1969.

972. LINOFF, MARIAN G. "An Investigation of Attitudes of Teachers Toward Student Problem Behavior Using Behavior Modification and Consultation Groups." Unpublished doctoral dissertation. Coral Gables: University of Miami, 1972.

973. LYNTON, ROLF P. "The Consulting Process in New Institutions." Unpublished doctoral dissertation. Buffalo: State University of New York, 1970.

974. MAASARANI, ALY M. "The Role of American Management Consultants in Some of the Middle Eastern and Adjacent Countries." Unpublished doctoral dissertation. Austin: University of Texas, 1962.

975. MAIERHOFER, RICHARD A. "Pupil Behavior Change Through Group Counseling and Teacher Consultation." Unpublished doctoral dissertation. Columbia: University of Missouri, 1970.

976. MALKIN, SAMUEL. "The Role of the Elementary Science Consultant." Unpublished doctoral dissertation. New York: Columbia University Teachers College, 1965.

977. MAZADE, NOEL, A. "An Analysis of Community Mental Health Consultation/Education Programs Originating from Three Organizational Structures." Unpublished doctoral dissertation. Pittsburgh: University of Pittsburgh, 1972.

978. NEWFIELD, NORBERT L. "An Evaluation of Mental Health Consultation for Public Health Nurses." Unpublished doctoral dissertation. Rochester: The University of Rochester, 1972.

979. NOOE, ROGER M., JR. "Therapeutic Consultation: Conceptualization and Evaluation of a Psychotherapeutic Approach." Unpublished doctoral dissertation. New Orleans: Tulane University of Louisiana School of Social Work, 1971.

980. OVERHEIM, R. DANIEL. "An Analysis of Selected Variables in Predicting Specified Teacher Performances and Teachers Opinions of Consultants Working with the Elementary Science Program, 'Science, a Process Approach.'" Unpublished doctoral dissertation. Buffalo: State University of New York at Buffalo, 1972.

981. POLENZ, GLEN D. "Supervision and Consultation in Child Care Licensing: Special Reference to Children's Institutions." Unpublished doctoral dissertation. Los Angeles: University of Southern California, 1970.

982. PRAZICH, GEORGE D. "Impact of Inter-District Cooperative Programs and Special Education Regional Consultant Efforts on Programming for the Handicapped in Minnesota." Unpublished doctoral dissertation. Minneapolis: University of Minnesota, 1971.

983. PURSLEY, LUCY A. "Rationale and Design of an Open Educational Setting Incorporating the Role of Instructional Consultant." Unpublished doctoral dissertation. Pittsburgh: University of Pittsburgh, 1971.

984. REES, IRA J. "The Role of the Attorney-Consultant in Labor Relations in a Southern Metropolitan Area." Unpublished doctoral dissertation. University: University of Alabama, 1970.

985. SAVAGE, WILLIAM W. "An Examination of Consultative Services Provided by Eight State Departments of Education." Unpublished doctoral dissertation. Chicago: University of Chicago, 1955.

986. SCOTT, CHARLES A. "The Consultative Role of the Teacher in the Decision Making Processes of Selected New Jersey School Systems." Unpublished doctoral dissertation. Philadelphia: Temple University, 1972.

987. TEITELBAUM, DEENA I. "An Evaluation of an Experimental Program of Assistance for Newly Appointed Teachers in Certain Elementary Schools of New York City." Unpublished doctoral dissertation. New York: New York University, 1961.

988. THURLOW, BRUCE H. "A Comparative Analysis of the Elementary Counseling Role and the Elementary Consultant Role with Selected Anxious Fifth Grade Students." Unpublished doctoral dissertation. Orono, Maine: University of Maine, 1971.

989. TIEDEMAN, G.H. "Psychiatric Consultation in Medical Setting: Intraprofessional Differentials and Resolutions." Unpublished doctoral dissertation. Chapel Hill: University of North Carolina, 1968.

990. TIEMAN, PHILIP EDWARD. "A Survey of Educational Consultants and Their Role in the Recruitment and Selection of School Superintendents." Unpublished doctoral dissertation. Columbus: The Ohio State University, 1968.

991. TILLES, SEYMOUR. "An Exploratory Study of the Emerging Relationship Between Executives of Small Manufacturing Companies and Their Con-

sultants." Unpublished doctoral dissertation. Cambridge: Harvard University Graduate School of Business Administration, 1960.

992. TOWSON, ROBERT FENN, JR. "An Analysis of Outside-Staff Services Available to Management." Unpublished doctoral dissertation. Washington, D.C.: George Washington University, 1958.

993. TROYER, RAYMOND E. "The Principles of Consultative Work in Education." Unpublished doctoral dissertation. Chicago: University of Chicago, 1951.

994. TYLER, MILTON M. "A Study of Some Selected Parameters of School Psychologist-Teacher Consultation." Unpublished doctoral dissertation. Lawrence: University of Kansas, 1971.

995. VANETTEN, GLEN D. "A Study of the Prediction of Learning Disability Students' Responsiveness to Treatment in a Special Consultant Plan." Unpublished doctoral dissertation. Lawrence: University of Kansas, 1970.

996. VONDERHEIDE, AGATHA C. "The Use of Consulting Services by Private Colleges and Universities." Unpublished doctoral dissertation. Washington, D.C.: The Catholic University of America, 1970.

997. WATSON, WARREN K. "The Use of Management Consultants by the United States Air Force." Unpublished doctoral dissertation. Washington, D.C.: George Washington University, 1958.

998. WILDMAN, GEORGE F. "A Study of the Competencies Needed by External Curriculum Consultants in Order for Them to Work Effectively as Educational Advisors to Public Schools as Perceived by Selected Groups of Superintendents, Principals, Teachers, and Consultants in the Eight-County Region of Southern New Jersey." Unpublished doctoral dissertation. Philadelphia: Temple University, 1969.

999. WILLIAMS, GEORGIA M. "The Child Development Consultant Project, Urban Program in Education: A Case Study of the Humanistic Model for Planned Change in Inner City Schools." Unpublished doctoral dissertation. Ann Arbor: The University of Michigan, 1971.

1000. WRIGHT, FRED B. "Sex and Style of Consultants as Variables in Self-Study Groups." Unpublished doctoral dissertation. New York: The City University of New York, 1972.

1001. YOUNG, CARL E. "The Effects of Three Consultation Models on Individuals and Group Decision Making." Unpublished doctoral dissertation. Nashville: George Peabody College for Teachers, 1971.

Articles and Periodicals

1002. ABRAHAMS, DAVID, and GOLDEN, J.S. Psychiatric consultations on a medical ward. *Archives of Internal Medicine*, 112:766–774, November 1963.

1003. ADELSON, DANIEL, and LURIE, LAWRENCE. Mental health education: Research and practice. In: Golann, Stuart E., and Eisdorfer, Carl, eds. *Handbook of Community Mental Health*. New York: Appleton-Century-Crofts, 1972. pp. 509–539.

1004. ALTROCCHI, JOHN. Mental health consultation. In: Golann, Stuart E., and Eisdorfer, Carl, eds. *Handbook of Community Mental Health*. New York: Appleton-Century-Crofts, 1972. pp. 477–508.

1005. BARCLAY, JAMES R. Evaluating behavior changes in school psychologists. *Psychology in the Schools*, VII(4):320–324, 1970.

1006. BARKER, WARREN J. The psychiatric consultation. *U.S. Armed Forces Medical Journal*, 3:243–251, February 1952.

1007. BARRY, JOHN R. Criteria in the evaluation of consultation. *Professional Psychology*, 1(4):363–366, Summer 1970.

1008. BARRY, JOHN R. Effects of consultation in model cities program. *Professional Psychology*, 2(4):325–329, Fall 1971.

1009. BEIGLER, JEROME S.; ROBBINS, FRED P.; LANE, ELI W.; MILLER, ARTHUR A.; and SAMELSON, CHARLES. Report on liaison psychiatry at Michael Reese Hospital. *American Medical Association Archives of Neurology and Psychiatry*, 81(6):733–746, 1959.

1010. BERGAN, JOHN R., and CURRY, DAL R. Psychological Services: The Pilot Year. Tucson: Arizona University, Arizona Center for Early Childhood Education, 1971. (EDRS).

1011. BINDMAN, ARTHUR J. Bibliography on consultation. *Journal of Education*, 146(3):56–60, February 1964.

1012. BLAIN, DANIEL, and GAYLE, R.F. Distribution, form and extent of psychiatric consultations. *Journal of the American Medical Association*. 154:1266–1271, April 10, 1954.

1013. BLUMBERG, ARTHUR. A selected annotated bibliography on the consultant relationship with groups. *Journal of Social Issues*, 15(2):68–74, 1959.

1014. BOLIAN, GEORGE C. Psychiatric Consultation Within A Community of Sick Children—Lessons From a Children's Hospital. Paper presented at the American Orthopsychiatric Association Convention, San Francisco, California, March 23–26, 1970. New York: American Orthopsychiatric Association. (EDRS).

1015. BOLMAN, W.M.; HALLECK, S.L.; RICE, D.G.; and RYAN, M.L. An unintended side effect in a community psychiatric program. *Archives of General Psychiatry*, 20:508–513, 1969.

1016. BREYER, NORMAN L.; CALCHERA, DAVID J.; and CANN, CHRISTINE. Behavioral consulting from a distance. *Psychology in the Schools*, VIII(2):172–176, April 1971.

1018. BROSKOWSKI, ANTHONY; KHAJAVI, FARROKH; and MEHRYAR, AMIR. An evaluation of an in-service training seminar on community consultation and education. *Journal of Community Psychology*, 1(2):174–176, April 1973.

1019. BROWN, JEANNETTE A., and MacDOUGALL, MARY ANN. The Impact of Teacher Consultation on Elementary School Children. Paper presented at the American Personnel and Guidance Association Convention, March 25–30, 1972, Chicago, Illinois. (EDRS).

1020. BROWN, JEANNETTE A., and MacDOUGALL, MARY ANN. Teacher consultation for improved feelings of self-adequacy in children. *Psychology in the Schools*, X(3):320–326, 1973.

1021. CHAPMAN, RICHARD F. Group mental health consultation—report of a military field program. *Military Medicine*, 131(1):30–35, January 1966.

1022. CONNER, DARYL R., and THORESEN, A. ROBERT. Observations of a mental health command consultation program. *Military Medicine*, 137(4):152–155, 1972.

1023. CORNEY, ROBERT T. The efficacy of a liaison psychiatric consultation programme. *Medical Care*, 4:133–138, 1966.

1024. COWAN, EMORY L. Social and community interventions: Consultation. In: Mussen, P.H., and Rosenzweig, M.R., eds. *Annual Review of Psychology*, New York: University of Rochester, 1973. pp. 440–443.

1025. DAVIDSON, P.O., and SCHRAG, A.R. Factors affecting the outcome of child psychiatric consultations. *American Journal of Orthopsychiatry*, 39(5):774–778, October 1969.

1026. DELOUGHERY, GRACE WIEST; NEUMAN, BETTY M.; and GEBBIE, KRISTINE M. Mental health consultation as a means of improving problem-solving ability in work groups: A pilot study. *Comparative Group Studies*, 3(1):89–97, 1972.

1027. DENNEY, DUANE. A record keeping system for a psychiatric consultation. *Journal of Nervous Mental Disease*, 141(4):474–477, 1965.

1028. DOKU, H.D.; RITVO, M.R.; and CALISTI, T.J. Student advisory program: Solution to dental student dropout? *Journal of Dental Education*, 3(3):330–334, 1967.

1029. DORSEY, JOSEPH R.; MATSUNAGA, G.; and BAUMAN, G. Training public health nurses in mental health. *Archives of General Psychiatry*, 11(2):214–222, August 1964.

1030. EDELMANN, ANNE M. A Pilot Study in Exploring the Use of Mental Health Consultants to Teachers of Socially and Emotionally Maladjusted Pupils in Regular Classes. Philadelphia: Mental Health Association of Southeast Pennsylvania, 1966. (EDRS).

1031. EISENBERG, LEON. An evaluation of psychiatric consultation service for a public agency. *American Journal of Public Health*, 48:742–749, 1958.

1032. EMLEN, ARTHUR C., and WATSON, EUNICE L. Matchmaking in Neighborhood Day Care: A Descriptive Study of the Day Care Neighbor Service. Portland: University of Oregon, 1970. (EDRS).

1033. Erie County Board of Cooperative Educational Services. The Training and Utilization of Child Behavior Consultants in the Schools. Final Report. Buffalo, New York. (EDRS).

1034. FOSTER, JOHN T., and HARTMANN, JANE. A project in voluntary consultation for hospitals. *Public Health Reports*, 74(7):607–614, 1959.

1035. FRIEDLANDER, FRANK. A comparative study of consulting processes and group development. *The Journal of Applied Behavioral Science*, 4(4):377–399, October-December 1968.

1036. GILBERTSON, ESTHER C,. and WILLIAMSON, EVA M. The consultation process in public health nursing. *Public Health Nursing*, 44:146–147, 1952.

1037. GOLANN, STUART; WURM, CAROLYNA; and MAGOON, THOMAS M. Community mental health content of graduate programs in departments of psychology. *Journal of Clinical Psychology*, 20(4):518–522, 1964.

1038. GOLDSTEIN, STEVEN G., and MARSHALL, NANCY R. Diagnostic consultations: An explanatory model. *American Journal of Mental Deficiency*, 76(1):5–11, July 1971.

1039. GORDON, DOROTHY E. A study of the functions of consultants—with special reference to cancer nursing. *Nursing Research*, 1(2):41–42, 1952.

1040. HALE, M.L., and ABRAM, H.S. Patients attitudes toward psychiatric consultations in the general hospital. *Virginia Medical Monthly*, 94(6):342–347, June 1967.

1041. HALL, T. Experiment in cooperation: An account of health-visitor/general practitioner liaison. *Lancet*, 1:1325–1327, June 1965.

1042. HARTY, HAROLD. Perceptions of Consultant Utilization. Statistical Report. First Draft. Syracuse, N.Y.: Eastern Regional Institute for Education, 1970. (EDRS).

1043. HENDERSON, RONALD W. Research and consultation in the natural environment. *Psychology in the Schools*, 7(4):335–341, 1970.

1044. HUNTER, WILLIAM F., and RATCLIFFE, ALLEN W. The Range mental health center: Evaluation of a community oriented mental health consultation program in northern Minnesota. *Community Mental Health Journal*, 4(3):260–267, June 1968.

1045. ISCOE, IRA; PIERCE-JONES, JOHN; FRIEDMAN, S. THOMAS; and McGEHEARTY, LOYCE. Some strategies in mental health consultation: A brief description of a project and some preliminary results. In: Cowen, E.L.; Gardner, E.A.; and Zax, M., eds. *Emergent Approaches to Mental Health Problems.* New York: Appleton-Century-Crofts, 1967. pp. 307–330.

1046. JANES, ROBERT G., and WEISZ, ALFRED E. Psychiatric liaison with a cancer research center. *Comprehensive Psychiatry*, 11(4):336–345, 1970.

1047. KAUFMAN, RALPH N. A psychiatric unit in a general hospital. *Journal of Mount Sinai Hospital*, 24(5):572–579, 1957.

1048. KELLAM, SHEPPARD G., and SCHIFF, SHELDON K. Adaptation and mental illness in the first-grade classrooms of an urban community. In: *Psychiatric Research Report No. 21: Poverty and Mental Health.* Washington, D.C.: American Psychiatric Association, January 1967. pp. 79–91.

1049. KELLY, JAMES G. The quest for valid preventive interventions. In: Spielberger, C., ed. *Current Topics in Clinical and Community Psychology.* Volume 2. New York: Academic Press, 1970. pp. 183–207.

1050. KEUTZER, CAROLIN S.; FOSMIRE, FRED R.; DILLER, RICHARD; and SMITH, MARY DELL. Laboratory training in a new social system: Evaluation of a consulting relationship with a high school faculty. *Journal of Applied Behavioral Science*, 7(4):493–501, 1971.

1051. KISEL, JOHN G. Command consultation: A practice modality used by Army mental hygiene consultation service staff; Part A. *Dissertation Abstracts International*, 31(5), November 1970.

1052. KLINE, MILTON V., and CUMINGS, RUTH. A study of the learning characteristics of public health nurses in relation to mental health education and consultation. *Journal of Social Psychology*, 42:43–60, 1955.

1053. KOOLEN, MARTIN F. Evaluation Summary for the Cooperative Mental Health Service. Washington, D.C.: Office of Health, Education, and Welfare, Division of Plans and Supplementary Centers, 1968. (EDRS).

1054. LAKE, DALE G.; RITVO, MIRIAM R.; and O'BRIEN, GREGORY M. Applying behavioral science: Current projects. *Journal of Applied Behavioral Science,* 5(3): 1969.

1055. LAMBERT, NADINE M. Similarities and differences between school-based and community-based consultation. *American Journal of Orthopsychiatry,* 41(2):314, 1971.

1056. LEWIS, MICHAEL D. The effects of counseling and consultation upon the sociometric status and personal and social adjustment of third grade pupils. *Elementary School Guidance Counseling,* 5(1):44–52, October 1970.

1057. LEWIS, MICHAEL D. Elementary school counseling and consultation: Their effects on teachers' perceptions. *School Counselor,* 18(1):49–52, September 1970.

1058. LIPOWSKI, Z.J. Review of consultation psychiatry and psychosomatic medicine: I. General principles. *Psychosomatic Medicine,* 29(2):153–171, March-April 1967.

1059. LIPOWSKI, Z.J. Review of consultation psychiatry and psychosomatic medicine: II. Clinical aspects. *Psychosomatic Medicine,* 29(3):201–224, May-June 1967.

1060. LIPOWSKI, Z.J. Review of consultation psychiatry and psychosomatic medicine: III. Theoretical issues. *Psychosomatic Medicine,* 30(4):395–422, July-August 1968.

1061. LIPOWSKI, Z.J.; RAMSAY, R.A.; and VILLARD, H.P. Psychiatric consultations in medical and surgical outpatient clinics. *Canadian Psychiatric Association Journal,* 14(3):239–245, 1969.

1062. LIPPITT, GORDON L. A study of the consultation process. *Journal of Social Issues,* 15(2):43–50, 1959.

1063. LUBETSKY, J.; KISEL, J.G.; and BLUME, R.M. An exploratory evaluation of a mental hygiene consultation service field program. *Military Medicine,* 128:1212–1216, 1963.

1064. McIVER, PEARL. Survey of consultant nurses in health agencies. *Public Health Report,* 68(5):519–526, May 1953.

1065. MACAROV, DAVID; AKBAR, A.; KULKARNI, D.V.; and WERTHEIMER, M. Consultants and consultees: The view from within. *Social Service Review,* 41 (3):283–297, September 1967.

1066. MACHT, LEE B.; SCHERL, D.J.; and ENGLISH, J.T. Psychiatric consultation: The Job Corps experience. *American Journal of Psychiatry,* 124(8):1092–1100, February 1968.

1067. MANN, PHILIP A. Accessibility and organizational power in the entry phase of mental health consultation. *Journal of Consulting and Clinical Psychology,* 38(2):215–218, 1972.

1068. MANN, PHILIP A. Student consultants: Evaluations by consultees. *American Journal of Community Psychology,* 1(2):182–193, April-June 1973.

1069. MANNINO, F.V. Task accomplishment and consultation outcome. *Community Mental Health Journal,* 8(2):102–108, May 1972.

1070. MANNINO, FORTUNE V.; ROONEY, HERBERT L.; and HASSLER, F.R. A study of clergy referrals to a mental health clinic. *Journal of Religion and Health,* 6(1):66–73, January 1967.

1071. Mannino, Fortune V.; Rooney, Herbert L.; and Hassler, Ferdinand R. Distance and the use of the mental health clinic by community professionals. *Mental Hygiene*, 54(1):73–78, 1970.

1072. Mannino, Fortune V., and Shore, Milton F. Research in mental health consultation. In: Golann, Stuart E., and Eisdorfer, Carl, eds. *Handbook of Community Mental Health*. New York: Appleton-Century-Crofts, 1972. pp. 755–777.

1073. Mariner, Allen S.; Brandt, Edith; Stone, Edmund C.; and Mirmow, Esther L. Group psychiatric consultation with public school personnel: A 2-year study. *Personnel and Guidance Journal*, 40(3):254–258, November 1961.

1074. Marshall, Nancy R., and Goldstein, Steven G. Effects of three consultation procedures on maternal understanding of diagnostic information. *American Journal of Mental Deficiency*, 74(4):479–82, January, 1970.

1075. Mendel, Werner M. The education of the consultant. In: Mendel, Werner M., and Solomon, Philip, eds. *The Psychiatric Consultation*. New York: Grune and Stratton, 1968. pp. 49–58.

1076. Mendel, Werner M. Psychiatric consultation education—1966. *American Journal of Psychiatry*, 123(2):150–155, August 1966.

1077. Monnelly, Edward P.; Ianzito, Benjamin M.; and Stewart, Mark A. Psychiatric consultation in a children's hospital. *American Journal of Psychiatry*, 130(7):789–790, July 1973.

1078. Mumford, Emily; Balser, Benjamin H.; and Rucker, Malcolm. Ambiguities in a secondary school mental health project. *American Journal of Psychiatry*, 126(12):53–59, 1970.

1079. Nagler, Sylvain, and Cook, Patrick E. Some ideological considerations underlying a mental health consultation program to the public schools. *Community Mental Health Journal*, 9(3):244–252, Fall 1973.

1080. Norman, Edward C., and Forti, Theresa J. A study of the process and the outcome of mental health consultation. *Community Mental Health Journal*, 8(4):261–270, November 1972.

1081. Noy, P.A.; De-Nour, A. Kaplan; and Moses, R. Discrepancy between expectations and service in psychiatry consultation. *Archives of General Psychiatry*, 14(6):651–657, June 1966.

1082. Papastamou, Peter A. Psychiatric consultations in a general hospital: Meaningful characteristics of referral patterns. *Psychosomatics*, 11(1):57–62, 1970.

1083. Parker, Pauline E., and Terranova, Barry D. Indirect Services: The Bridge Between Mental Illness and Mental Health, Including Programming and Reporting Models. Sacramento, California State Department of Mental Hygiene, Sacramento Division of Local Programs, 1969. (EDRS).

1084. Payne, A. Achievement in sixth grade science associated with two instructional roles of science consultants. *Journal of Educational Research*, 57:350–354, March 1964.

1085. Pings, Vern M. The Medical Library Consultant—A Proposal for Investigation and Evaluation. Papers and Reports, No. 12. Detroit: Michigan Regional Medical Library, 1972. (EDRS).

1086. Regional Curriculum Project. Consultant Role Study: Regional Perceptions and Practice. Report No. ESEA. Title 5. Washington, D.C.: Office of Education, Department of Health, Education, and Welfare, Bureau of Elementary and Secondary Education, 1968. (EDRS).

1087. Robbins, Paul R., and Spencer, Esther C. A study of the consultation process. *Psychiatry*, 31(4):362–368, November 1968.

1088. Robbins, Paul R.; Spencer, Esther C.; and Frank, Daniel A. Some factors influencing the outcome of consultation. *American Journal of Public Health*, 60(3):524–534, 1970.

1089. Robinson, Shirley E. Problems in replacing a consultant. *Mental Hygiene*, 56(11):48–56, 1972.

1090. Rossi, A.M.; Klein, D.C.; Von Felsinger, J.M.; and Plant, T.F.A. A survey of psychologists in community mental health. *Psychological Monographs*, 75(4):1–38, 508, 1961.

1091. Rossi, A. Michael; Akins, K.B.; and Solomon, P. Psychiatric consultation requests in a general hospital. *Hospital and Community Psychiatry*, 17:144–146, May 1966.

1092. The Royal Medico-Psychological Association. Report on the questionnaire on postgraduate experience and training of consultants in adult psychiatry. *British Journal of Psychiatry*, 115(519):225–231, 1969.

1093. Ryker, Millard, and Vierkant, Arlyn. Community mental health and the schools: Perceptions of educational personnel. *Community Mental Health Journal*, 8(2):87–91, 1972.

1094. Sandt, John J., and Leifer, Ronald. The psychiatric consultation. *Comprehensive Psychiatry*, 5(6):409–418, December 1964.

1095. Schmuck, Richard A. Helping teachers improve classroom group processes. *The Journal of Applied Behavioral Science*, 4(4):401–435, October-December 1968.

1096. Schwab, John J., and Clemmons, Roy S. Psychiatric consultations: The interface between psychiatry and medicine. *Archives of General Psychiatry*, 14(5):504–508, May 1966.

1097. Schwab, John J.; Clemmons, Roy; Freeman, F.; and Scott, M. Differential characteristics of medical in-patients referred to psychiatric consultation: A controlled study. *Psychosomatic Medicine*, 28(2):112–118, March-April 1965.

1098. Schwab, John J.; Clemmons, R.; Scott, M.; and Freeman, F. Problems in psychosomatic diagnosis: II. Severity of medical illness and psychiatric consultations. *Psychosomatics*, 6(2):69–72, 1965.

1099. Schwab, John J.; Clemmons, R.; Scott, M.; and Freeman, F. Problems in psychosomatic diagnosis: III. Physical examinations, laboratory procedures, and psychiatric consultations. *Psychosomatics*, 6(3):147–149, 1965.

1100. Schwab, John J.; Clemmons, R.S.; Valder, M.J.; and Raulerson, J.D. Medical inpatients' reactions to psychiatric consultation. *Journal of Nervous and Mental Disease*, 142(3):215–222, March 1966.

1101. Schwab, John J.; Clemmons, R.; Valder, M.; and Raulerson, J. Medical patients' reactions to referring physicians after psychiatric consultations.

Journal of the American Medical Association, 195:1120–1122, March 28, 1966.

1102. SHAPIRO, DAVID S., and MAHOLICK, LEONARD T. Study III: A venture into interprofessional training and consultation. In: Shapiro, David S., and Maholick, Leonard T., eds. *Opening Doors for Troubled People.* Springfield, Illinois: Charles C Thomas, 1963. pp. 41–48.

1103. SMITH, PHILIP A. Evaluating Mental Health Consultation: Problems in Research Appraisal. Paper presented at Western Psychological Association, San Francisco, California, April 19, 1971. Northridge, California: San Fernando Valley State College. (EDRS).

1104. SPENCER, ROGER F. Medical patients: Consultation and psychotherapy. *Archives of General Psychiatry,* 10(3):270–275, 1964.

1105. STEPHENSON, P. SUSAN. Judging the effectiveness of a consultation program to a community agency. *Community Mental Health Journal,* 9(3):253–259, Fall 1973.

1106. STEWART, JOHN T. Patterns of dependency as related to projected responses of clergymen to mental health consultation. *Massachusetts Journal of Mental Health,* 2(4):28–29, 1972.

1107. STEWART, M.A.; TEASON, V.B.; GUZE, S.B.; and SATTERFIELD, J.H. A study of psychiatric consultations in a general hospital. *Journal of Chronic Diseases,* 15:331–340, April 1962.

1108. SWENSON, CLIFFORD H. Social impact of consultation. *Professional Psychology,* 2(4):324, 1971.

1109. TAGGART, MORRIS. AAPC membership information project: Part 3. Patterns in the receiving and offering of consultation among pastoral counselors. *Journal of Pastoral Care,* 26(4):240–244, 1972.

1110. TALMADGE, MAX; HAYDEN, BENJAMIN S.; and MORDOCK, JOHN B. Evaluation: Requisite for administrative acceptance of school consultation. *Professional Psychology,* 1(3):231–234, Spring 1970.

1111. TOBIESSEN, JON, and SHAI, AMNON. A comparison of individual and group mental health consultation with teachers. *Community Mental Health Journal,* 7(3):218–226, 1971.

1112. TOWNES, BRENDA D.; LYTLE, C.E.; WAGNER, N.N.; and WIMBERGER, H.C. The diagnostic consultation and rural community mental health programs. *Community Mental Health Journal,* 4(2):157–163, April 1968.

1113. TRIONE, VERDUNE. The school psychologist, teacher change and fourth grade reading achievement. *California Journal of Educational Research,* 18(4): 194–200, 1967.

1114. ULMER, RAYMOND A., and KUPFERMAN, SAUL. An empirical study of the process and outcome of psychiatric consultation. *Journal of Clinical Psychology,* 26(3):323–326, 1970.

1115. WAITE, MARJORIE. Consultant surgeons and vasectomy. *British Medical Journal,* pp. 629–634, June 16, 1973.

1116. WARDASZKO-LYSKOWSKA, HALINA. Psychiatric consultation in the departments of a general clinical hospital. *Psychiatria Polska (Warszawa),* 5(5): 525–531, 1971.

1117. WHYBROW, PETER C., and SPENCER, ROGER F. Changing characteristics of psychiatric consultation in a university hospital. A study of outcome. *Canadian Psychiatric Association Journal*, 14(3):259–266, 1969.

1118. ZACKER, JOSEPH; RUTTER, ELLIOT; and BARD, MORTON. Evaluation of attitudinal changes in a program of community consultation. *Community Mental Health Journal*, 7(3):236–241, 1971.

See also:　173, 309, 371, 372, 373, 378, 404, 405, 419, 422, 552, 555, 574, 575.

FILMS AND TAPES RELATED TO CONSULTATION PRACTICE

Accompanying the increase in the consultation literature and the development and expansion of training programs in the area of consultation are a number of tapes and films which relate to various aspects of consultation practice. Confined pretty much to the fields of mental health and psychiatry, the films are primarily oriented to professional training, intended for use by experienced and qualified professional teachers. Because of this, some of them are available only to bona fide training programs and institutions. They are included here, not only to broaden the overall scope of this guide as a resource to consultation, but to encourage the use of films as a new and potentially valuable dimension in the training of consultants and perhaps to stimulate the development of other films by professionals involved in educational programs from related fields of practice.

FILMS AND TAPES

1119. THE ART OF CONSULTATION. (No. 35 in series—42 minutes, 1968). Produced by Martin Grotjahn, M.D. Obtainable from AAP Tape Library, 1040 Woodcock Road, Orlando, Florida 02115. Rental: $10, extra scripts, $0.50.

1120. AN EXAMPLE OF MENTAL HEALTH CONSULTATION (44 minutes, black and white, 1968). Produced by Edward A. Mason, M.D., Mental Health Training Film Program, Laboratory of Community Psychiatry, Harvard Medical School. Accompanying discussion guide. Available from Mental Health Training Film Program, Harvard Medical School, 33 Fenwood Road, Boston, Mass. 02115. Rental: $15.

1121. CAREGIVERS IN CONSULTATION (Session I—23 minutes; Session II —26 minutes, 16mm. black and white, 1968). Produced by Edward A. Mason, M.D., Mental Health Training Film Program, Laboratory of Community Psychiatry, Harvard Medical School. Obtainable from Mental Health Training Film Program, Harvard Medical School, 33 Fenwood Road, Boston, Mass. 02115. (Limited availability.) Rental: $25 for both films, for 3 days use.

1122. THE CLERGY, A CASE OF FAMILY BREAKUP (16 minutes, color, 1968). Produced by Don Heath. Obtainable at present on loan from the Project Office, Mental Health Services Division, County of San Mateo,

Department of Public Health and Welfare, 225 37th Avenue, San Mateo, Calif. 94403.

1123. COUNTY JAIL, A MANAGEMENT PROBLEM (14 minutes, color, 1968). Produced by Don Heath. Obtainable at present on loan from the Project Office, Mental Health Services Division, County of San Mateo, Department of Public Health and Welfare, 225 37th Avenue, San Mateo, Calif. 94403.

1124. DR. ERICH LINDEMANN, PROGRAM CONSULTATION TO THE CENTER (24 minutes, color, 1968). Produced by Don Heath. Obtainable at present from the Project Office, Mental Health Services Division, County of San Mateo, Department of Public Health and Welfare, 225 37th Avenue, San Mateo, Calif. 94403.

1125. EMOTIONAL FACTORS IN GENERAL PRACTICE (43 minutes, 16 mm. black and white, 1961). Produced by Robert Anderson Associates. Available from Geigy Pharmaceuticals, Box 430, Yonkers, N.Y. Free loan.

1126. ENLISTING THE RESOURCES (47 minutes, color, 1967). Written and produced by Don Heath. Obtainable at present from the Project Office, Mental Health Services Division, County of San Mateo, Department of Public Health and Welfare, 225 37th Avenue, San Mateo, Calif. 94403.

1127. MAKING AN ASSESSMENT (28 minutes, 16mm., black and white, 1965). Available with 1128, listed below.

1128. DELIVERING THE MESSAGE (20 minutes, 16mm., black and white, 1965). Produced by Edward A. Mason, M.D., Mental Health Training Film Program, Laboratory of Community Psychiatry, Harvard Medical School. Obtainable from Mental Health Training Film Program, Harvard Medical School, 33 Fenwood Road, Boston, Mass. 02115. (Limited availability.) Rental: $25 for both films for three days use.

1129. ONE DAY A WEEK (33 minutes, black and white, 16mm. sound film, 1967). Produced by Edward A. Mason, M.D., Mental Health Training Film Program, Laboratory of Community Psychiatry, Harvard Medical School. Discussion guide supplied. Rental: $9 from New York University Film Library, 26 Washington Place, New York, N.Y. 10003. Purchase: $135 from Columbia University Press, 440 West 110 Street, New York, N.Y. 10025.

1130. PSYCHIATRIC CONSULTATION WITH THE GERIATRIC NURSING HOME (12 minutes, black and white, 1968). Produced by World Wide Medical News Service in cooperation with the American Psychiatric Association under a grant from Roche Laboratories. Available on free loan from Roche Laboratories, Division of Hoffmann-LaRoche, Inc., Nutley, N.J. 07110.

1131. THE PSYCHIATRIST IN THE COMMUNITY (22 minutes, black and white, 1968). Produced by Edward A. Mason, M.D., Mental Health Training Film Program, Laboratory of Community Psychiatry, Harvard Medical School. Accompanying discussion guide. Available from Mental Health Training Film Program, Harvard Medical School, 33 Fenwood Road, Boston, Mass. 02115. Rental: $10.

1132. FRONTIERS OF PSYCHIATRY ON CAMERA: PSYCHIATRIC CONSULTATION AT THE NURSING HOME OF THE AGED. (12 minutes, 16mm., black and white, 1968). Produced by the Roche Film Library, c/o Association-Sterling Films, Inc., 600 Grand Avenue, Ridgefield, N.J. 07657.

1133. SPECIAL EDUCATION. A TEACHER'S RELATIONSHIP PROBLEMS

(31 minutes, color, 1968). Produced by Don Heath. Obtainable at present from the Project Office, Mental Health Services Division, County of San Mateo, Department of Public Health and Welfare, 225 37th Avenue, San Mateo, Calif. 94403.

1134. SUPERVISION (28 minutes, black and white, 1968.) Produced by Edward A. Mason, M.D., Mental Health Training Film Program, Laboratory of Community Psychiatry, Harvard Medical School. Accompanying discussion guide. Available from Mental Health Training Film Program, Harvard Medical School, 33 Fenwood Road, Boston, Mass. 02115. Rental: $15.

1135. THEME EXPLORATION (27 minutes, 16mm., black and white, 1966). Available with 1136, listed below.

1136. DEALING WITH THE THEME (36 minutes, 16mm., black and white, 1966). Produced by Edward A. Mason, M.D., Mental Health Training Film Program, Laboratory of Community Psychiatry, Harvard Medical School. Obtainable from Mental Health Training Film Program, Harvard Medical School, 33 Fenwood Road, Boston, Mass. 02115. (Limited availability). Rental: $25 for both films for 3 days use.

AUTHOR INDEX

A

AAP Tape Library, 1119
Abidin, R.R., 305
Abma, G., 534
Abrahams, D., 1002
Abram, H.S.., 750, 1040
Abramovitz, A.B., 751
Abrams, S., 264
Abramson, H., 228
Abramson, M.F., 380
Adams, R.S., 866
Adamson, C., 37
Adamson, F.K., 630
Adelson, D., 1003
Adland, M., 245
Adler, P.T., 180
Ahern, M.S., 631
Ahr, A.E., 324, 595
Aikin, D., 531, 941
Aird, G., 277
Akbar, A., 1065
Akins, K.B., 1091
Albini, J.L., 426
Albornoz-Ruiz, J.M., 427
Albright, D.E., 942
Aldrich, C.K., 246, 247, 370, 867
Alford, R.L., 943
Allen, H., 38
Alt, E.S., 342
Altrocchi, J., 609, 773, 1004
American Association of Junior Colleges, 832
American Association of Medical Social Workers, 337
American Nursing Association, 211
American Psychological Association, 859
Anadam, K., 79
Anderson, F., 683
Anderson, J.R.., 457
Anderson, T.I., 394
Anderson, V.E., 80
Andrews, J.E., 863
Anshin, R.N., 475
Anstel, N.I., 156

B

Anton, T.A., 944
Argyris, C., 752
Armstrong, R.M., 664
Arnold, M., 343
Arnold, R., 406
Arrington, W.W., 856

Babcock, C.G., 248, 585
Bach, G.R., 686
Bach, P.B., 458, 460
Badowski, P., 671
Baer, D.M., 868
Bailey, R., 39
Baizerman, M., 571
Balinsky, B., 451
Balser, B.H., 1078
Banister, R.E., 945
Barcai, A., 249
Barclay, J.R., 1005
Bard, M., 306, 1118
Barker, W.J., 1006
Barman, A.S., 476
Barnes, L.B., 633
Barnes, R.H. 869
Barrett, C.F., 459
Barrett, R., 4, 452
Barry, J.R., 1007, 1008
Bartemeier, L.H., 753
Bartlett, H.M., 344
Bates, R.C., 157
Batman, R.H., 870
Batton, L., 774
Baudry, F., 250
Bauman, G., 1029
Bavelas, A., 725
Bayer, C.A., 381
Beasley, F., 220
Beaumont, J.A., 632
Beckhard, R., 610
Beckman, G., 332
Beigler, J.S., 1009
Benedek, E., 575
Benne, K.D., 611

☆ U.S. GOVERNMENT PRINTING OFFICE: 1975 O—552-490